Rebirth and the Stream of Life

Rebirth and the Stream of Life

A Philosophical Study of Reincarnation, Karma and Ethics

Mikel Burley

Bloomsbury Academic
An imprint of Bloomsbury Publishing Inc

B L O O M S B U R Y
NEW YORK · LONDON · OXFORD · NEW DELHI · SYDNEY

Bloomsbury Academic
An imprint of Bloomsbury Publishing Inc

1385 Broadway	50 Bedford Square
New York	London
NY 10018	WC1B 3DP
USA	UK

www.bloomsbury.com

BLOOMSBURY and the Diana logo are trademarks of Bloomsbury Publishing Plc

First published 2016

© Mikel Burley, 2016

All rights reserved. No part of this publication may be reproduced or transmitted in any form or by any means, electronic or mechanical, including photocopying, recording, or any information storage or retrieval system, without prior permission in writing from the publishers.

No responsibility for loss caused to any individual or organization acting on or refraining from action as a result of the material in this publication can be accepted by Bloomsbury or the author.

Library of Congress Cataloging-in-Publication Data
A catalog record for this book is available from the Library of Congress.

ISBN: HB: 978-1-6289-2225-7
      PB: 978-1-6289-2226-4
      ePub: 978-1-6289-2227-1
      ePDF: 978-1-6289-2228-8

Typeset by Fakenham Prepress Solutions, Fakenham, Norfolk NR21 8NN

CONTENTS

Acknowledgements	vii
Abbreviations	ix
Introduction	
THINKING ABOUT REBIRTH	1
'Stream of Life'	3
Terminological Matters	5
An Expanded Conception of Philosophy of Religion	9
Chapter Summaries	11
Chapter 1	
VARIETIES OF REBIRTH	15
Soteriological Orientations	18
Retributive Correlations	26
Affinitive and Consanguineous Continuities	33
Concluding Remarks	37
Chapter 2	
REMEMBERING HAVING LIVED BEFORE?	39
'Infamous Puzzle Cases'	40
Rebirth and Remembering	43
Remembering and Merely *Seeming* to Remember	47
Lived Examples	52
Concluding Remarks	58
Chapter 3	
FINDING MEANING IN MULTIPLE LIVES	61
Allegedly Fatal Objections to a Belief in Rebirth	63
The Ethical Significance of 'Same Person'	67
Simultaneous Multiplicity	71
Rebirth and the Spirit World	75
Concluding Remarks	77
Chapter 4	
INTEGRATING REBIRTH AND ETHICS	81
Transmigration and Moral Outlooks in Ancient Greece	84

Eschatologies and 'Ethicization'	92
Instances of Non-Karmic Ethical Integration	98
Concluding Remarks	102

Chapter 5
DEMYTHOLOGIZING REBIRTH?   105
'Demythologizing' in Theology and the Study of Religions	106
Karma and Rebirth without Personal Continuation	108
Critical Discussion	116
Concluding Remarks	125

Chapter 6
KARMA AND EVIL   129
Karma as a Principle of Moral Guidance	131
Is the Doctrine of Karma Incoherent?	134
The Problem of 'Blaming the Victim'	139
A Deep Disagreement	144
Alternative Aspects of Karma	148
Concluding Remarks	153

Chapter 7
CONCLUSIONS   155
Disrupting Assumptions	156
Diversity and Dispute	158
Methodological Reflections	161

Bibliography	163
Index	191

ACKNOWLEDGEMENTS

As someone who aims to combine elements from several areas of philosophy and the study of religions in my work, I am fortunate to be part of the School of Philosophy, Religion and History of Science at the University of Leeds. The School offers a fertile environment for sustained engagement both within and across disciplines, and I have benefited especially from my involvement with the School's Centre for Philosophy of Religion and Centre for Religion and Public Life, each of which facilitates ongoing discussions on themes relevant to my research.

Much of the work on this book was carried out during a period of study leave from September 2013 to June 2014. I am grateful both to my School and to the University of Leeds' Faculty of Arts for granting me that valuable research time. Staff at Leeds University Library also deserve my thanks for dealing so efficiently with numerous interlibrary loan requests. Many friends and colleagues both at Leeds and elsewhere have been supportive of the project out of which this book has emerged, by commenting on drafts or presentations, reviewing research proposals, sending me relevant pieces of their own work or by participating in stimulating and encouraging conversations related to the book's themes. I wish in particular to thank Amber Carpenter, Brian Clack, David Cockburn, David Cooper, Tyron Goldschmidt, Dave Green, Kim Knott, Gerald Larson, Antonia Mills, Rachel Muers, Campbell Purton, Catherine Rowett, Kevin Schilbrack, Stephen Shenton, Emma Tomalin, Matthew Treherne, Adriaan van Klinken, Kevin Ward, Mark Wynn, Renatus Ziegler and two anonymous readers for the publisher.

Some chapters draw upon, rework and develop themes or material from papers that I have presented or published elsewhere. Chapter 2 expands ideas I began exploring in a paper entitled 'Memory and Reincarnation', presented at the 36th International Wittgenstein Symposium at Kirchberg am Wechsel, Austria, in August 2013, and which appears in the conference proceedings published by the Austrian Ludwig Wittgenstein Society. Chapter 3 utilizes portions of my 'Believing in Reincarnation', *Philosophy* 87 (2012), by kind permission of Cambridge University Press. Chapter 4 is adapted from my article 'Reincarnation and Ethics', *Journal of the American Academy of Religion* 81 (2013); I thank Oxford University Press for permission to do so. Chapter 5 elaborates elements from a paper entitled 'Is Demythologizing Buddhism a Wittgensteinian Project?', which I presented at the *Philosophy in Cross-Cultural Perspective* workshop at Durham University in July 2013. I am grateful to Ian James Kidd, who organized that event, and to other participants for their fruitful questions and discussion. Themes from that paper found a place in my 'Karma and Rebirth in the Stream of Thought and Life', *Philosophy East and West* 64 (2014), parts of which also bear a family resemblance to Chapter 5; I thus extend my gratitude to the University of Hawai'i Press. Finally, Chapter 6 draws upon bits of two of my articles, namely 'Retributive Karma and the Problem of Blaming the Victim', *International Journal for Philosophy of Religion* 74 (2013), and 'Karma, Morality, and Evil', *Philosophy Compass* 9 (2014); for these permissions I thank Springer Science and Business Media B.V. and Wiley-Blackwell respectively.

In addition to the conference and workshop mentioned above, material that has made it into this book was also aired in papers presented to audiences at the University of Exeter, University of Leeds, University of Liverpool and University of Manchester between March 2013 and July 2014. I benefited enormously from discussions on these occasions and am indebted to the respective organizers for the opportunities to try out my ideas.

Haaris Naqvi, Mary Al-Sayed and their colleagues at Bloomsbury Publishing have again been thoroughly genial, supportive and diligent in seeing this book through to publication. I am deeply appreciative of all their good work. Finally, Sue Richardson has, as always, been a constant source of love, reassurance and advice throughout this project; even given many lifetimes I could not thank her enough.

Mikel Burley
Leeds, April 2015

ABBREVIATIONS

AN *Aṅguttara Nikāya* (Morris, Warder and Hardy 1885–1900)
DN *Dīgha Nikāya* (Rhys Davids and Carpenter 1890–1911)
MN *Majjhima Nikāya* (Trenckner and Chalmers 1888–1902)
SN *Saṃyutta Nikāya* (Feer 1884–98)

References to the Buddhist Pāli Nikāyas are to the above Pali Text Society editions, using these editions' respective volume and page numbers. Full publication details are given in the bibliography. In cases where the text is quoted in English, the English edition is also cited.

Introduction

THINKING ABOUT REBIRTH

> It seems clear to me that the philosophy of religion is not properly just the philosophy of the Christian (or Judaeo-Christian) tradition, but in principle of religion throughout history and throughout the world.
>
> (Hick 2010: 12–13)

The present study is a work of cross-cultural interdisciplinary philosophy. It seeks to cover a particular area of inquiry in depth and at the same time to exemplify an expanded conception of philosophy of religion, a conception in keeping with John Hick's vision of a historically and geographically unrestricted discipline. The book's several chapters, both individually and taken as a whole, are endeavours to get clearer about what it means to believe in rebirth (or reincarnation), how holding this belief – or some version of it – bears upon and manifests in believers' lives and hence also how the belief relates to ethical behaviour and values. My purpose is not to establish whether rebirth 'really happens' or whether anyone ought to believe that it happens; it is to explore the meanings and significances of believing that it does. In this respect what I have written is a work of philosophical hermeneutics. More specifically, it could be described as participating in the 'hermeneutics of contemplation', a phrase coined by D. Z. Phillips to designate methods that analyse and elucidate 'possibilities of sense' without trying either to advocate those possibilities as true or to impugn them as false (see Phillips 2001: esp. ch. 1).

My hope is that by the end of the book the reader will feel better informed about beliefs in rebirth, not because I have offered anything approximating to a comprehensive theory or definition but rather because I have brought out something of the multiplicity of aspects that the phenomenon – or syndrome – of believing in rebirth displays.[1] The

---

1. I here use 'syndrome' in the sense not of a set of pathological symptoms, but merely of a *concurrence* or *assemblage* (though, of course, many philosophers

aim is not to concoct an artificial and orderly idealization of rebirth (smoothing over the ragged edges, as it were); it is to examine the concept in its roughness. In doing so, we may see a richness of intelligibility that is often submerged when belief in rebirth is treated as though it were in every case aspiring to be a precisely formulated theory about the trajectories of our lives.

Conceptions of and discourse about rebirth occupy a prominent place in the thought and life of millions of people in the world today and have done throughout all recorded human history. These conceptions and modes of discourse occur, with particular variations, in numerous cultural and religious milieus. Often associated with religions originating in South Asia – notably Hindu, Buddhist, Sikh and Jain traditions – ideas of rebirth also abound in many other geo-cultural and historical settings, from ancient Greece to modern-day Africa and from Melanesia to Native American and Inuit communities.

Thinking about rebirth immediately immerses us in profound questions concerning the meaning and purpose, and indeed the very nature, of life. As the editor of a volume of essays by Indian philosophers put it in the 1960s, contemplating rebirth 'offers an opportunity for the metaphysician, the ethical philosopher, the conceptual analyst and the philosopher of science alike'. He adds that 'this theme may prove to be a fruitful basis for cross-fertilization of ... different types of philosophical reflection' (Mahadevan 1967: 16). I intend the present study to offer a confluence of at least some of those types of reflection, within the overall context of an investigation in the philosophy of religion (or 'philosophy of *religions*'[2]).

The remainder of this introduction divides into four sections: first, I outline some of the salient resonances of the phrase 'stream of life' that make it apt for inclusion in the book's title; second, I offer some thoughts on the terminology surrounding my central topic; third, I elaborate how this study connects with, while also venturing to broaden

---

have been inclined to view belief in rebirth as a pathological epistemic condition).

2. Though tempted by this plural form of the locution – 'philosophy of religions' – I am minded in the end to regard it as redundant, concurring with Kevin Schilbrack that the singular form – 'philosophy of religion' – can itself denote 'the philosophical study of religions in all their diversity, in all their aspects, and as a contributing part of a family of approaches in the study of religions' (Schilbrack 2014: 14).

the scope of, the philosophy of religion; and finally I adumbrate the book's structure by way of a summary of its chapters.

'Stream of Life'

The image, invoked in the title of this study, of a stream associated with life is a recurring motif in many areas of human thought. In the 1920s, for instance, Julian Huxley spoke of biological science as painting a picture 'of the continuity of life – a picture of life as essentially one, a great stream which is in reality single although advancing along myriads of channels' (1926: 1). Seventy years later, Richard Dawkins remoulded the image into that of 'a river of DNA ... a river of information, not a river of bones and tissues' (1995: 4). In a more explicitly poetic register, Rabindranath Tagore has written: 'The same stream of life that runs through my veins night and day runs through the world and dances in rhythmic measures' (1917: 64). And still other deployments of the notion of a stream or river of life have been plentiful.[3]

Ludwig Wittgenstein uses the metaphor of an active and ever-flowing current within which the things that we, human beings, do and say have their sense. 'Only in the stream of thought and life', he writes, 'do words have meaning' (1981: §173).[4] Elsewhere, he speaks of the 'weave', 'pattern' or 'hurly-burly' (*Gewimmel*) of life, again emphasizing our interconnectedness within a socio-cultural world.[5] The life that each of us is living is woven together with the lives of others; it is amid that interpersonal flux that the thoughts and words with which we, collectively and individually, articulate the meanings of our lives gain their purport.

In traditions of thought rooted in South Asia the image of life or the world 'as a stream of happenings, a perpetual flow of events' has been closely associated with rebirth and karma (Radhakrishnan 1952: 27). These ideas coalesce in the concept of *saṃsāra*, which is central to Hindu, Buddhist, Jain and Sikh traditions. Though commonly understood to denote the cycle or succession of rebirths, scholars occasionally point out that 'cycle of rebirth' is not a precise translation.

---

3. The many available examples include Milton (1864), Bogart (1866), Lispector (1989).
    4. See also Wittgenstein (1982: §913; 1992: 30e) and Malcolm (1984: 75).
    5. Wittgenstein (1967: 174e; 1982: §211; 1980: §629; 1981: §§567–8).

'[D]erived from the root sar- "run, hasten, flow, stream"', writes Jan Gonda, 'it means "going about, faring on, streaming continually". To exist in the saṃsāra means to go along ... with the beginningless and endless stream, without interruption, without rest, without being alone with oneself' (1975: 310). As is hinted in this latter description, saṃsāra has generally been conceived by the relevant Asian traditions as an unsatisfactory condition; it is the form of existence from which, ultimately, liberation is sought.

In western philosophy and psychology William James popularized the notion of a 'stream of thought' or 'stream of consciousness'. 'Consciousness', he writes,

> does not appear to itself chopped up in bits. ... It is nothing jointed; it flows. A 'river' or a 'stream' are the metaphors by which it is most naturally described. *In talking of it hereafter, let us call it the stream of thought, of consciousness, or of subjective life.* (1890: 239, original emphasis)

Similar metaphors have enjoyed extensive currency in the Indian-derived traditions. Most conspicuously in Buddhism, the image of life as a stream commingles with that of the stream of thought or consciousness in various ways. Our immersion in the stream of dissatisfactory life is construed as a consequence of the flow of desires, 'the craving for and enjoyment of sense-pleasure as an uncontrollable force, a current by which one is drowned or carried along helplessly in the round of rebirth, *saṃsāra*' (Collins 1982: 249).[6]

The purpose of this book is to investigate philosophically the belief in rebirth in its abundant diversity. Inevitably, Buddhist and Hindu versions of the belief feature prominently in many parts of the discussion, but examples are also drawn from elsewhere, including Native American and African traditions, ancient Greek philosophy and, at one place in Chapter 1, some strands of New Age and Neo-Pagan thought. The guiding theme throughout the inquiry is, expressly, that of the stream of thought and life, both in Wittgenstein's sense (i.e., the context in which our words have the meanings that they do) and in the sense displayed in rebirth traditions themselves, of lifetimes flowing

---

6. See also Dhammananda (1973: 23): 'This life-stream or *samsara* flows *ad infinitum*, as long as it is fed by the muddy waters of ignorance and craving. When these two are completely cut off, then only does the life-stream cease to flow; then rebirth ends.'

on from one to another. I seek to explore the significance that these fluidities and multiplicities have for one's experience and conception of what it is to be human. More will be said about the purpose and structure of the study below. First, however, it is worth pausing to consider some matters pertaining to terminology, which inevitably arise in a project that is as historically, culturally and linguistically wide-ranging as this one.

Terminological Matters

A dauntingly large array of terms has, over time, been used for the phenomenon that is the subject of this study. This may be one important indicator that there is not merely a single phenomenon here at all but rather a heterogeneous constellation of concepts and beliefs. English terms that have, historically, been pertinent to the topic include several derived from either classical Greek or Latin. Among those from the Greek are *metempsychosis* and *metensomatosis*, both denoting transference of the soul (*psuchē*) from one human or animal body (*sōma*) to another,[7] and *palingenesis*, 'coming into being again'.[8] From Latin are derived the terms *transmigration* (from *transmigrāre*, 'to migrate across')[9] and *reincarnation* (from *reincarnatio*, 'again in flesh').[10] From the mid-nineteenth century the term 'reincarnation' gained increasing recognition, and was further popularized by the Theosophical Society from the 1880s onwards.[11] Votaries of the Theosophical movement, treating 'reincarnation' as implying a specifically progressive spiritual

---

7. See, e.g., Plotinus, *Enneads* 4.3.9: 'there is the entry – metensomatosis – of a soul present in a body by change from one (wholly material) frame to another' (1956: 267–8). See also Werblowsky (1987: 21).

8. See Ogren (2009: 134). Schopenhauer, for one, adduces the term 'palingenesis', preferring it to 'metempsychosis' on the grounds that it better accommodates his theory of its being the will alone, and not the intellectual aspects of the soul, that persists from one bodily life to the next (1966 II: 502; 1974 II: 276).

9. Sandford, Thomson and Cunningham (1841: 789), Skeat (1882: 325, 568).

10. Cf. Werblowsky (1987: 21). Also compare Hoynacki (1993: 12) and Langmead (2004: 16) on the etymology of 'incarnation'.

11. Early Theosophical sources include Blavatsky (1888) and Besant (1892). However, *pace* Goudey (1928: 13), it is not the case that 'reincarnation' was

evolution, have generally distinguished it from earlier terms such as 'transmigration'; the latter, owing to its allowing for 'devolution' from human to animal forms of life, they take to represent 'a vulgarization of the greater truth of reincarnation' (Goudey 1928: 13). This allegedly vulgarized version of the doctrine, Theosophists maintain, is 'irrational, for such retrogression would contradict the fundamental laws of nature' (Walker 1923: 13).

While the exclusive association of the *word* 'reincarnation' with unidirectional progress has not been consistently adhered to outside Theosophy, the *concept* of a strictly progressive movement through multiple lives has received widespread approval. Those by whom it has been taken up include influential Hindu intellectuals – especially proponents of Neo-Vedānta philosophy such as Swami Abhedananda, Sri Aurobindo and Sarvepalli Radhakrishnan[12] – and some notable modern interpreters of Buddhism.[13] For Buddhists, regardless of whether a progressive model is accepted, the distinction that is commonly made is between terms such as 'reincarnation', 'transmigration' and 'metempsychosis' on the one hand, and 'rebirth' on the other. Terms of the former sort are typically held to be misleading in a Buddhist context on account of their seeming to imply 'the existence of an immortal soul (ātman) that is periodically incarnated in a fleshly host' (Keown 2004: 235). In view of Buddhism's characteristic – indeed, often self-defining – denial of a persisting self, Anglophone exponents of Buddhist teachings have generally opted for 'rebirth' as an approximation of the Pāli *punabbhava* or Sanskrit *punarbhava*, with 'renewed becoming' or 're-becoming' also occasionally figuring among the proposed translations of these terms.[14] In place of the idea of a reincarnating or transmigrating soul, these exponents, often drawing on early Pāli sources, speak of a dynamic 'stream of becoming' (*bhavaṅga-sota*) or 'stream of consciousness' (*viññāṇa-sota*) 'consisting of karmic energy that renders the rebirth or rebecoming possible'

'coined by ... Blavatsky in 1883'. The earliest occurrences of 'reincarnation' (or 're-incarnation') recorded in the *Oxford English Dictionary* are from 1845.

12. See, e.g., Abhedananda (1957), Aurobindo (1978), Radhakrishnan (1937). The term 'Neo-Vedānta' has come to be used to designate modern formulations, normally of Advaita ('non-dualist') Vedānta, that have arisen from the nineteenth century onwards (see Mukerji 1983).

13. Evans-Wentz (2000: 39–61), Humphreys (1983), Rhys Davids (1942), Roos (1967). For a critique of these interpretations, see Story (2000: 52–79).

14. Nimanong (1999: 240–1), Keown (2004: 224), Harvey (2013a: 52).

(Nimanong 1999: 241).[15] 'Rebirth' has also come to be favoured in scholarship concerning Hindu traditions as a convenient translation of the Sanskrit *punarjanman*,[16] and has been generally accepted by scholars of Jainism and Sikhism as well.[17]

The contention often advanced by Buddhists is that the word 'reincarnation' carries with it metaphysical commitments that 'rebirth' avoids. Yet, as Francis Story aptly notes, 'rebirth' too 'implies that there is a *something* which is born again'. For this reason, Story adds, 'rebirth' itself must be regarded as merely a term of convenience as opposed to one that precisely tracks reality; from the perspective of absolute truth (*paramattha-sacca*) 'there is nothing that is born again' (Story 2000: 89). This may be somewhat overstating the point, for even when the ever-changing nature of the 'stream of becoming' is emphasized, there nevertheless remains a sense in which this stream is indeed a 'something' that is born again from one life to another.[18]

From a Neo-Vedānta point of view, Aurobindo declares a preference for the term 'rebirth' because, in the case of 'reincarnation', 'the idea in the word leans to the gross or external view of the fact and begs many questions'. 'Rebirth', by contrast, 'commits us to nothing but the fundamental idea which is the essence and life of the doctrine' (1978: 1).[19] Aurobindo's misgivings about 'reincarnation', unlike those of Buddhists, do not derive from the categorical denial of a soul; rather, he maintains that the soul itself is evolving and that 'rebirth' expresses this evolutionary orientation whereas 'reincarnation' implies that there is simply an unchanging 'psychic entity getting into a new case of flesh' (1978: 17). One response to these suggestions would be to submit that Aurobindo himself is begging some questions when he assumes that 'reincarnation' must have the associations just mentioned and that these associations necessarily entail the rejection of an

15. Cf. Nyanatiloka (1980: 68) on *bhavaṅga*: 'having the nature of a process, lit. a flux or stream (*sota*)'. See also Matthews (1986: 125).

16. Monier-Williams (1899: 633). Also relevant is *pūrvajanman*, 'former birth, previous state of existence' (Macdonell 1954: 167).

17. Jaini (1980), McLeod (1984: 48–52 *et passim*), Singha (2005: 133).

18. Relevant to this issue is the question of whether – or the extent to which – the notion of rebirth is to be understood figuratively in Buddhism. This will receive closer attention in Chapter 5.

19. Cf. MacIntosh (1989: 154): 'Of course, the very word "reincarnation" is etymologically question begging, carrying with it, as it does, its load of dualistic baggage.'

evolutionary model. After all, as I noted above, the term 'reincarnation' has readily been used by Theosophists when articulating their own conceptions of progressive spiritual evolution, and several advocates of (Neo-)Vedānta, both before and after Aurobindo, have done the same.[20] Ironically, a South Indian poet named Padmashree Bendre has adopted almost exactly the opposite terminological position to that of Aurobindo. As reported by Kalghatgi (1972: 73), Bendre rejects the term 'rebirth' on the grounds that 'the old self is not born in its old form' but 'is in the process of evolution towards the Transcendental Spirit', Bendre's own preferred locution being 'new incarnation'.

The present study makes use of both 'reincarnation' and 'rebirth'. I take the view that, rather than words carrying their meanings around with them like a halo or an aura that remains unchanged in every context (to paraphrase Wittgenstein 2009a: §117), it is the uses to which the words are put that imbue them with life: '*Practice* gives the words their sense' (Wittgenstein 1998: 97e). *Pace* Aurobindo, I hold it to be misleading to speak of 'the idea *in* the word' (emphasis added) or to imply that the etymology of a word somehow determines its meaning for all time. There is no reason why talk of reincarnation must commit the speaker to belief in a 'psychic entity' getting out of one 'case of flesh' and into another. And even when imagery of souls inhabiting fleshly bodies does occur, it would be ill-advised to assume that such imagery is tied necessarily to any particular metaphysical theory. There are many meanings that the imagery might convey, and these cannot be known in advance, prior to an investigation of the contextual surroundings.

Notwithstanding these doubts about the charge that 'reincarnation' is burdened with unhelpful metaphysical baggage, the general terminological preference among contemporary scholars of Buddhism and South Asian religions will be borne in mind; accordingly, I employ 'rebirth' more frequently than 'reincarnation' when discussing these traditions in particular. Older terms such as 'metempsychosis', 'metensomatosis', 'palingenesis' and 'transmigration', having dropped out of common usage, are best reserved for treatments of specifically historical interest, such as when ancient Greek thought is under consideration (as it will be in parts of Chapter 4).[21]

---

20. See, e.g., Abhedananda (1957 [1899]: esp. ch. 3), Coomaraswamy (1946).

21. There are also many terms from non-Indo-European languages that, though pertinent to the topic, will not be discussed directly in this study. These

An Expanded Conception of Philosophy of Religion

Philosophers of religion in western countries have been rather slow to take a serious interest in traditions outside the three major Abrahamic faiths. There have, however, been exceptions, one of the most notable being John Hick (1922–2012), whose work routinely incorporates reflections upon Buddhist and Hindu ideas and whose expansive conception of philosophy of religion is intimated in the epigraph to this introduction. Developing a more globally aware philosophy of religion is an end worth pursuing if this area of philosophical inquiry is to achieve a comprehensive understanding of the myriad phenomena that go by the name 'religion'. But the obstacles remain considerable. Engaging in astute philosophical analysis of religious beliefs and practices requires a detailed acquaintance with the religious traditions concerned; hence it is hardly surprising that philosophers from countries in which Christianity has for centuries been the dominant religion tend to gravitate towards the investigation of, principally, Christian-related concepts and doctrines, and secondarily concepts and doctrines pertaining to religions that have important historical connections with Christianity, notably Judaism and Islam.

But the situation is gradually changing. Anthologies on the philosophy of religion are increasingly including substantial entries on Hinduism, Buddhism, African traditional religions, Confucianism, Daoism and occasionally on particular thinkers or concepts within these traditions.[22] There have also been anthologies making a deliberate effort to extend the remit of philosophy of religion,[23] as well as essay collections and textbooks that take a fully integrated comparative approach.[24] The present work endeavours to make a significant contribution to these developments by exemplifying a conception of philosophy of religion that expands its scope both methodologically and with respect to its subject matter. Methodologically, it aims to bring philosophy into meaningful and mutually informing dialogue with disciplines such as anthropology, theology and religious studies (including the latter's

include *gilgul* (Hebrew), *taspikha* (Syriac) and *tanāsukh* (Arabic). For a concise overview and some further reading suggestions, see Werblowsky (1987).

22. Indicative anthologies include Taliaferro, Draper and Quinn (2010), Meister and Copan (2013).

23. Kessler (1999), Eshleman (2008).

24. Clayton (2006), Griffith-Dickson (2005), Vroom (2006). For further discussion and references, see Schilbrack (2014: 25–6).

philological, historical and sociological dimensions). This interdisciplinarity facilitates an investigation of religious beliefs and practices that deepens our understanding of their place in human life as opposed to examining them in virtual isolation from their humanly lived contexts. I do not intend or expect to mimic the work of ethnographic fieldworkers; my task is not to immerse myself in a single religio-cultural milieu in order to meticulously elucidate its interconnecting strands. But I shall be drawing extensively on published ethnographic studies to inform my discussion of philosophically salient topics.

With regard to subject matter, the phenomenon of rebirth beliefs provides a theme in relation to which multiple religious traditions and a wide variety of textual sources can be discussed. In addition to ethnographic studies and work by philosophers and theologians (both western and non-western and from the ancient past to the present), other sources that I have consulted include: religious, ethical and legal texts, especially from South and East Asian traditions; biographies, autobiographies and memoirs of people from communities in which rebirth beliefs play a significant part; collections of and commentaries upon narrative folklore, poetry and literary fiction; works of religious, cultural and philosophical historiography; and summaries of case studies compiled by researchers into professed memories of previous lives.

A small number of philosophers in western countries have, over recent decades, pondered the idea of rebirth because of its bearing upon questions of personal identity; some have discussed the credibility of purported empirical evidence for past-life memories; and a further area of curiosity has been the question whether the combined doctrine of rebirth and karma can usefully be applied to the so-called 'problem of evil'. Each of these domains of inquiry is of interest and importance in its own right, and all of them will receive consideration over the course of this study. As noted earlier, however, my underlying concern is with the logically prior question of what it *means* to believe in rebirth, a question that, in turn, calls for careful attention to the place that the belief occupies in believers' lives: how it connects with other beliefs and values that they hold, cohering with and making a constitutive contribution to their outlook on life and the world. Such questions tend to elude concise answers or simple forms of argumentation. They call for reflection upon particular cases and an eye for conceptual connections and distinctions. Moreover, if the nuances of any particular case are to be highlighted, a comparative approach is required; for it is by placing examples in close proximity to one another that opportunities are afforded for bringing both their similarities and their dissimilarities – and hence their particularities – into view. Although one of my tasks is to explicate the diversity of forms that rebirth beliefs can and do take, it would be unrealistic for any single project to aim for completeness. Given the vast historical and geographical spread of these beliefs, selectivity is necessary. In Chapters 1 to 6, which constitute the main body of this study, topics have been covered that I take to be of deep philosophical interest. In most instances my discussion cites and responds to existing philosophical work related to the topic while at the same time endeavouring to move the discussion in novel directions, prompting further thought rather than striving for definitive conclusions.

Chapter Summaries

Chapter 1, 'Varieties of Rebirth', offers an indication of the heterogeneity displayed by rebirth beliefs while also drawing attention to some common elements. Following an extensive, though by no means exhaustive, list of peoples who recognize some form of rebirth, the chapter makes a number of typological distinctions. These concern, first, how the belief in rebirth coheres with the broader spiritual or soteriological orientations of certain religious traditions, and second, the kind of connection that is held to exist between the lives that make up a succession of rebirths or reincarnations. I highlight three kinds of connection, one of which is the idea of retributive karma that is especially closely aligned with the doctrine of rebirth in traditions deriving from South Asia.

Chapter 2, 'Remembering Having Lived Before?', examines the philosophical debate surrounding empirical research purportedly suggesting that significant numbers of people, mostly children, have remembered one or more previous lives. Such claims raise conceptual questions relating to the intelligibility of personal identity and the continuity of memory across distinct lifetimes, bringing these questions out of the realms of abstract thought experiments or science fiction stories and into real life. While aiming to do justice to the arguments of those who preclude past-life recollection on *a priori* conceptual grounds, I argue that a high degree of fluidity concerning the concept of memory needs to be acknowledged; moreover, it is to the cultural contexts in which claims to remember former lives are made that we need to look in order to understand the sense that these claims have in the lives of believers.

Chapter 3, 'Finding Meaning in Multiple Lives', pursues further some central tacks of the preceding chapter, especially that of contesting the adequacy of philosophical thought experiments for resolving issues concerning the alleged absurdity of belief in rebirth. A well-known thought experiment, devised by Bernard Williams and intended to demonstrate the logical impossibility of personal identity without bodily continuity, is taken as a starting point, and two main types of response are explored. One of these involves careful consideration of the emotional and ethical significance of believing someone now alive to be a reincarnation of someone who previously died; the other draws upon ethnographic studies that appear to illustrate beliefs about personhood that are at odds with certain assumptions underlying Williams' argument.

Chapter 4, 'Integrating Rebirth and Ethics', critically appraises some theoretical contentions regarding the relation between rebirth beliefs on the one hand and ethical values on the other. While it has often been assumed that the 'metaphysical' belief in rebirth logically supports and explains particular values and practices, this assumption has been disputed by Catherine Osborne, who argues with reference to certain ancient Greek philosophers that the order of priority is the other way round; that is, that the belief in rebirth is in fact generated by ethical values. By engaging with this proposal of Osborne's and also with ideas from anthropologist Gananath Obeyesekere, this chapter places in question the deeper presupposition that there must be an order of priority at all. I also raise objections to Obeyesekere's model of how South Asian ideas of karma evolved from 'non-ethicized' conceptions of rebirth, arguing that Obeyesekere's notion of ethicization runs the risk of obscuring the pervasiveness of ethics within supposedly non-ethicized forms of rebirth belief in small-scale traditional societies.

Chapter 5, 'Demythologizing Rebirth?', explores the phenomenon of reinterpreting karma and rebirth in ways that emphasize their ethical and psychological significance without committing the believer to a conception of individuals' continued existence beyond the present life. After comparing three main examples of such interpretations, I discuss whether they can be defended against the charge of illegitimate reductionism that is often brought against them. I also consider whether some modes of defence in fact involve an abandonment of a thoroughly demythologized interpretation.

Chapter 6, 'Karma and Evil', takes a closer look at ethical issues surrounding the retributive dimension of the doctrine of karma. I examine three criticisms that have been central to recent debates:

first, that the doctrine offers no practical moral guidance; second, that it faces a dilemma between free will and fatalism; and third, that it involves a morally repugnant form of blaming victims for their own misfortunes. Seeking to elucidate rather than to resolve the debate, the chapter indicates the radical divergence of ethically imbued perspectives that underlies the disagreements at issue while also illustrating forms of belief in karma that at least partially avoid what some would see as its morally unpalatable implications.

The concluding chapter, drawing together various points that have emerged over the course of the book, accentuates both the disruptive and the constructive aspects of the study. On the disruptive side, the study challenges certain assumptions or 'pictures' that tend to vitiate a full recognition of the possibilities of sense that find expression in rebirth beliefs. One of these assumptions consists in an unduly constrained picture of concept-formation, a picture that militates against seeing how particular culturally and religiously suffused forms of life open up space for meaningful talk both of rebirth and of remembering former lives. Another assumption concerns the relation between metaphysics and ethics, leading us to overlook the often deeply integrated nature of these aspects of a worldview. On the constructive side, meanwhile, the study foregrounds the diversity of forms that rebirth beliefs take, highlighting also the existence of ongoing interpretive debates within both the scholarly literature and certain rebirth traditions themselves. While the study's central purpose is to illuminate the meanings and ethical implications that believing in rebirth can and does have, we should not expect these meanings and implications to be neatly summarizable; rather, we see them embodied in examples distributed throughout the study as a whole.

Chapter 1

VARIETIES OF REBIRTH

Belief in rebirth, in one form or another, has been around for millennia. Some scholars have speculated that it may have arisen 'contemporaneously with the origins of human culture per se' (Long 1987: 265).[1] So, too, is it geographically diffuse, some version of it being present among myriad peoples, in numerous religions and philosophical schools of thought. Besides the major traditions deriving from South Asia, those who have professed a belief in rebirth (or at least to whom such a belief has commonly been attributed) include the following: Orphics, Pythagoreans and Platonists in ancient Greece;[2] Manichaeans, who flourished from Europe to southern China between the third and seventh centuries CE;[3] Chinese Daoists influenced by Buddhism during the fifth century CE and thereafter;[4] certain Jewish sects, especially Kabbalists from the twelfth century onwards;[5] several

---

1. See also Eylon (2003: 10): 'The belief in reincarnation seems to be as ancient as human civilization on earth.' Aurobindo conjectures that the doctrine of rebirth, 'even as it is in all appearance well-nigh as old as human thought itself, is likely also to endure as long as human beings continue to think' (1978: 1).
2. Long (1948), Guthrie (1993: esp. 164–75).
3. Williams Jackson (1925), Casadio (1992).
4. Kohn (1998; 2003: ch. 3).
5. Nemoy (1940), Scholem (1974: 344–50), Pinson (2004). Josephus (37–c. 100 CE) appears to ascribe a belief in reincarnation to the Pharisees as early as the first century CE, though the interpretation of the ascription is contentious; see the translator's commentary in Josephus (2008: 133 n.1012). According to the tenth-century Karaite exegete Jacob al-Kirkisani, reincarnation was endorsed by Anan ben David, widely regarded as the founder of Karaite Judaism, in the eighth century. The belief became a central component of Kabbalistic thought only after the appearance of the *Sefer ha-Bahir* ('Book of the Brightness') around 1180 CE. See Ogren (2009: 12, 14–15).

religious traditions largely rooted in Islam, notably the Alevis, Druze, Ismāʿīlīs and Nuṣayrīyah (or 'Alawites);[6] adherents of the syncretic Ahl-e Haqq religion based in Iranian Kurdistan;[7] Gnostic-influenced forms of Christianity, including the so-called Cathars of the eleventh to fourteenth centuries;[8] many Native American and Inuit communities;[9] a number of peoples from Africa, such as the Yorùbá, Igbo and Beng of West Africa, the Nandi of East Africa and the Betsileo of Madagascar;[10] the Jívaro people of eastern Ecuador;[11] Brazilian Spiritist and Umbanda movements from the second half of the nineteenth century onwards;[12] Melanesian peoples such as the Trobriand Islanders;[13] various followers of Pagan or Neo-Pagan paths;[14] a large number of New Age groups

6. Gimaret (2000), Werblowsky (1987: 24), Stevenson (2001: 271–4). For some cautionary remarks on terminology related to these groups, see Hodgson (1962: 5 n.4).
7. Mir-Hosseini (1994), During (1998: 116).
8. MacGregor (1978: esp. ch. 4), Quispel (2000: 190–4). I say 'so-called' because the term 'Cathars' has been used rather indiscriminately by many historians of religion to refer to a disparate collection of Christian groups who were regarded as heretical by the Inquisition. For critical analysis, see Pegg (2001; 2008: 22–6, 169–71).
9. Mills and Slobodin (1994).
10. Besterman (1930), Parrinder (1951: 115–31), Stevenson (1985, 1986), Awolalu (1996: 59–60), Sadiku (1996), Gottlieb (1998), Creider (1986), Evers (2002: 44–5). Driberg remarks that, although 'in certain areas [of Africa] the belief in reincarnation appears to have faded ... we may reasonably hold that it was formerly universal' (1936: 14). As others have noted, however, generalizations about African peoples need to be treated with extreme caution owing to Africa's immense cultural diversity (Heijke 1993: 46).
11. Stirling (1938: 114), Service (1978: 213).
12. Warren (1968), van Rossum (1993), Cavalcanti (2006).
13. Malinowski (1932: 145–52), Obeyesekere (2002: 28–37).
14. Farrar and Farrar (1985: 115–34); Hutton (1999: 392–3); Berger, Leach and Shaffer (2003: 47–8). The terms 'Paganism' and 'Neo-Paganism' generally encompass such movements (or 'paths') as Wicca, Druidry, Ásatrú (a.k.a. Heathenry, Odinism, the Northern Tradition) and Shamanism; see, e.g., York (1995) and Jennings (2002). See also the description of Paganism on the website of the Pagan Federation (2013).

and practitioners;[15] and a plethora of New Religious Movements.[16] Furthermore, it has been claimed that belief in rebirth is growing in popularity among people who would not typically associate themselves with any of the foregoing cultural or religious groups, and is becoming a 'mainstream option' in the United Kingdom and other western countries.[17]

A single book, let alone a single chapter, can hardly do justice to even a small proportion of these multifarious traditions, groups, movements and individuals; hence I do not propose to attempt a comprehensive or systematic survey. Rather, in order to provide a basis from which to venture into more specific philosophical inquiries, the present chapter sets out to offer an overview of salient themes in rebirth traditions and to introduce some useful conceptual distinctions. Without presuming to have devised an exhaustive typology, I cite selected examples to illustrate a range of similarities and differences that obtain across the traditions concerned, thereby building up a nuanced picture of the multiplex phenomenon that constitutes the subject of this book. Types of rebirth belief can be distinguished from one another along several dimensions. In this chapter I distinguish between them first in terms of their *soteriological orientations*, and then, over two further sections, in terms of the kind of connection or correlation that they suppose to exist between lifetimes in any particular succession of

15. Hanegraaff (1998: 262–75), Hammer (2004: 455–94). 'New Age' has been 'described as an umbrella term for a wide collection of phenomena' (Kemp 2004: 7). Heelas, seeking a more determinate definition, highlights the emphasis within the New Age movement upon 'inner spirituality – embedded within the self and the natural order as a whole', but admits that 'New Agers differ in how they portray the inner life' (1996: 16, 19).

16. The term 'New Religious Movement' is notoriously flexible. A representative sample of groups that are commonly placed in this category and which purport to believe in reincarnation or rebirth include: the Ancient Mystical Order of the Rosy Cross, the Association for Research and Enlightenment, Brahma Kumaris, Brotherhood of the Cross and Star, Church Universal and Triumphant, Great White Brotherhood, International Church of Ageless Wisdom, International Society for Krishna Consciousness, Kofuku-no-kagaku, Liberal Catholic Church, Radhasoami, Sathya Sai Baba movement, Self-Realization Fellowship, Soka Gakkai, Spiritual Science Church and the Theosophical Society. See Clarke (2006a, 2006b) and Chryssides (2012).

17. Waterhouse (1999). See also Toolan (1993: 34): '[T]he belief in past lives is being mainlined into [European and North American] culture at large.'

rebirths. Of the many modes of connection that could be mentioned, I have opted to highlight those which I term *retributive, affinitive* and *consanguineous* respectively. Each of these forms a broad category which could be subdivided beyond the degree of conceptual refinement that I have brought into play. But rather than try to capture every quirk and peculiarity of the traditions discussed, my aim is simply to point towards the diversity that exists, thereby guarding against any premature suppositions concerning what rebirth beliefs 'must' be like.

Soteriological Orientations

Rebirth beliefs are typically closely aligned with specific conceptions of the value and purpose of life, and these latter conceptions often envisage all of life, or human life in particular, as having a direction or goal. When the goal is conceived as a kind of salvation, or as a spiritual liberation or fulfilment, then we may meaningfully speak of a vision of life as having a *soteriological orientation*.[18] A rebirth belief need not necessarily be accompanied by such an orientation; it might simply comprise the idea that people, or other living beings, are in some sense reborn after they die, without this entailing that the process of ongoing death and rebirth is directed towards a salvific end. In this section I shall consider two main types of soteriological orientation, which I call *cessative* and *affirmatory* respectively; these will then be compared and contrasted with a third type of orientation, which is in effect *non-soteriological*. I readily admit that talk of 'types' carries with it dangers of over-simplification. However, while the glossing over of some details and idiosyncrasies is unavoidable, this can be mitigated by grounding the discussion in particular examples rather than letting it float off into 'ideal typical' abstractions.

I am borrowing the term 'cessative' from Stuart Sarbacker, who distinguishes between the '*numinous* and *cessative* dimensions of yoga and meditative practice in the Hindu and Buddhist context' (2005: 1). For my purposes the 'numinous' can be set aside, and although Hinduism and Buddhism are of central importance, it need not be with these traditions alone that the term 'cessative' is associated.

---

18. 'Soteriological' derives from the Greek *sōtēria*, 'salvation'. For previous uses of the term 'soteriological orientation', see Halbfass (1980: 288); Christiano, Swatos and Kivisto (2008: 308).

Sarbacker is concerned specifically with meditative discipline, but the idea of a cessative dimension – one that 'emphasizes the attainment of freedom through separation from phenomenal existence' (ibid.) – can be applied to a soteriological orientation to life more generally. In the context of conceptions of rebirth, it becomes the view that the flow or cycle of existence from life to death to rebirth – known as *saṃsāra* in the South Asian traditions – is not an end in itself but something ultimately to be brought to cessation.

It is sometimes assumed that a belief in rebirth is motivated by 'the instinctive love of life and desire for continued existence after death' (Dasgupta 1965: 212). Although in some cases this may be true, cessative soteriologies portray the succession of our lives as an arduous and meandering trudge that must be ended sooner or later; and if one is a spiritual adept who has dedicated one's existence to the soteriological quest, then in principle the sooner it is ended the better. This ostensibly pessimistic apprehension of worldly life is vividly depicted in a passage from the Indian *Mārkaṇḍeya Purāṇa* (*c*. third to ninth centuries CE), wherein an embryo in the womb is imagined as becoming dispirited by the recollection of its numerous previous lives. 'I won't ever do *that* again', it thinks, vowing to take precautions in its imminent lifetime to avoid having to return on any future occasion. Each of us, the text adds, 'wanders on the wheel of rebirth [*saṃsāra-cakra*] like the bucket on the wheel of a well' (11.13–15, 21, trans. O'Flaherty 1988: 98).[19] From this point of view, the goal is not to remain on the wheel, feeling thankful for yet another opportunity to experience the wonders of life, but rather to strive for 'release' (*mokṣa, mukti*).[20]

How this release or liberation is conceptualized varies between different South Asian traditions, as do understandings of how it is most effectively to be secured. One tendency is found in certain devotional movements, in which what is aimed at is an ecstatic encounter with the divine, or 'total absorption' therein, achieved by means of an intensification of amorous emotionality and the grace of one's beloved deity (McDaniel 1989; Talib 1979). An alternative tendency is towards detachment from and the progressive diminution of affective impulses.

19. See also Pargiter (1904: 70). For estimates of the *Mārkaṇḍeya Purāṇa*'s antiquity, see Pargiter (1904: xx) and Hazra (1940: 12–13).

20. The terms *mokṣa* and *mukti*, along with variants such as *vimokṣa* and *vimukti*, are common to the major traditions deriving from South Asia; see, e.g., van Buitenen (1957), Zydenbos (1983), Singh (2005) and Keown (2004: 330, 331).

In Buddhism the culmination of this process is conceived as the 'blowing out' (*nirvāṇa* in Sanskrit, *nibbāna* in Pāli) of the three fires, namely passion, hatred and delusion.[21] In 'non-dualist' Vedānta liberation is held to be precipitated by an 'immediate knowledge' of *brahman* and *ātman* – that is, by knowledge of the depth of universal being and the depth of the self, and of the identity or 'non-difference' between them – which is gained 'through proper understanding of sacred texts, not by devotion or works' (Fort 1998: 5).[22] In classical Sāṃkhya and Yoga it consists in the 'aloneness' (*kaivalya*) of the conscious subject (*puruṣa*), having realized through sustained meditation its *non*-identity with everything that constitutes the world of its experience (*prakṛti*) (Burley 2004, 2012b). In Jainism it is said to take the form of 'perfect knowledge' or 'unlimited, absolute, direct omniscience' (*kevala-jñāna*);[23] achieved by adhering to a stringent regime of ethical conduct and contemplation, this knowledge remains latent in the living soul until various contaminating factors, known as *karma*s, have been eradicated.[24]

When reflecting upon these conceptions of a final 'release' from the stream of life we should not overlook differences between the normative soteriological injunctions of a given religious tradition on the one hand and the daily lived activity of most followers of that tradition on the other. Some theorists make a distinction along these lines when they distinguish highly dedicated practitioners or 'religious virtuosos', who are often monastics or wandering mendicants, from the great majority of religious adherents, comprising various types of lay followers.[25] We should be

21. See esp. the Buddha's 'Fire Sermon' (SN IV: 19–20). As a translation of *nirvāṇa/nibbāna*, Richard Gombrich has proposed 'going out' instead of 'blowing out', 'to make it clear that the term is intransitive: the fires (of passion, hate and delusion) must go out but the term does not imply an agent who extinguishes them' (2006: xv; see also 65–70).

22. See, e.g., *Upadeśasāhasrī* 11.7 (generally attributed to Śaṅkara, c. eighth or ninth century CE): 'I am Ātman, i.e., the highest *Brahman*; I am Pure Consciousness only and always non-dual' (Mayeda 1992: 126); see also Deutsch (1966). For the idea of 'depth' in this context, see Nakagawa (2010: 333).

23. Gelblum (1986: 229), Glasenapp (2003: 44).

24. '*Karman* [or *karma*] does not here mean "deed, work", nor invisible, mystical force (*adṛṣṭa*), but a complexus of very fine matter, imperceptible to the senses, which enters into the soul and causes great changes in it' (Glasenapp 2003: 3). Cf. Jaini (1980).

25. For the distinction between 'virtuoso' (or 'heroic') religiosity and 'mass' religiosity, see Weber (2009). For discussion, see Sharot (2001).

wary, however, of assuming that the 'virtuosic' practitioners consistently do what their sacred scriptures say they ought to be doing. In particular, it would be unwise to assume that textual descriptions of recondite 'states of consciousness' necessarily correspond to the achievements of most monks and nuns or even to those of the authors of the texts themselves; these authors might simply have been basing their accounts on accepted formulations in the absence of any first-hand experience.[26]

Pertinent to these considerations is a distinction, introduced by Melford Spiro in his study of Buddhism in Burma, between what he designates *nibbanic* and *kammatic* Buddhism.[27] The first of these is so called because it is 'an ideology of radical salvation' that vigorously advocates striving for the final goal of *nibbāna* (Spiro 1982: 66). Whether the members of the monastic order who do the advocating are themselves following a strict ethical and meditative regime is a further question, but that the diligent monk (*bhikkhu*) represents the normative ideal of Burmese Buddhism and of Theravāda Buddhism more generally is hardly in doubt. *Kammatic* Buddhism, meanwhile, is 'a religion of proximate salvation'; while frequently giving lip service to the radical goal of final cessation, it in fact seeks to advance the practitioner's condition *within* the wheel of rebirth by means of prescribed ritual and ethical action (*karman* in Sanskrit, *kamma* in Pāli). 'Buddhism for most Buddhists', writes Spiro,

> is a means not so much for the extinction of desire as for its satisfaction; not so much for the cessation of rebirth as for a better rebirth; not so much for some kind of absolute Deliverance ... as for the persistence of the individuated ego in a state of sensate happiness. (67)

Nor is this situation unique to Buddhism; a comparable distinction between a normative soteriological ideal, symbolized by (even if not fully realized in) a monastic elite, and the actual day to day practice and aspirations of the society at large obtains equally prominently in other rebirth traditions (Carrithers 1989; Sharot 2001: ch. 5).

The notion of a cessative soteriological orientation is thus closely connected with the perceived normative goal of particular Indic, or more broadly South and East Asian, worldviews. For these traditions there is a

26. For some valuable words of caution in this vein, see Sharf (1995).
27. Spiro also identifies two other forms of Buddhism, namely *apotropaic* and *esoteric*, but these are not directly relevant to my present discussion.

sense in which the *process* of rebirth is indeed held to be perpetuated by 'the instinctive love of life and desire for continued existence after death' (Dasgupta, quoted above); but it would be misleading to claim that this was the motivation for the belief itself, given that the belief is integral to worldviews in which, for the most part, the succession of rebirths is conceived not as something desirable in itself but as a necessary evil to be undergone as a prelude to its eventual termination. This aim of bringing the cycle to an end contrasts with what I am calling an *affirmatory* soteriological orientation, from the perspective of which the cycle of rebirth is celebrated as something of intrinsic spiritual value. A contrast of this kind has occasionally been highlighted by placing the Indian notion of saṃsāra, conceived as 'a painful way', in opposition to what 'appears in the West, with its delight in evolution, as a way to personal consummation' (Häring and Metz 1993: ix). Such a binary opposition between 'India' and 'the West' oversimplifies both the geographical spread of the different conceptions and the intricacies internal to each of them, but the basic distinction between rebirth portrayed as a path of suffering to be decried and its portrayal as a path of spiritual evolution to be affirmed does offer a viable analytic starting point.

Among the places to look for examples of affirmatory soteriologies are certain strands of New Age and Neo-Pagan movements centred within contemporary Europe and North America. Wouter Hanegraaff identifies '*progressive spiritual evolution* considered as a process which started before birth and will continue after death' as 'the universal element in New Age ideas about survival' (1998: 262, original emphasis). Although, as Hanegraaff acknowledges, this progressive model should not be simply equated with ideas of rebirth or reincarnation, it undoubtedly provides a congenial ideological environment for such ideas. The contrast with cessative models is poetically voiced by George Trevelyan, who remarks (with allusion to a familiar biblical phrase) that 'the eastern "wheel of rebirth" is, in the West, transformed into a spiral staircase leading ultimately to "a new heaven and a new earth"' (2012: 31). Again, however, a more subtle analysis would recognize the misleadingly homogenizing implications of terms such as 'eastern' and 'the West', especially in view of the fact that certain Indian-born thinkers, most notably Aurobindo and Radhakrishnan, have been at the forefront of developing evolutionary or progressive models of rebirth.[28]

---

28. See esp. Aurobindo (1978; 2005: 659–1107), Radhakrishnan (1937: 122–3, 286–301; 1960: 183–207). See also Mukherjee (2004) and Minor (1986).

Affirmatory conceptions often characterize the series of rebirths as a 'pathway' or 'ongoing journey' without a final destination (Bloch 1998: 35; Mantin 2004: 162). Commenting on recent revivals of Pagan movements, Barbara Jane Davy writes that, 'Like Buddhists, many Pagans believe in reincarnation, but without the goal of release from rebirth' (2007: 84), an observation that need not preclude the possibility that some modern Pagans derive many of their ideas about rebirth directly or indirectly from Buddhist and other Asian traditions (Green 2001–2: 141). From a Pagan perspective each successive lifetime is held to be 'a new adventure' (Jennings 2002: 30), offering opportunities for fresh experiences, the healing of emotional wounds and the learning of new lessons either on earth or on another 'plane' (Farrar and Farrar 1985: 121). Given the absence of a final goal, the claim that these conceptions amount to a *soteriological* orientation could be disputed. Insofar as they involve a sense of progressive evolution, however, they do at least suggest an orientation *towards* increased spiritual awakening even if there is no endpoint envisaged.

The therapeutic and educational rewards of rebirth are conspicuously emphasized in New Age circles, frequently being combined with the idea that a degree of choice is exercised over the type and speed of learning that occurs and over the circumstances into which one is reborn. As one author of popular spiritual self-help books puts it, 'We have chosen to come here to learn a particular lesson that will advance us upon our spiritual, evolutionary pathway' (Hay 2004: 4). In accounts such as this, the South Asian notion of karma is either excluded entirely or reconfigured as a principle of 'education' and 'development', which enables individuals to increase knowledge and understanding 'through experience' and 'to do what should be done' (Roberts 1970: 151).

Although these New Age modifications of karma and rebirth may be relatively recent innovations, the idea that we in some sense choose the life into which we are reborn has a long pedigree, occurring among many traditional peoples as well as being vividly depicted in the final book of Plato's *Republic* (c. 380 BCE). There, in Socrates' narration, the story is told of a warrior named Er, who undergoes what in today's parlance would be called a 'near-death experience', during which he witnesses the process of souls selecting particular features of their subsequent lifetime. Socrates draws a moral lesson from the story, urging that we should choose as our next life that which will lead 'the soul to become more just'; it is by opting for a life that avoids extremes 'that a human being becomes happiest' (*Republic* 10.618d–e, 619b). In much New Age thought the motif of choosing one's rebirth is retained, though the criteria for the choice that one allegedly made are more likely to be articulated in terms of the 'patterns' that one needs to 'work on' or 'work with' (Hay 2004: 4; Cayce 2006: 9). Distinguishable from both the cessative and the affirmatory orientations that I have outlined above are various conceptions of rebirth that, since they contain neither the idea of a final spiritual goal nor that of incremental spiritual progress, seem not to be soteriological orientations of any kind. The conceptual boundaries are not well defined, however, for the sorts of non-soteriological orientations that I have in mind are often affirmatory in the sense of perceiving life on earth as something to be affirmed and celebrated rather than to be lamented as a vale of tears. Several African varieties of belief in rebirth can be situated in this category, and hence commentators have tended to contrast these with forms of the belief derived from Asia. 'African and Eastern conceptions of reincarnation are poles apart', writes Robin Horton, 'the African ideal tend[ing] to be one of endless return', whereas 'the Eastern ideal is one of successive returns which nonetheless progress toward and culminate in escape from "the wheel"' (1993: 180).[29]

Some scholars have questioned whether terms such as 'reincarnation' are applicable to African contexts on the grounds that the African beliefs diverge too radically from more paradigmatic forms. 'It is almost certain', contends E. Bọlaji Idowu in a study of the Yorùbá of West Africa, 'that there is no belief in reincarnation in the classical sense among the Yoruba' (1966: 194). In a later book he makes the claim both broader and more categorical: 'In African belief, there is no reincarnation in the classical sense. One can only speak of partial or, more precisely, apparent reincarnation, if the word must be used at all' (1973: 187; cf. Mbiti 1990: 159). Innocent Onyewuenyi has gone further, complaining of the 'imposition of the "belief in reincarnation" on Africans' by western academics and administrators, and also by '"educated" Africans' (1996: 44). There is, of course, no reason why words such as 'reincarnation' or 'rebirth' *must* be used. But we might

---

29. See also Parrinder's claim that 'the African's attitude is world-affirming not world-renouncing' (1974: 138), a claim that has been endorsed by others with reference to particular African communities (Stevenson 1985: 15–16; Awolalu 1996: 59–60). Similar points have been made in connection with Native American beliefs. As Warren Jefferson observes, 'Among [North American] Indian people there was no desire for escape or salvation. To the contrary, their goal was to be reborn and to have their ancestors return to live among them' (2008: 51).

wonder why their use should be precluded in deference to some presumed 'classical sense'. Idowu and Onyewuenyi are deriving their definition of reincarnation from an encyclopaedia entry, according to which 'Reincarnation is the passage of the soul from one body to another ... the lot of the soul on earth being determined by its behaviour in a former life' (Thomas 1921: 425).[30] It is the divergence of African forms of belief from this definition that generates the concerns typified by Idowu and Onyewuenyi. But there is no obvious reason why this definition should be treated as normative for all varieties of belief in rebirth or reincarnation. Part of my purpose in this chapter is to bring out the heterogeneity of forms that rebirth beliefs take, thereby assuaging the impulse to adopt an unduly restrictive understanding of what counts as such a belief.

A striking feature of the outlooks of several African peoples is that a notion of rebirth – or, at any rate, a notion that comes very close to one of rebirth – exists alongside the idea that the spirits of the dead reside permanently in a 'spirit world' or 'afterlife'. The Beng of Ivory Coast, for example, maintain that, 'Once someone dies, the *neneŋ*, or soul, is transformed into a *wru*, or spirit. Yet when that person is reincarnated as someone else, the *wru* nevertheless continues to exist as an ancestor [in the spirit world]' (Gottlieb 2004: 81). It is the co-existence of beliefs of this sort that prompts Idowu to suggest, with reference to Africa, that we can at most 'speak of partial or, more precisely, apparent reincarnation'. Onyewuenyi responds by asserting that 'Reincarnation cannot be partial or apparent. Either it is or it is not' (1996: 39). Instead of describing someone as an ancestor's reincarnation, he proposes alternative descriptions, such as 'the "vital influence" or the "life-share" or "personal ray," or "living-perpetuation" of the ancestor' (44). Meanwhile, Gottlieb, again referring to the Beng, speaks of their positing 'a dual, rather than an either/or, existence' and thereby allowing 'that a being may exist simultaneously at two very different levels of reality – the one visible and earthly, the other invisible and ghostly' (2004: 81–2). Similarly, Jane Tapsubei Creider, who was raised among the Nandi of East Africa, avows the belief that 'each person has a counterpart in the spirit world' and yet is also the reincarnation of that spirit; hence spirits reincarnate on earth while nevertheless remaining

30. The passage is slightly misquoted in Idowu (1966: 194), 'on earth' being erroneously replaced with 'in each', and the misquotation is repeated by Onyewuenyi (1996: 29). The passage is quoted accurately and at greater length in Parrinder (1951: 115), from which Idowu may have derived it.

in the spirit world. As if that were not already complicated enough, she adds that 'you may choose to come back as more than one new baby, for one spirit may have a number of reincarnations' (1986: 2). These issues of parallel existence and multiple simultaneous rebirth will receive further attention in Chapter 3. At the present juncture it is sufficient to observe that this conception of ongoing exchange between earth and the spirit world is not bound up with any obviously progressive or soteriological orientation. Rather, there is 'a cyclical trajectory, with no beginning and no end, and death itself is another kind of life' (Gottlieb 2006: 152).

Retributive Correlations

Already, in the above discussion of soteriological orientations, the concept of karma has been introduced. Almost synonymous with the idea that morally relevant actions have retributive repercussions for the agent (either in the present life or in a future one), this concept has become closely aligned with that of rebirth in the popular imagination. The intermingling of these concepts is a consequence of the predominant association of rebirth beliefs with the major religious traditions deriving from South Asia, especially Hinduism and Buddhism, in which retributive karma has been a prevalent motif. So influential has this association been that even when it is admitted that other, non-retributive, conceptions of rebirth obtain elsewhere, these other conceptions are often equated with relatively 'crude' or 'primitive' prototypes out of which the more ethically 'advanced' and philosophically 'systematic' versions – evinced especially in South and East Asia but also in ancient Greece – 'must' have evolved.[31] A speculative historical thesis along these lines, developed in considerable detail by Gananath Obeyesekere, will be discussed at length in Chapter 4. For our present purposes two points are worth emphasizing: first, that the doctrine of retributive karma is only one of several formulations of the connection between lifetimes in rebirth traditions, a point that will be brought out in the present chapter as a whole; and second, that even the doctrine of retributive karma itself is not a uniform phenomenon, but comes with different understandings of the correlation between acts performed in one lifetime and consequences experienced in

---

31. See, e.g., Mead (1912: esp. 162, 170), Tatacharya (1967: 48).

another. Elaborating this latter point is the purpose of the present section.

Debate over when and where the first indications of a combined doctrine of karma and rebirth are to be found in the South Asian sources is ongoing. The question of the doctrine's origin has long been described as 'one of the most difficult questions in the religious history of India' (Whitney 1874: 61).[32] Some scholars argue that it can be traced to Vedic compositions prior to the Upaniṣads (Horsch 1971; Tull 1989). Others maintain that it originated outside Vedic Brahmanism among religious groups from the eastern region of the Gangetic plain and was gradually incorporated into mainstream Brahmanical religion from around the time when the earliest Upaniṣads were being composed (Bronkhorst 2007: Part 2). Although I shall not be trying to resolve such troublesome historical questions in this study, the task of highlighting the diversity of the doctrine's articulations will be served by citing a few of the early sources.

It remains a live question whether a doctrine of rebirth is discernible in the oldest known text of the Vedic religion, the Ṛgveda (c. 1400–1000 BCE). While most exegetes have assumed that its 'Funeral Hymn' calls upon the crematory fire to return the deceased individual *to* his ancestors (Ṛgveda 10.16.5),[33] it has recently been argued that the hymn's grammar allows for it to be read also as a request for the deceased to be released *from* the ancestors to inhabit the earth again (Jurewicz 2004: 52–3). Since both readings are grammatically viable, the interpretive issue is unlikely to be definitively resolved.[34] Less contentious is the idea that a somewhat later Vedic source, the Śatapatha Brāhmaṇa (c. sixth century BCE), contains a passage in which rebirth on earth is linked with imagery of the succession of the seasons: 'Now the spring, assuredly, comes into life again out of the winter, for out of the one the other is born again: therefore he who knows this, is indeed born again in this world' (1.5.3.14, trans. Eggeling 1882–1900 I: 148).[35] Here

32. See also Salomon (1982: 410) and Bodewitz (1997: 583).
33. See, e.g., Jamison and Brereton (2014 III: 1395).
34. The operative term in the hymn is *pitṛbhyo*, which can indeed be read either as the dative (literally, 'to the fathers', meaning 'to the ancestors') or as the ablative ('from the fathers', 'from the ancestors').
35. For the Sanskrit text, see Gippert (2008: Part 5). The sixth or seventh century BCE is the most common scholarly dating for the Śatapatha Brāhmaṇa (see, e.g., Dasgupta 1927: 424), though much earlier dates have also been proposed. For discussion, see Bryant (2001: 246–8, 256–7).

it is by knowledge and not as a consequence of karma or the petitions of one's mourners that rebirth is precipitated, though the context of ritual instruction in which the passage appears affords few resources for further interpretation. Some commentators have conjectured that it probably signifies a father's being 'reborn' in his male heir (Bodewitz 1997: 592–3; Horsch 1971: 120).

It is in the earliest of the major Upaniṣads that more explicit references to rebirth emerge, but still the doctrine of karma is not always evident. While the dating of these texts remains only approximate, it is generally agreed that the two earliest Upaniṣads, the Bṛhadāraṇyaka and Chāndogya, can be placed in the seventh or sixth century BCE, 'give or take a century or so' (Olivelle 1998: 12).[36] Images designed to illustrate the idea of rebirth in the Bṛhadāraṇyaka Upaniṣad include that of a caterpillar reaching out from the tip of one blade of grass to another. In an analogous way, it is said, the 'self' (ātman), when the body has been discarded, 'reaches out to a new foothold and draws itself onto it' (4.4.3, trans. Olivelle 1998: 121). Immediately following this passage is one containing a different analogy, according to which the self, like a weaver making another garment after finishing the previous one, 'makes for himself a different figure that is newer and more attractive – the figure of a forefather, or of a Gandharva, or of a god, or of Prajāpati, or of brahman, or else the figure of some other being' (4.4.4, trans. Olivelle 1998: 121).

Though divergent in some respects, these images of the caterpillar and the weaver are similar insofar as they both depict the one who is reborn as playing an active role in determining the form of the next rebirth: the caterpillar reaches for another blade of grass, the weaver creates a new garment. As in the passage from the Śatapatha Brāhmaṇa, however, neither image suggests that the newly acquired bodily form depends on the ethical quality of past-life actions. Indeed, as Bronkhorst notes (2007: 122), the idea of the weaver constructing ever more attractive garments for himself would be at odds with that of subjection to an ineluctable law of retribution. Not only are none of the types of 'figure' (rūpa) named in the passage human beings, but all of them would be regarded as spiritually higher forms of existence – 'heavenly' rather than earthly beings. Thus, although the theme of weaving one's own destiny has been fused with that of retributive

36. This, of course, would make them roughly contemporaneous with, or even earlier than, the Śatapatha Brāhmaṇa (provided we accept the most common dating of the latter).

karma in more recent popular accounts of the doctrine,[37] there is no indication in these particular excerpts from the *Bṛhadāraṇyaka Upaniṣad* that inauspicious behaviour will result in a 'lower' rebirth. In this respect they are in tension with other passages from the same Upaniṣad in which the sage Yājñavalkya is said to declare that one 'turns into something good [*puṇya*] by good action and into something bad [*pāpa*] by bad action' (3.2.13, 4.4.5, trans. Olivelle 1998: 81, 121).[38]

Even this latter declaration is ambiguous and, as one scholar has recently put it, 'frustratingly terse' (Lindquist 2011: 44). Does it mean that one becomes a more virtuous person by doing good and a more vicious one by doing evil; or does it mean instead that those who do good will be blessed with a 'pleasant' rebirth, characterized by such things as health, status and prosperity, whereas those who act badly will be plagued by illness, ignominy and poverty? Though not referring explicitly to this particular passage, Aurobindo highlights a more general ambiguity in the doctrine of karma when he complains of a pervasive conflation between the concepts of *moral* goodness and badness on the one hand, and those of *hedonic* goodness and badness (i.e., pleasure and pain) on the other (1978: 111). There is, we might suppose, an obvious sense in which doing good is morally edifying and doing evil has a tendency to corrupt, but to contend that a necessary connection exists between morality and pleasure is to exhibit a very different line of thought. Yet it is precisely this latter contention that is built into the long tradition of belief in retributive karma.

The term *karma* is the nominative singular form of the Sanskrit noun *karman*, denoting, in its widest sense, 'any action, whether moral or immoral, intended or unintended, voluntary or involuntary'

---

37. See, e.g., Blavatsky (1888 I: 639): 'Those who believe in *Karma* have to believe in *destiny*, which, from birth to death, every man is weaving thread by thread around himself, as a spider does his cobweb.' See also other Theosophical and Anthroposophical literature, such as Blavatsky (1987: 210), Leslie-Smith (1990: 41), Steiner (1977: 36). The spider motif echoes *Śvetāśvatara Upaniṣad* 6.10 (Olivelle 1998: 431), only there it is the 'one God' (*ekā devaḥ*) who surrounds himself with his own threads.

38. See also *Bṛhadāraṇyaka Upaniṣad* 4.4.6: 'A man who's attached goes with his action [*karman*], to that very place to which his mind and character cling. Reaching the end of his action, of whatever he has done in this world – From that world he returns back to this world, back to action' (Olivelle 1998: 121, line breaks omitted).

(Pappu 1987b: 2). In the context of what has come to be known as the *doctrine* of karma it designates, more narrowly, a morally evaluable action plus the potential of that action to engender repercussions for the experience or well-being of the agent. As Aurobindo puts it, 'our action has in some degree the motion of recoil of the boomerang and cycles back towards the will that has cast it on the world' (1978: 112), this recoil effect being liable to happen sometime after the action's commission, often in a future life (Krishan 1997: 4). Analogies of sowing seeds by one's actions and later reaping the fruits thereof are pervasive in traditional expositions.[39]

In Buddhist traditions the term *karma* is explicitly understood to encompass the intention behind or volition with which the action is performed; hence it has been defined as 'volition and that which is effected by it' (*Abhidharmakośa* 4.1, quoted in Griffiths 1982: 281).[40] Since one's good (or 'wholesome') actions are held to produce merit and one's bad ('unwholesome') actions to produce demerit, the analogy of a 'bank account of karma' has often been invoked as a model (Schlieter 2013). In Hindu, Jain and Sikh traditions, as well as in Buddhism, the fructifying of merit in pleasant and of demerit in unpleasant experience is commonly regarded as an operation intrinsic to the very structure of the universe, and hence the phrase *law of karma* is widely used to denote it.[41]

The forms of correlation that are conceived as obtaining between actions and retributive consequences are manifold. Everyday expressions of the belief usually leave the nature of the supposed offence vague; it is declared simply that the one who is now suffering some disadvantage or misfortune must have done *something* to deserve it, if not in this life then in a former one.[42] Scriptural sources, meanwhile,

---

39. See, e.g., SN I: 227: 'By you ... has the seed been sown; / Thus you will experience the fruit' (Bodhi 2000: 328). See also Keyes (1983b: 262–3), *Dhammapada* 1 (Carter and Palihawadana 1987: 13, 89–94), Krishan (1983).

40. Vasubandhu, the author of the *Abhidharmakośa*, is here following AN III: 415, which reads: 'It is volition ... that I call kamma. For having willed, one acts by body, speech, or mind' (Bodhi 2012: 963). See also McDermott (1980: 182).

41. 'Whatever the ontological constitution of *karman* may be, the law of *karman* is a universal law; it pervades the whole universe and is coextensive with it almost by definition' (Panikkar 1972: 34). See also Lopez (2008: 21–2).

42. Relevant anthropological accounts include Sharma (1973: 351), Dalal (2000), Staples (2011: 547).

have been more meticulous in associating specific conditions with specific misdeeds. There are in such texts various degrees of 'proximity' or 'symmetry' discernible between the deed and its consequences; or, to use other metaphors, there are different extents to which the consequences 'echo' or 'mirror' the deed. In some instances the agent is said to suffer a fate that closely resembles the harm he or she inflicted upon someone else; in other instances the form of retribution, or in some cases reward, is more distantly related. An illustrative story from Buddhist legend is that of the Buddha's disciple Moggallāna, who allegedly died at the hands of highway robbers because he, in a previous life, had killed his blind parents while pretending to be a highway robber himself. Despite having acquired supernatural powers through resolute spiritual practice in his life as the Buddha's disciple, he was obliged to accept the just deserts of the law of karma.[43]

Another Buddhist source offering an exceptionally rich supply of examples to illustrate the idea of symmetry between deed and consequence is the Chinese *Zuiye yingbao jing* (c. fifth or early sixth century CE).[44] The text's setting is the familiar one of the Buddha sermonizing to a large audience, which, since this is a work of Mahāyāna Buddhism, comprises 'bodhisattvas, dragon kings, and gods' in addition to the standard retinue of monks, nuns and lay followers (Kohn 1998: 26). Unusually for such a text, the Buddha is depicted as responding with a specific answer to each of twenty questions asked by a bodhisattva, instead of merely presenting a number of lists in response to a single question. The bodhisattva's questions concern the relation between actions in an earlier and experiences in a later life. At one point, for example, he asks why someone might encounter a situation in which he suffers from severe exposure at high altitude, 'the cold wind blowing, and his skin and flesh getting cut and torn, wishing for death but unable to die' (*Zuiye yingbao jing* 17.451b, quoted in Kohn 1998: 27). The Buddha's reply is that the person in question was a bandit in a past life, 'obstructing the road, cutting and tearing the clothes off people and leaving others to die from exposure in the cold months of winter'. He

---

43. This version of the story appears in Buddhaghosa's commentary (fifth century CE) on *Dhammapada* 137 (Warren 1896: 222–5). For discussion, see Keown (1996: 341–2).

44. This is an abbreviated version of the title, the full title being *Foshuo zuiye yingbao jiaohua diyu jing* ('Sūtra Preached by the Buddha on Retribution for Sinful Actions and the Religious Transformation of These in Hell') (Kohn 1998: 26).

adds that such a person 'will be reborn again as an ox or sheep, suffering unbearable pain from the cutting of its skin',[45] before ending the reply with a moral injunction: 'Thus be warned and abstain from this sin!' Evidently, the emphasis on desisting from prohibited behaviour is central to this text, as it is to many other genres of expository literature concerning karma and rebirth.

Analogous affirmations of relatively symmetrical correlations between act and consequence are found outside South and East Asian sources in the Neoplatonist tradition.[46] Plotinus (third century CE), who typifies this tradition, asserts that rulers who abuse their power become slaves, misusers of money become poor and murderers are themselves destined to be murdered. Moreover, men who murder their mothers will become women and be murdered by their own son, and 'one who has raped a woman will be a woman in order to be raped' (*Enneads* 3.2.13; 1979: 83). Elsewhere, Plotinus, like Socrates in Plato's *Phaedo* (81e–82c), avers that people who have lived in servitude to their sensual desires will become animals 'corresponding in species to the particular temper of the life – ferocious animals where the sensuality has been accompanied by a certain measure of spirit, gluttonous and lascivious animals where all has been appetite and satiation of appetite' (*Enneads* 3.4.2; 1956: 186).[47] This way of thinking, which abounds also in Hindu and Buddhist sources, combines the theme of retribution with that of dominant character traits. The theme of retribution is present inasmuch as, within the traditions concerned, being reborn as an animal instead of a human being is construed as a kind of punishment; yet the type of animal that one will become is determined by an affinity of character. A form of poetic justice is thus envisaged.

The motif of retributive animal rebirth is especially prominent in the genre of Brahmanical Hindu law books known as the Dharma Śāstras (Rocher 1980). In the best known of these, the *Mānava Dharmaśāstra* (*c.* second or third century CE), we find examples of various kinds of

45. The text leaves it unclear whether these animal rebirths are to be endured prior or subsequent to the human life in which exposure on a mountain is suffered.

46. For discussion of possible Indian influence on Neoplatonism, see Tripathi (1982).

47. Plotinus, unlike Plato, also explicitly affirms the idea of rebirth as a plant for those in whom 'only or mainly the vegetative principle was active' (*Enneads* 3.4.2; 1956: 186).

correlation, some of which are 'substantive', drawing upon stereotypical character traits or modes of behaviour associated with particular animal species, and others of which are 'purely formal and poetic', relying on punning wordplay or invented etymologies (Yelle 2010: 187). The substantive variety includes such claims as that grain thieves become rats, stealers of meat become vultures, stealers of deer or elephants become wolves, horse thieves become tigers, thieves of fruit and flowers become monkeys, and so on (*Mānava Dharmaśāstra* 12.63–67). In these and other cases the relevant associations are forms of dietary and predatory behaviour in which the named animals characteristically engage.

Of numerous instances of karma-related wordplay that could be mentioned, an especially pithy example is the pronouncement that '"Me he (*mām sa*) will eat in the next world, whose meat (*māmsa*) I eat in this world" – this, the wise declare, is what gave the name to and discloses the true nature of "meat" (*māmsa*)' (5.55, trans. Olivelle 2005: 140).[48] Here the purported correlation exploits the homophony between the Sanskrit term for 'flesh' or 'meat' (*māmsa*) and the conjunction of 'me' and 'he' (*mām sa*).[49] Similar verbal devices are ubiquitous in Indian and other classical sources in connection both with rebirth and with other themes.[50] They contribute, we might say, to the 'poetry of life', dissolving boundaries between imaginative *jeux de mots* and serious moral and legal instruction.[51]

Affinitive and Consanguineous Continuities

Of the various non-retributive forms of connection between lives to which certain rebirth traditions subscribe, I shall here draw attention to two broad categories, which I call *affinitive* and *consanguineous*

---

48. This verse is quoted with approval in, among other places, *Yogaśāstra* 3.26 by the Jain scholar Hemacandra (2002: 53–4). An almost identical passage occurs at *Mahābhārata* 13.117.34a. See also *Mānava Dharmaśāstra* 5.33.

49. The homophony is ingeniously mimicked in an English idiom by Doniger and Smith in their rendering of the verse (1991: 104): 'He whose *meat* in this world do I eat will in the other world *me eat*.'

50. For examples, see Gonda (1955–6), Bronkhorst (2001), Yelle (2011).

51. I here borrow the phrase 'poetry of life' (*die Poesie des Lebens*) from Goethe (1998: 20, maxim no. 171). Cf. Clack (1995: 114).

respectively. They are not mutually exclusive, and neither are they necessarily incompatible with retributive conceptions of the connection between lives. Indeed, we have already seen in the previous section notions of retribution being blended with notions of the continuity of predominant character traits and behaviour patterns across lifetimes, and continuities of these latter sorts are among those for which I am using the term 'affinitive'. I shall say more about this category before coming to that of consanguineous rebirth.

Relevant to affinitive rebirth is a distinction between *retributive* and *developmental* karma, made by Ian Stevenson, who devoted much of his long career to investigating alleged memories of previous lives (a topic to be discussed in Chapter 2). By 'developmental karma' Stevenson means 'the carry-over from one life to another of personality traits', which 'include not only a particular body of cognitive information, but also behavioral qualities including aptitudes in the moral sphere' (1977: 323). From his copious case studies it is evident that the types of traits Stevenson holds to be transferable from one lifetime to another are plentiful. They include not only psychological, emotional and behavioural characteristics, such as phobias, obsessive interests, talents and skills, but also bodily features such as birthmarks, scars, congenital abnormalities and diseases.[52] The term 'developmental karma' is thus somewhat narrow for his purposes in two respects. First, the sorts of characteristics purportedly transferred from one lifetime to the next do not themselves invariably undergo any development and neither do they necessarily constitute a development of the individual concerned; in some instances they are merely repeated. For example, a phobia or a bodily impairment can allegedly be 'carried over' without this implying that any development (in the condition or in the person) has taken place. Second, the term 'karma', having become virtually synonymous with the idea of ethically significant actions generating retributive consequences for the agent, is liable to be misleading when what is at issue is the continuation of traits that have no distinctively ethical bearing. It would thus be more felicitous to speak of trans-life *correspondences* or (as I am suggesting) *affinitive continuities* between lifetimes, and then to specify in particular cases what the salient affinities are.

Rather than trying to discuss all the kinds of affinity between lives that are instantiated in rebirth traditions, I shall here cite an example

---

52. Stevenson has written about these matters in numerous places: e.g., Stevenson (1974, 1977, 2001 and esp. 1997a).

that illustrates one way of conceptualizing the relation between rebirth and bodily impairment, a way which, taken on its own, leaves aside the question of moral desert that arises in connection with retributive conceptions. Instead of seeing, for instance, a malformed or missing limb as a punishment for some sin performed in a previous life, the impairment may be regarded as an inheritance or, to use Stevenson's term, a 'carry-over' from a life in which an accident resulted in the limb being damaged or severed. A case in point is that of a Burmese girl who, having been born with the lower part of her right leg missing, was believed by her parents to be the reincarnation of another Burmese girl, who had died when she was run over by a train. It was maintained within the community that the train had severed the girl's right leg before crushing her trunk and that this mutilation was reprised, or reiterated, in the succeeding life (Stevenson 1997b: 122–3).

The compatibility between an affinitive connection of the sort just described and retributive conceptions of rebirth is clear from the fact that there would be no incongruity in the parents of the child with a partially formed leg supposing that what has been 'carried over' is in fact the residue of a karmic consequence; that is, they could maintain that the girl's having been hit by a train in her previous life was itself a retributive effect of something done, perhaps in a life prior to that one, and that the 'debt' is still being 'paid off' in the present life. The important point to note, however, is that there is no necessity for the retributive view to get a foothold here. There are, as we might put it, multiple aspects under which belief in rebirth enables a bodily impairment or any other human characteristic to be comprehended, though the conceptual possibilities will inevitably be constrained by the surrounding cultural assumptions.

Consanguineous rebirth is the phenomenon of being reborn within one's own immediate or extended family (McClelland 2010: 229). Belief in rebirth of this sort is remarkably common, being especially prevalent in certain African, Native American and Inuit communities (Parrinder 1951: ch. 10; Mills 1994b: 27).[53] A well-documented custom practised by the Yorùbá of West Africa is that of naming the first male child born after the death of its grandfather *Babátúndé*, literally 'father returns'; correspondingly, the first female child born after the death of its grandmother will be named *Ìyábò* or *Yétúndé*, 'mother returns'

---

53. Bronkhorst notes that this belief 'is attested in ethnographic literature pertaining to all the continents' (1998: 9). See also Mauss (1969: 137–8), a passage from which is translated into English in Allen (1985: 33).

(Idowu 1966: 195–6).⁵⁴ The Igbo, too, have traditionally given to their children names such as *Nne-Nna* ('mother of her father') and *Nna-Nna* ('father of his father'), indicating 'the return of specific ancestors' (Onyewuenyi 1996: 22–3). It is not only in names but also in other terms of address that the rebirth belief shows itself. In the case of the Nandi of East Africa, for instance, 'a man may call his son (named after a deceased brother of the man's father) "father," and the child may call his father "my child"' (Creider and Creider 1984: 539). Aside from tending to create a confusing impression for outsiders, such practices have significant implications for the community's awareness of and relationship with its own past. The names and epithets accorded to children go along with a perceived presence of former generations in the living population, thereby serving to keep alive the biographies of those former generations; consequently, a deeper recollection of shared history is perpetuated among the Nandi than among nearby communities who lack the belief in rebirth. 'By making the past a part of the everyday interactional present, it is not simply remembered, but is continually made real and relived' (ibid.: 542).

The process of establishing which ancestor has been reincarnated in a given child varies from one cultural group to another. Looking for indicative birthmarks or other bodily signs is one widespread practice among both African and a number of other indigenous peoples (Stevenson 1985; Mills 1994a). Creider describes how the fact that her younger brother's left eye was closed when he was born was understood by the Nandi as a sign of his being the reincarnation of his deceased grandmother, who 'had been blind in her left eye since childhood' (1986: 4). A similar example is given by Peter Freuchen, who lived for many years with a Greenland Inuit community. When his Inuit wife gave birth to a son, it was generally accepted that the mother's grandfather, having died a few months earlier, had now been reborn. The telltale signs included 'a slight squint in the very same eye that [the child's great-grandfather] had lost to the cannibals in Baffin Land' (Freuchen 1961: 207). Among these and many other peoples for whom belief in consanguineous rebirth has a place, characteristics of a given ancestor are held to be exhibited in a child's behaviour as well as in its bodily appearance. Members of these communities, unlike people from cultures in which the concept of rebirth does not obtain, are apt to view physical and behavioural resemblances not as – or not *merely*

54. See also Parrinder (1956–7: 265), Awolalu (1996: 60), Sadiku (1996: 134).

as – instances of genetically inherited traits, but as manifesting a more pervasive continuity. As Creider witnesses her brother growing up, she notices such things as his placid temperament and gentle voice, his 'way of casting aspersions with his eyes when you said something he didn't like or didn't believe', and recognizes these as expressions of the grandmother reborn in him (1986: 5).[55]

A consequence of such a belief, displayed in these ways of perceiving likenesses in people, is the strengthening of webs of connection between members of a family and a wider kin network, the interweaving of biographical narratives across multiple generations. With reference to certain Native American cultures, Mills speaks of their being 'honeycombed with cases [of rebirth], linking families and "individuals" back and forth generation after generation, or reincarnation after reincarnation' (2001: 322 n. 4). Children are conceptualized as possessing layered personalities, harbouring complex histories of lives previously lived (cf. Gupta 2002: 36). Often, in African societies and elsewhere, it is by older members of the community that children are informed of the details of their former lives (Oboler 1985: 49; Creider 1986: 10), though in some instances a child is regarded as already possessing knowledge of these details (Stevenson 1986: 209). Unsurprisingly, the ways in which children are conceptualized within a culture have implications for, and are actualized in, the kinds of treatment they receive from those around them, a theme that will be given further attention in Chapter 3 and towards the end of Chapter 4.

Concluding Remarks

By delving into the vast gamut of rebirth beliefs that have existed in various times and places the present chapter has begun to show some of the diversity within that gamut. The lines of demarcation between what is and what is not a belief in rebirth are porous, and the terminology concerning this area of human religious and cultural life is fluid. Notwithstanding the assumption of some commentators that there is a 'classical' sense of the notion of rebirth or reincarnation, deployable as a conceptual paradigm, it remains highly questionable whether any such tightly circumscribed sense could usefully be delineated. Trying to pin

---

55. For insightful discussion of Creider's autobiography in relation to notions of cross-cultural identity, see Hogan and Hogan (1998).

down a definition that would suffice for all cases is unlikely to be either viable or helpful, yet by attending to the range of phenomena that have, in popular or scholarly discourse, been referred to as beliefs in rebirth, we notice amid the variety certain 'family resemblances', 'a complicated network of similarities overlapping and criss-crossing', to borrow a well-known analogy from Wittgenstein (2009a: §§66–7).[56]

Recognizing the multiplicity of rebirth beliefs is not a license for brushing aside contentious issues, such as those which surround the application of the term 'reincarnation' in the context of traditional forms of African religion. On the contrary, it prompts us, when seeking to understand the nature of the beliefs in question, to look and see how they manifest in the lives of those who hold them rather than placing all the weight on whether the beliefs conform to some imagined precise sense of the term. The danger in discussions of rebirth or reincarnation is often that of presuming too quickly that we know perfectly well what this concept must consist in. The present chapter has been an attempt to open up and explicate some important aspects of the concept in ways that make room for the philosophical inquiries that are to follow.

---

56. Cf. Hick (1976: 388): '[T]he notion of rebirth is a family of concepts.'

Chapter 2

REMEMBERING HAVING LIVED BEFORE?

Remembering, like believing, is a variegated phenomenon. There are many ways of remembering and we remember many kinds of things. In some instances we recall something voluntarily; in others a memory just comes to us, or we 'relive' an episode from our past. We may, on occasions, *try* to remember but the attempt is not always successful. Remembering sometimes involves mental imagery – visual, auditory or perhaps in another sensory modality – though it would be a mistake to suppose that it must always do so; as Gilbert Ryle was apt to say, 'there is no "must" about it' (2009: 250). We frequently make assertions on the basis of memory, though sometimes our remembering consists simply in *doing* something competently: singing a song (remembering the words), playing a game (remembering the rules), dancing the tango (remembering the steps). A common temptation for philosophers is, as Norman Malcolm observes, 'to concentrate on a portion of the total range and fix on it as "memory in the fullest sense" or as "genuine" memory. But these stipulations are unjustified' (1977: 79).

The claims of certain people to remember having lived another life are normally far from philosophers' minds when reflecting upon the various forms that remembering takes. But these claims add a further reminder that we should not take it for granted that we know what it means to say that someone is *remembering*. Since remembering can be many kinds of things, attention needs to be paid to the context in which terms such as 'memory' and 'remember' are at work if we are to comprehend the meaning of relevant utterances. In the absence of that attentiveness, the philosophical temptation that Malcolm highlights, to pick out only 'a portion of the total range' and stipulate that this is what memory *is*, is liable to lead to hasty judgements concerning past-life memory claims. It is liable, in fact, to lead to the very polarization of debate that we find in much of the philosophical literature on this topic. On one side are those who see no sense in the claim to remember a previous life, because (they suppose) 'our concept' – or '*the* concept' – of memory cannot meaningfully be applied in such cases. On the other side are those who assume that the concept can in principle be applied without any difficulty, the only question – or the main question – being that of how strong the evidence is to show whether certain people do indeed remember previous lives; the logically prior question of what it *means* to claim, or to believe, that someone (perhaps oneself) is remembering a previous life then gets pushed aside in the rush to make pronouncements on the quality and quantity of the 'evidence'.

This chapter will examine the debate over the intelligibility of claims to remember having lived before, highlighting the central points of divergence. It is a debate that, having historically been tightly bound up with questions of personal identity and of the criteria for regarding someone as the same person over time, has for the most part been conducted through the medium of philosophical thought experiments. Despite being intended to sharpen the issues by disentangling them from messy cultural and doctrinal matters, the use of such thought experiments tends, for that very reason, to allow precisely the factors that give sense to a belief in rebirth to drop out of sight. To counter such abstractive strategies, I shall in the penultimate section of the chapter examine two particular cases that illustrate certain features of beliefs in rebirth, this approach of attending to particulars being one that will recur in subsequent chapters.

'Infamous Puzzle Cases'

The heavy reliance on more or less imaginative thought experiments has been a central feature of debates over the metaphysics of personal identity since the inception of this area of philosophical inquiry in the seventeenth century. Constituting a distinctive genre of philosophical thought experiments, they have been dubbed 'the infamous puzzle cases of the personal identity literature' (Martin 1992: 182).[1] Some philosophers take a dim view of such thought experiments, comparing them to the construction of fantasy or science fiction stories, from which little or nothing of philosophical value can be inferred. One such critic, Peter Hacker, consigns the sorts of thought experiment

---

1. The use of the term 'puzzle cases' in this context goes back at least as far as Flew (1951). See also Shoemaker (1959: 870–1).

in question, along with extravagant narratives from literary fiction, to the same category as the belief in reincarnation itself. 'Since time immemorial', he writes, 'human beings have fantasized about metempsychosis, the transmigration of souls. A variant of the idea is patent in Locke's supposition of the intelligibility of the prince awakening "in the body" of the cobbler, having retained all his memories' (Hacker 2007: 301). While observing that this notion of a mind being transferred 'from one body to another' may be used for comic effect or as an eerie or terrifying theme in a fictional story, Hacker doubts whether these fictions make sense.

Regardless of whether the term being used is 'metempsychosis', 'transmigration', 'reincarnation' or 'rebirth', it might be deemed premature to lump the associated beliefs together with philosophical and narrative 'fantasies' and to dismiss the whole bag as confused or nonsensical, especially if one has not taken much trouble to examine how the beliefs in question are integrated into the lives of those who hold them. Indeed, we might suspect that when a philosopher concludes (or assumes) that what millions of people believe to be true is actually precluded on *a priori* logical grounds, there is a good chance that the philosopher and the believers are not talking about the same thing (cf. Daniels 1990: 501). To voice this suspicion need not be to propose an argument *ad populum* (*pace* MacIntosh 1992: 247); that is, it need not involve assuming that the mere number of believers adds weight to the case for a belief's veracity. But if we subscribe to anything like a principle of hermeneutical charity, we should take pains to ensure that we are not rashly dismissing as unintelligible a belief or form of discourse whose sense would become clearer to us when considered in its surrounding cultural milieu.[2]

Since a good deal of philosophical thinking about the intelligibility or possibility of rebirth has been guided, or misguided, by the 'infamous puzzle cases', it will be necessary to dwell a little longer on the sorts of cases that some philosophers have held to be relevant. John Locke, to whom Hacker refers, is widely acclaimed as having initiated the philosophical debate over personal identity in its recognizably modern form,[3] a form that makes abundant use of the puzzle cases. In his *Essay concerning Human Understanding*, Locke famously deploys

2. A version of the principle of charity is pithily formulated by Quine (1975: 304) as follows: 'The more absurd the doctrine attributed to someone, *ceteris paribus*, the less the likelihood that we have well construed his words.'

3. See, e.g., Kolak and Martin (2001: 142) and Megill (1998: 40).

certain imaginary scenarios in arguing for conscious memory's being criterial for personal identity.[4] One such scenario is that of someone who, despite claiming to have the same soul as Nestor at the siege of Troy, has no recollection of performing any of Nestor's actions. Under these circumstances, Locke maintains, the person cannot rightly profess to be the same person as Nestor (Locke 1979: Bk 2, ch. 27, §14). If, however, the soul of a cobbler were to depart from his body and be replaced by that of a prince, 'carrying with it the consciousness of the Prince's past Life', then 'every one sees, he would be the same Person with the Prince' (§15). The contention that this is what everyone sees might imply that, for Locke, the relation between 'consciousness of [one's] past Life' and one's personal identity is so intimate that it becomes little more than a truism to say that if someone has consciousness of A's past life, then the person in question must be A. However, given that Locke tells us very little about the kind of consciousness he is interested in, or about the features of the prince's past life of which the cobbler-bodied person now *is* conscious, it remains difficult to discern exactly what it is that, according to Locke, everyone sees.

Other philosophers have devised thought experiments resemblant of Locke's prince-and-cobbler, though with the emphasis more squarely on the capacity to recall particular facts that, allegedly, only the person in the prince's position could have known. Alfred Ayer, for instance, imagines someone who, purporting to be Julius Caesar, is able not only to describe experiences generally known to have been had by Caesar, but also to provide details of events in Caesar's life that are confirmed only afterwards by new discoveries (Ayer 1956: 194). We might suspect that Locke, faced with such a situation, would readily grant that this person is indeed Caesar, provided that what little Ayer tells us about the person's ability to recall features of Caesar's life comes at least close to what Locke means by someone's having 'consciousness' of the life in question. Other philosophers, including Derek Parfit, have maintained that, were a case such as the one Ayer adumbrates to occur,

---

4. Locke's *Essay* was first published in 1689 and the chapter on personal identity was added in the 1694 edition (Nidditch 1979: xvi). Although Locke himself does not use the terms 'criteria' or 'criterial', these have become common in more recent discussions, especially since the publication of Shoemaker (1963). As Perry (2008: 12) puts it, some philosophers, following Shoemaker, regard a 'criterion of identity' as privileged evidence furnishing a conceptual guarantee that 'the unity relation holds' across the appearances of a person at different times.

it would give us some evidence in support of the existence of 'Cartesian Egos' – 'some purely mental entity' that could undergo reincarnation in successive bodies – and the more frequently such cases were to arise, the stronger this evidence would become (Parfit 1984: 227).[5] Ayer is more circumspect than this, observing that in the scenario he imagines, 'we should hardly know what to say' (1956: 194), his point being that, since our concepts – including, crucially, our concept of a person – have evolved in circumstances where cases of this sort do *not* arise, the concepts are ill-adapted to deal with them. Ayer's contention is that if cases of this sort *did* arise, then a decision would be called for over whether to extend the scope of the concept of personal identity to encompass them or not (Ayer 1956: 194; 1963: 127).[6]

It is curious that Ayer does not pause to consider of whom he is speaking when he declares that, under the circumstances he outlines, '*we* should hardly know what to say' (my emphasis), or who, within any given linguistic community, should be called upon to make a 'decision' about what to say. We might legitimately wonder what significance the cultural context would have for the question of whether the interlocutors involved do or do not know what to say, a point to which I shall return later. Initially, however, let us consider how philosophical advocates of reincarnation have contributed to the debate.

Rebirth and Remembering

I mentioned briefly in Chapter 1 the research of Ian Stevenson and his associates, much of which examines cases of people, mostly children, who purport to have memories of previous lives. Philosophers who take seriously the results of this research have argued that many of the cases examined provide evidence for reincarnation that is at least as convincing as would be the real-life instantiation of the sorts of imaginary situations envisaged by philosophers such as Ayer and

---

5. Although Parfit does not refer specifically to Ayer's Caesar case, he devises a thought experiment of his own that is structurally similar to it, involving a Japanese woman who claims to recall 'living a life as a Celtic hunter and warrior in the Bronze Age' (1984: 227).

6. Cf. Rundle (2009: 164): '[I]f we should speak of "the same person", this would not represent a discovery ... ; it is simply a decision to extend a certain way of speaking.'

Parfit. Occasionally philosophers go further in their conclusions than does Stevenson himself. While Stevenson maintains only that there are many cases *'suggestive* of reincarnation',[7] certain philosophers have contended that, in the light of the most impressive cases, it would be 'unreasonable' or indeed 'positively irrational' to deny that there is overwhelming support for the reincarnation 'hypothesis' (Almeder 1992: 62; 2001: 354; Preuss 1989: 131).[8]

In arguing for the conclusion that it would be unreasonable to accept anything other than reincarnation as an explanation of the data, Robert Almeder invokes Ayer's reflections on the Julius Caesar thought experiment and attributes to Ayer a stronger claim than that which Ayer in fact makes. As noted above, Ayer's contention is that our concepts concerning personhood are unsuited to deal with cases of the sort imagined and that, for this reason, a decision would be needed as to whether the person in question should be regarded as (the same person as) Caesar. Almeder, however, assumes – apparently like Locke – that our concepts are already capable of handling cases of the sort at issue and that what Ayer has done is to specify the conditions sufficient for establishing that the person truly is Caesar reincarnated (Almeder 1992: 60–1). While Ayer in fact maintains that 'we should hardly know what to say' in the circumstances described, Almeder, eager to find a philosophical ally, takes him to have asserted that we should know exactly what to say (or ought to know, at any rate), namely that the person is a reincarnation of Caesar. Asserting that 'it will be sufficient for the truth of reincarnation that the memory conditions laid out by Ayer ... be satisfied', Almeder adds that these conditions have indeed already been satisfied in a number of the cases documented by Stevenson and his associates (61–2).

It is important to remember that when Ayer observes that 'we should hardly know what to say', he is thinking specifically of the concept of diachronic personal identity. He means that we should hardly know whether to say that the person in front of us is the same person as Caesar or not. Although Ayer does proceed to suggest that what is at

7. 'I would only here reiterate that I consider these cases *suggestive* of reincarnation and nothing more. ... Neither any case individually nor all of them collectively offers anything like a proof of reincarnation' (Stevenson 1974: ix–x, original emphasis).

8. See also Almeder (2000): 'My claim was ... that it's irrational to disbelieve it [reincarnation]. ... if you have a very commanding argument that you can't refute, not to accept the argument is to act irrationally.'

stake here is 'the possibility of reincarnation' (1956: 194; 1963: 127), it should not be assumed that 'same person as' and 'reincarnation of' are universally interchangeable expressions. Someone might, for instance, envisage reincarnation in terms of the 'transmigration of souls' without thereby implying that the transferral of a soul from one body to another is equivalent to the transferral of a person. When Locke denies that someone with none of Nestor's memories could be the same person as Nestor, he does not deny that such a person could nevertheless have Nestor's soul. Given that Locke's primary acquaintance with rebirth beliefs will have derived from his knowledge of Platonic thought, in which there obtains the idea of a 'River of Forgetfulness' that souls must cross between incarnations (*Republic* 10.621a–c),[9] it is unsurprising that he allows for the possibility of soul-transference without memory of previous lives – and hence, by Locke's own lights, without personal identity.

Whatever we think of Locke's particular contentions in this area, it is evident that denying the possibility of retaining personal identity across biologically distinct lifetimes need not entail the denial of rebirth. As Raymond Martin has argued, much of the work in the philosophy of personal identity since the late 1960s has 'motivated the belief that identity may not be what matters primarily in survival', suggesting 'that identity, even under normal circumstances, has been overrated' (1992: 183).[10] Even if *identity* is not the crucial thing, however, many philosophers, and not only philosophers, will maintain that what *matters* includes remembering; this is why it has been common to dismiss the desirability, if not the intelligibility, of surviving the death of one's body if there is no form of memory that persists. G. W. Leibniz concisely captures this thought when, in his *Discourse on Metaphysics*, he invites us to imagine someone suddenly being transformed into a Chinese king while simultaneously forgetting everything that he has been up to that point. Asking rhetorically whether, in practical terms, this would not be equivalent to the person's having been 'annihilated and a king of China created at the same instant in his place', Leibniz concludes that this is something the person in question 'would have no reason to desire' (1991: §34).

If we turn to the traditions deriving from South Asia in which belief

---

9. For discussion of other Platonists on this theme, see Chrétien (2002: 34). For discussion of Platonic influence on Locke, see Rogers (2008).

10. Martin specifically points to a book by David Wiggins (1967) as a pivotal moment.

in rebirth has been prevalent, we find that the capacity to remember elements of one's previous lives is also held to be important, but not for the sake of rebirth's *desirability*. In the South Asian context the very idea of desirability would have to be reformulated, for as we saw in Chapter 1, the common normative position is that the perpetuation of rebirth is not ultimately desirable at all; on the contrary, the ongoing flow of rebirths is to be brought to cessation.[11] One of the principal methods of expediting that cessation is, precisely, the relinquishing of the desire for continuation. Remembering one's previous lives gains its importance from the fact that it is widely perceived as a spiritual achievement, the outcome of sedulous meditative discipline or 'of a self-denying and pious life' (Cowell 1895: vii). The foremost manual of classical yoga, popularly known as the *Yoga Sūtra* (*c.* second or third century CE), lists 'knowledge of previous births' (*pūrva-jāti-jñānam*) among the 'special powers' obtainable by means of sustained meditation (3.18, trans. Bryant 2009: 343–4),[12] and the *Mānava Dharmaśāstra* declares that recollection of former births is enabled by constant recitation of the Veda, purificatory practices, asceticism 'and by showing no hostility to any creature' (4.148, trans. Olivelle 2005: 131).

In Buddhist traditions, too, the ability to recall one's own previous lives and also to gain insight into the former lives of others are counted among the special powers attained by means of meditative training or as 'fruits of the homeless life'.[13] Of the Buddha himself, it is said that after gaining these powers on the night of his spiritual awakening, he then recalls not just one or two of his former lives, but 'a hundred thousand'. So too does he see, with his 'divine eye', the 'passing away and being reborn' of beings other than himself; as he does so, he understands how their actions in one life contribute to the conditions experienced in the next (SN II: 213–14, trans. Bodhi 2000: 673–4). If a monk should wish to attain such depth of understanding, the Buddha advises, 'let him fulfil the precepts, be devoted to internal

---

11. 'Rebirth or regeneration is a fundamental evil of phenomenal life and Indian philosophy seeks to determine its cause in order to escape from it. To have another life or to be born again is neither an encouraging prospect nor a consolation' (Chattopadhyaya 1967: 50).

12. See also *Yoga Sūtra* 2.39, which states that 'knowledge of the whys and wherefores of births manifests' when the principle of 'refrainment from covetousness becomes firmly established' (Bryant 2009: 266).

13. *Sāmaññaphala Sutta* in DN I: 47–110 (Walshe 1995: 91–109); cf. Willson (1987: 20–1).

serenity of mind, not neglect meditation, be possessed of insight, and dwell in empty huts' (MN I: 35, trans. Ñāṇamoli and Bodhi 2009: 117). While later compendia of Buddhist teachings, such as Buddhaghosa's *Visuddhimagga* (fifth century CE), offer detailed instructions on how to cultivate one's recollection of former lives by means of meditative techniques,[14] a place has also been made in Buddhism for the idea that such recollection may occur even in the absence of spiritual and ethical mastery, especially 'if one's past life contained particularly powerful events that left deep imprints' (Powers 2007: 188).

Many who do not already subscribe to the doctrine are likely to hear signs of over-enthusiastic exaggeration in declarations that the 'supernormal' capacity of yogins to report on their past lives 'proves conclusively the doctrine of Rebirth' (Sen Gupta 1967: 111). Nevertheless, the existence of such reports, along with anthropological inquiries of the sort undertaken by Stevenson and others, does tell us something about the status within certain South Asian communities of the belief that previous lives can be recalled. It is the discourse of these communities, and the lives into which that discourse is woven, that provide a conceptual richness and nuance that tends to be lacking in the thought experiments and literary fictions which philosophers such as Hacker regard as incoherent. With this in mind, it will be fruitful, shortly, to consider some illustrative case studies from Stevenson's files. In order to sharpen the contrast with extant philosophical debates, however, let us first dig a little deeper into the literature on the concept of remembering and its relation to personal identity.

Remembering and Merely Seeing *to Remember*

There is a well-worn objection to Locke's memory criterion of personal identity which, if sound, would have significant repercussions for the intelligibility of claims to remember previous lives. Briefly put, it is that our rightly describing someone as remembering having performed some action or undergone some experience *presupposes* the identity of that person with the one who did in fact perform the action or undergo the experience, and therefore cannot itself be a criterion of identity.[15] Commonly attributed to Joseph Butler (1736), the objection

---

14. See esp. *Visuddhimagga* 13.13–71. For discussion, see Collins (2009).
15. This point has been much discussed in the philosophical literature on

involves distinguishing between remembering and merely seeming to remember, or, as some more recent philosophers have put it, between a strong and a weak sense of 'remember' (Penelhum 1970: 55; Shoemaker 1970: 281). Clearly, merely seeming to remember doing or experiencing something cannot be criterial for one's having done or experienced it, for we know only too well the fallibility of human memory; we sometimes misremember or fail to remember things, or feel certain that we remember something which, as it turns out, we could not possibly have been remembering. So if remembering is to be a criterion of personal identity at all, it is real remembering, as opposed to merely apparent remembering, that is the viable candidate. But, the argument goes, this very distinction between real and merely apparent remembering implies that there is some further criterion – a criterion for distinguishing, at least in principle, the one type of remembering from the other. Many philosophers have concurred that this further criterion is bodily continuity.

Thus, as Terence Penelhum puts it,

> There has to be some independent way of determining that the person who did or experienced what Smith believes he remembers doing or experiencing was, or was not, Smith himself. And this, it seems, has to be his physical presence at the occasion in question. (1970: 56)[16]

If this point is accepted, then an obvious difficulty is generated for the very intelligibility of a claim to remember a previous life, this difficulty being that one's physical presence – that is, the presence of the human being that one now is – at any time earlier than one's current biological lifetime is logically precluded.[17]

---

personal identity; see, e.g., Parfit (1984: 217–22), Wiggins (2001: 213–14), Noonan (2003: 11).

16. See also Shoemaker (1959: 877): '[In] establishing whether a person remembers something without taking his word for it that he does ... we could not use memory as our criterion of personal identity, and it is difficult to see what we could use if not bodily identity.'

17. This logical preclusion would have to be modified if one were willing to accept as coherent certain religious conceptions of bodily resurrection. Although Penelhum is in some places rather circumspect on this issue (e.g., 1970: ch. 9), in the argument of his to which I am here referring he unequivocally regards bodies as 'spatio-temporally continuous' (66). For philosophical

Almeder has responded to arguments of this sort by asserting that they merely beg the question against believers in reincarnation: they propose 'an a priori interpretation of memory that would make reincarnation ... conceptually impossible when in all other respects the hypothesis of reincarnation fits an important body of data not otherwise capable of explanation' (1992: 84–5). Proponents of such arguments, meanwhile, would maintain that they are not offering an *interpretation* of memory; rather, they are simply reminding us of an essential feature of the concept of memory, namely the fact that internal to the concept is a distinction between remembering and merely seeming to remember, and that distinguishing the one from the other requires at least the possibility of verification by reference to bodily continuity.

Almeder clearly wants to deny that bodily continuity is a necessary condition for genuine memory. This denial is implicit in the point that he draws from Ayer's thought experiment, which is that the possession of accurate information apparently on the basis of memories is, in the absence of any other means of having acquired the information, sufficient to show that the memories are genuine – even in cases where the memories concern actions and events that occurred before the birth of the biological human being who is now having them. Thus, according to Almeder, if someone, Smith, claims to remember where a certain object such as a pocket knife is hidden, and no one other than the person who hid the knife could know this,

> then we are certainly at liberty, upon finding the knife where Smith says it is, to conclude that Smith remembers where the knife was hidden – even if the knife is determined to have been hidden many years before Smith, as we know him, was born. (1992: 84)

From the perspective advocated by Penelhum, however, the problem with this response is its assumption that an argument concerning the constitutive criteria of a given concept can be refuted by bringing forward empirical data or, in this particular case, by imagining a scenario involving empirical data. We are 'at liberty' to conclude something on the basis of evidence, it might be said, only if it makes sense to do so, and it is the intelligibility of regarding someone as remembering an action or experience that occurred before she was

discussion of resurrection, which lies beyond the scope of my own present study, see Gasser (2010).

born – as opposed to merely imagining that she remembers it – that is at issue. Since Almeder has simply assumed that it makes sense to speak of real remembering in the sort of case he imagines, his opponents might contend that it is he who is begging the question in the debate. But there is undoubtedly something right about Almeder's concern that Penelhum and others are operating with an unduly constrained conception of what remembering is, a conception that by concentrating on only a portion of the total range of instances of remembering does indeed rule out, *a priori*, the intelligibility of believing that some people can and do remember previous lives. The urge to resist such conceptual imperialism is understandable. One way of resisting it is to turn away from definitions or criteria stipulated on the basis of highly attenuated 'puzzle cases' and towards real-life scenarios in which claims to remember previous lives are made. The data provided by anthropologists and reincarnation researchers such as Stevenson thus constitute a valuable resource for a conceptual inquiry into what it means to claim to remember having lived before. The problem with a response such as Almeder's, however, is that it gives insufficient attention to the fact that it is precisely this question of what it means to claim to remember a previous life – and, moreover, of whether it means anything at all – that lies at the heart of the disagreement. Once the centrality of this question is recognized, then the focus can shift from the mere parading of 'evidence' – which the other party in the dispute will not accept as evidence of a relevant sort – to careful exposition of how talk of reincarnation acquires the sense that it has.

A significant observation made by several participants in the debate is that our concepts – any concepts – are formed within particular cultural environments, and that if those environments change substantially the concepts will either need to change with them or become redundant. Ayer, as we have seen, makes a point of this kind with regard to the concept of a person, and Penelhum, too, avers that '[c]ircumstances might arise that made us change our concepts so that certain sorts of discontinuities, such as bodily exchanges, were allowed under the concept of a person' (1970: 60). Hacker, likewise, acknowledges that 'our concept of a person is tailored to creatures like us' and that 'all manner of circumstances' are imaginable 'in which it would lose its grip, circumstances under which we would no longer know what to say' (2007: 308). Other philosophers have formulated the point by saying that our concepts might not apply, without modification, in other possible worlds (Shoemaker 1970: 284; Perry 2002: 110). Such circumstances, or altered worlds, might include ones in which dissociative identity disorder became ubiquitous or where complete 'portfolios' of our memories became instantaneously 'transferable from one human being to another' (Hacker 2007: 308).

Whether circumstances of the latter sort can indeed coherently be imagined is not something we should simply take for granted, but the important point to note here is the difference between this use of exotic thought experiments and the use to which philosophers such as Locke put them. While Locke supposes that, by coming to see how our concepts apply to fanciful scenarios, we discover something about the concepts themselves, Hacker and others are proposing that the fanciful scenarios they cite are ones in which our concepts *do not apply*. Though we may speculate about how our concepts – our ways of thinking and speaking – might change if one or other of the imagined scenarios were to eventuate, we can be fairly sure that such speculations would illuminate our current concepts only by way of *contrast* and not by showing us how, without our having noticed it, they actually applied to those scenarios all along.[18]

In the light of this observation about ('our') concepts, any sweeping assertion that beliefs in rebirth, or claims to remember having lived before, do not make sense seems out of place. In response to such an assertion one would be entitled to ask: Do not make sense *to whom*? If it is true, as the research cited by Almeder suggests, that there are cultures in which many instances of people claiming to remember previous lives have occurred, and these claims seem to be accommodated fairly well within the ways of thinking and speaking of the people concerned, then it is unclear on what grounds it should be denied that the claims are intelligible. Are we to suppose that there is a concept of remembering that floats free of the cultural contexts within which it functions and whose meaning is an aura or atmosphere that accompanies the word ('remembering') on every occasion of its use?[19] Philosophical talk of *the* concept or *our* concept of a person, or of *the* concept of memory and so forth, may rely on an unduly rigid picture of what these concepts

18. Cf. Wittgenstein (2009b: §366): 'I am not saying: if such-and-such facts of nature were different, people would have different concepts (in the sense of a hypothesis). Rather: if anyone believes that certain concepts are absolutely the correct ones, and that having different ones would mean not realizing something that we realize – then let him imagine certain very general facts of nature to be different from what we are used to, and the formation of concepts different from the usual ones will become intelligible to him.'

19. Here I have adapted a sentence from Wittgenstein (2009a: §117).

consist in, when in fact the uses of language that involve talk of persons and remembering are far more fluid than that picture suggests. When the scope of the inquiry is extended further to encompass multiple cultural traditions, the likelihood of conceptual fluidity – or 'conceptual amorphousness', to borrow a phrase from Julia Tanney (2013a: ch. 16) – becomes greater still. In this light, it would be presumptuous to proscribe talk of rebirth and of remembering previous lives as nonsensical in advance of careful cross-cultural conceptual investigation.

Ironically, the pretensions of Ian Stevenson, and of advocates of his work such as Robert Almeder, to be presenting *scientific* evidence in support of reincarnation inclines them to downplay the significance of cultural context for the understanding of the case studies they cite. Almeder in particular argues for what he describes as a 'minimalist reincarnation thesis', the formulation of which is intended to capture an idea 'that would be accepted minimally by all major forms of the belief in reincarnation' (1997: 503). By paring down the notion of reincarnation and abstracting away from any specifically religious or cultural characteristics, Almeder ends up with something so schematic as to bear only a tenuous resemblance to any actual reincarnation beliefs. Such an approach is unlikely to deepen our understanding of what it means to believe that rebirth is a reality or of how maintaining that some people remember their previous lives connects with other aspects of this belief. For Almeder, the aim is not to deepen our understanding of these things, but instead to isolate an essence that transcends any cultural surroundings. In effect, the approach assumes that we already know what it means to believe in rebirth and that the only question to be addressed is whether it really occurs, or whether we at least have good reason to believe that it does.

What I am proposing is that if we do wish to deepen our understanding of the meaning of talk of rebirth and remembering previous lives, we shall have to look more carefully at the place of such talk in the lives of those who hold the relevant beliefs. This task will be begun here by analysing a couple of salient examples, and will be complemented in Chapter 3 where different examples will be considered.

Lived Examples

Of the hundreds of cases 'of the reincarnation type' that Stevenson and others have documented I shall here select two that are representative in some respects but peculiar in others. These examples will serve to illustrate some important ways in which attention to the context of someone's purporting to remember having lived before can bring out the sense that the belief in rebirth has for that person and for the society to which he or she belongs.

The first example concerns a woman named Swarnlata Mishra, who was born in the central Indian state of Madhya Pradesh in 1948 (Stevenson 1974: 67–91; 2001: 202–3). From the age of three she claimed to remember two previous lives. One was as a woman named Biya Pathak, who, having lived in a small town approximately a hundred miles from Swarnlata's home, had died in 1939. The other was that of a girl named Kamlesh from the town of Sylhet, which has now been incorporated into Bangladesh but was then in the Northeast Indian state of Assam. Kamlesh had died around the age of nine shortly before the birth of Swarnlata. Among the notable features of Swarnlata's connection to the second of these two remembered lives is her ability to perform songs and dances that she claims to have learnt as Kamlesh, the songs being in Bengali, which is not Swarnlata's native language. In a letter written to Stevenson in 1972 she describes how singing the songs associated with life in Sylhet stirs in her memories of 'the environment of that place' (quoted in Stevenson 1974: 89). As a consequence of remembering her life as Biya, meanwhile, Swarnlata and her family were able to make contact with the Pathak family, and Swarnlata became intimately involved with their lives. 'I share with them ... in their pleasure and pain', she writes; and when she visited the Pathaks' home town to mourn the death of Biya's eldest brother, 'On this occasion all the events of the past life were fresh to me' (ibid.: 89–90). 'In short, environment is the greatest factor to remember the past lives' (89).

We are thus able to see the significance that Swarnlata's memories of her life as Biya have for her in the feelings that she expresses and in the way that she lives her life. While some philosophers would want to stipulate that she cannot *really* be remembering or that the 'concept of remembering' does not 'apply' in this case due to the absence of any possibility, even in principle, of verifying by reference to a bodily criterion that Swarnlata was in fact Biya, such stipulations would involve privileging only a portion of the uses of memory-related terms and fixing on it as the paradigm of 'genuine' remembering. What we *might* want to say, however, is that the concept of remembering that is operating in the Swarnlata case is not the same as that which occurs in certain other contexts, or that it *is* the same concept but that it is a different variety of it. One way of making the point would be to recall that there is a 'family of concepts of memory', that '[t]he words "memory" and "remember," as they are actually used, range over a huge spectrum of cases' (Malcolm 1977: 72, 79).

Relevant to these considerations is Wittgenstein's well-known discussion of 'aspect perception' or 'seeing-as', in which he proposes that there are different concepts of experience (Wittgenstein 2009b: ch. xi). In the case of some experiences, such as that of having toothache, there is no skill or technique required in order to have it: the experience is simply *had* (or undergone, suffered, endured, etc.). In other cases a technique needs to be learnt and applied, such as when, looking at a triangle, one deliberately sees first one corner and then another as its apex (2009b: §222). Wittgenstein's most famous example is that of seeing a certain drawing as, alternately, a duck and then a rabbit. To do this, one must already be 'conversant with the shapes of the two animals' (§216). The relevance of these observations for our present discussion is that, by being prompted to notice that certain conditions need to be fulfilled in order for a particular sort of experience to be had, we may come to appreciate that this is the case with experiences of remembering having lived before. Although putting it in terms of needing to have mastered a *technique* would be misleading, it remains true to say that one must have developed fluency with a certain range of concepts, a fluency that is enabled by participating in a particular community, culture or form of life.

It is to a large extent the surrounding cultural milieu, pervaded by Hindu beliefs and customs, that opened up the possibility of the Mishra and Pathak families acknowledging what had happened to Swarnlata, and indeed not only to her, for other members of the Mishra family also reported past-life memories (Stevenson 1974: 90). It is within that milieu that Swarnlata's describing her experiences as memories of her former life as Biya has the sense that it does. In other cultural circumstances there is likely to have been strong resistance on the part of her family and local community to a child's exhibiting such a close association with another family many miles away; moreover, the child's own envisaging of her relationship to the deceased Biya as one of reincarnation would have struggled to get a foothold within a different cultural environment. The central point here is that certain experiences can have a depth and richness of meaning in one cultural milieu that may be wholly or partially lacking in many others; consequently, the question whether talk of remembering previous lives has any sense, or what sense it has, is not one that can be answered abstractly on the basis of imaginary thought experiments alone.

Turning now to the second example to be reflected on here, this one is rather unusual in the literature, for it involves the concept not only of remembering a previous life, but also of retributive karma (which I introduced in Chapter 1). Despite its prevalence in religious traditions deriving from South Asia, this latter concept occurs surprisingly infrequently among the cases collected by Stevenson and his associates.[20] Speculations on why this is might begin with the observation that it is far from clear how mnemonic phenomenology alone – the mere remembering of occurrences in a previous life – could disclose the karmic connections between actions performed in that life and one's present-life experiences or state of well-being. If, within a single lifetime, one commits a crime and is punished for it, the connection between the two events is plain to see. But if the act for which one is now suffering the consequences was committed in a former life, it is not obvious how one would see that it is *that* act which is to blame, even if, as the belief in retributive karma tends to imply, one can be sure that the suffering is a consequence of *something* one did (or omitted to do). Although certain religious virtuosos, such as the Buddha, are deemed capable of perceiving these connections (with a 'divine eye'), such powers of insight are not expected of less enlightened individuals. Indeed, at least one Buddhist scripture lists the precise workings of karma and its consequences among the 'inconceivable matters', conjecturing about which is liable to induce 'either madness or frustration' (AN II: 80, trans. Bodhi 2012: 463).[21] Against the background of such warnings it perhaps appears less surprising that the case about to be examined is one of only a handful in which a karmic connection *is* taken to obtain between a serious crime committed in one life and a particular characteristic of a subsequent one.

20. In the context of a discussion of cases involving congenital impairments in particular, Stevenson notes that out of all the cases he has studied he has come across only four 'in which a birth defect has been said to derive from some wrongdoing on the part of the previous personality' (1997a II: 1372). For other remarks on the paucity of empirical data relating to retributive karma, see Stevenson (1977: 323; 2000: x) and Tucker (2009: 73–4).

21. See also Story (2000: 51): 'It is due to the multiplicity of contributing causes in the production of any given result that the operations of karma are classed as "unthinkables" (*acinteyya*), one of the subjects that are beyond the reach of thought, and if unwisely pondered over lead to "unhinging of the mind and disorganization of the personality."'

H. A. Wijeratne Hami was born into a Buddhist family in Uggalkaltota, Ceylon (now Sri Lanka), in 1947. Born with a congenital condition known as Poland syndrome, his symptoms included a severely underdeveloped pectoralis major muscle on the right side of his chest and a shortened right arm with stubby and partially conjoined fingers (Stevenson 1974: 149–71; 1997a II: 1366–73). It seems that Wijeratne's father, H. A. Tileratne Hami, surmised from the outset that Wijeratne was a reincarnation of Ratran Hami, who was Tileratne's deceased younger brother and hence would have been Wijeratne's uncle. This surmise was based on, or at least associated with, Wijeratne's sharing a relatively dark complexion with Ratran, exhibiting a facial resemblance and on Ratran's having allegedly predicted before his death that he would return as Tileratne's son. Ratran had been executed by hanging in 1928 after receiving a death sentence for fatally stabbing Podi Menike, a woman to whom he had recently got married but whom he suspected of having second thoughts.

Wijeratne's mother, E. A. Huratal Hami, claims in interviews with Stevenson and other researchers not to have known what had happened to her husband's brother until Wijeratne himself, sometime before the age of three, began attributing the malformation of his arm and chest to his having committed a murder in his previous life. Huratal informed Stevenson that her son had recounted to her and Tileratne in a piecemeal fashion the things he recalled from his former life, 'telling them one thing one day and then a little later speaking about some other episode or detail' (Stevenson 1974: 149–50). In his early twenties Wijeratne suffered from serious bouts of mental illness and was diagnosed with hebrephrenic schizophrenia in late 1969. Many critical observers would take this to indicate that the whole idea of his remembering a previous life as his uncle was a delusion, perhaps exacerbated by insinuations from his father. Stevenson, however, brings out a possible connection between the rebirth belief and Wijeratne's psychological troubles in a more sympathetic manner, remarking that a significant contributory factor to the illness seems to have been Wijeratne's difficult relationship with women to whom he was attracted, especially when they reminded him of the woman he believed himself to have murdered in his former life (ibid.: 166–8). Buddhist commentators might also draw attention to the traditional warning mentioned above, that madness is prone to result from too much speculation on karma and its effects.

A significant feature of the case of Wijeratne for our present purposes is its capacity to illustrate the nexus of interlaced beliefs that compose the framework in which a belief that one is remembering having lived before makes sense, even if the sense that it makes is far from morally complimentary to the one who claims to remember it. The belief that physical or intellectual impairment results from sinful behaviour in a former life has historically been pervasive in Buddhism, as it has in other traditions rooted in South Asia (Ghai 2010: 123–30; Burgess 2012). The doctrine of karma and rebirth can thus be seen as contributing to a worldview in which both the hypoplasia of Wijeratne's arm and chest and his mental health problems are conceptualizable as natural retributive consequences of past-life transgressions.

Wijeratne himself maintained 'that his hand was malformed because, in the previous life, he had killed his wife with his hand' and that his chest concavity was a karmic result of his having stabbed her in the right breast (Stevenson 1997a II: 1372). This explanation coheres with the kinds of accounts found both within popular Buddhism and in more specialized sources of Buddhist doctrine, which state that *kusala* (wholesome, meritorious) and *akusala* (unwholesome, demeritorious) deeds contribute to the likelihood of an auspicious or an inauspicious rebirth respectively. Notwithstanding the Buddha's cautionary remarks to the contrary, 'Buddhist thinkers', as David Burton points out, 'devote considerable resources to mapping the mechanics of karma, explaining the relative weights of various types of good and bad action and the repercussions of particular deeds' (2013: 22), the Abhidharma literature being especially prone to such speculations (e.g., Anuruddha 2007: ch. 5). The most inauspicious rebirths are those that involve the tortures of hell, and Wijeratne reported initially 'dropping into a pit of fire' immediately after the execution that ended his former life (Stevenson 1974: 158). In comparison with the prolonged agonies depicted in popular folk stories and temple art, Wijeratne may have considered himself to have got off fairly lightly, though others might interpret his mental illness as a figurative hell realm in itself.[22]

As it happens, the post-mortem record indicates that Podi Menike received stab wounds to her back and left axilla but not to her right breast. Stevenson responds to this incongruity with Wijeratne's account by mentioning the frequency with which people 'confuse left with right' and 'refer to the left side of someone facing them as "right," because it is right for them' (1997a II: 1372). Sceptics are apt to hear such rationalizations as special pleading on Stevenson's part. But, from another

---

22. Cf. Nagapriya (2004: 99): 'Hell beings are overwhelmed by suffering .... Conditions such as paranoid schizophrenia exemplify this kind of experience all too graphically.' See also Trungpa (2002: 24).

point of view, as a trained psychiatrist who has assumed the mantle of cultural anthropologist, Stevenson might be said to be making a genuine attempt to comprehend Wijeratne's perspective – the perspective of someone who is operating with the concepts of rebirth and retributive karma. Writing off that perspective as a delusional fantasy would be one way of explaining away the phenomenon of remembering previous lives; it would, however, hardly be doing conceptual justice to the stratified cultural texture that makes such a perspective possible. Doing conceptual justice need not, of course, involve endorsing or assenting to the beliefs in question, but it does require making an effort to examine the beliefs in their religiously and culturally imbued conceptual context.

Concluding Remarks

Ian Stevenson, who died in 2007, portrayed himself as a scientist seeking to 'expound the idea of reincarnation as a potentially unifying theory that can make intelligible a number of disparate and seemingly unrelated observations in the fields of psychology, psychiatry, biology, and medicine' (1977: 305). Almeder, too, has asserted that 'the belief in reincarnation offers the best available *scientific* explanation for certain forms of observable behavior not capable of explanation by appeal to any current scientifically accepted theory of human personality' (1992: 2, original emphasis). Philosophers such as Peter Hacker, meanwhile, would not merely doubt the scientific credentials of a purported theory or explanation based on the idea that we live, and can sometimes remember, many lives, but would doubt the intelligibility of the idea itself.

This chapter has sought to elucidate the conceptual dispute over the claim that some people do remember having lived before, a dispute about whether any sense can be made of such a claim. I have suggested that a danger with describing claims to remember previous lives as 'fantasies' is that one thereby appears to be dismissing whole religious and cultural traditions and ways of life as somehow rationally defective or at least permeated by rationally defective beliefs. Some philosophers will not balk at doing so, whereas others will, for good reasons, see such dismissals as premature unless preceded by careful attention to the specific cultural contexts in which the beliefs have the sense that they do (and hence are the beliefs that they are). Those contexts are apt to include actual or potential objections to the beliefs at issue that are *internal* to the cultures in which the beliefs principally flourish. It would be surprising if this were not the case, given that cultures tend to be neither homogeneous nor discrete. However, attentiveness to religio-cultural context remains imperative, along with a reflective awareness of the observer's own cultural assumptions.

I have argued that Almeder, in his hurry to defend rebirth beliefs as not merely rational but properly scientific, fails to fully recognize the conceptual point about memory that his philosophical opponents are making. That point is that attributing genuine remembering to someone makes no sense unless there is, at least in principle, a possibility of the attribution's being verified by reference to bodily continuity. Those who press this latter argument are not subscribing to a general verifiability criterion of meaningfulness; they are making a particular claim about the concept of remembering. I have also proposed, however, that there is something right about Almeder's complaint that the argument of his opponents is too quick to preclude, on *a priori* conceptual grounds, the possibility of remembering having lived before. Where Almeder goes wrong – indeed, where both parties in the dispute typically go wrong – is in assuming that there must be a single, unified 'concept of remembering' at work in human affairs, and that this either permits intelligible talk of remembering previous lives (as Almeder maintains) or it does not.

When we begin to consider the panoply of phenomena that count as some form of remembering, we notice how extensive talk of remembering can be. Whether we say that what is at issue is one concept with a number of ramifying aspects or several concepts with overlapping features is not the essential matter. What is important in the present debate is that we remain alert to the place that past-life memory claims have in the lives of those who make them and in the societies in which those claims are characteristically made. The importance of this inquiry into the roles and meanings of such claims can be missed if one concerns oneself purely or primarily with their 'evidential value', as defenders of the scientific credibility of rebirth are prone to do.[23] This chapter has begun the task of turning from philosophical thought experiments to doctrinally and ethnographically informed examination of lived beliefs. Needless to say, there remains much more that can usefully be explored by means of this approach. Chapter 3

---

23. For instances of the use of phrases such as 'evidential value' and 'evidential strength' in this context, see Stevenson (1974: 228), Almeder (1992: x), Haraldsson and Abu-Izzeddin (2004: 84).

will pursue further the inquiry into the meanings that people find in rebirth beliefs in spite of philosophical objections that question their very intelligibility.

Chapter 3

FINDING MEANING IN MULTIPLE LIVES

> What we may learn by studying other cultures are not merely
> possibilities of different ways of doing things, other techniques.
> More importantly we may learn different possibilities of making
> sense of human life, different ideas about the possible importance
> that the carrying out of certain activities may take on for a man,
> trying to contemplate the sense of his life as a whole.
>
> (Winch 1964: 321)

Among the possibilities of making sense of human life is the seeing of one's present lifetime as occupying a position within a longer trajectory of lives that stretches back, perhaps endlessly back, into the past and forward, perhaps endlessly forward, into the future. My central purpose in this book is to explore this possibility of sense-making without assuming that its implications, including its ethical implications, must be all of a kind. In Chapter 1 we saw that believing in rebirth is itself a phenomenon with many aspects; while pointing out a number of its varieties, I noted along the way that in some instances there continues to be contestation over whether a given belief should or should not be designated a belief in rebirth at all. Chapter 2 took up the idea that certain people remember having lived before, and critically examined what philosophers, especially those exercised by questions of personal identity, have made of this idea. I argued that the preoccupation in the philosophical literature with somewhat rudimentarily sketched thought experiments has severe limitations, and that attention to culturally inflected particular cases has the potential to disclose possibilities of sense that defy philosophical stipulations concerning the concepts of memory and personhood.

The present chapter develops further this confrontation between, on the one hand, philosophical thought experiments designed to reveal the rigid parameters of certain concepts, and on the other hand the intricacies and fluidity of those concepts, which come to light when we observe how they function in the lived vocabularies of people from diverse cultural backgrounds. The starting point for my discussion will be a thought experiment, well known to many philosophers, that was devised by Bernard Williams as part of an argument for the conclusion that bodily continuity is a necessary condition for personal identity. First published in 1957, the paper in which Williams' argument is presented made a stimulating contribution to the philosophical debate. The philosophers who were impressed by the argument include D. Z. Phillips, who endorses it in the context of a brief discussion of reincarnation. Phillips' endorsement involves using Williams' thought experiment specifically to discredit a conception of reincarnation whereas Williams himself had deployed it for the more general purpose of discrediting denials that bodily continuity is necessary for personal identity to be retained. But these two uses are closely connected and entirely mutually compatible.

After outlining the features of the thought experiment that are most salient for Phillips' purposes and noting Phillips' favourable response to Williams' conclusion, I shall then consider two alternative ways of responding. One of these is exemplified in a thoughtful essay by David Cockburn, in which Cockburn, with reference to a case described by Ian Stevenson, examines the ethical implications of regarding someone, specifically a child, as a reincarnation of a deceased individual, such as a sibling who died before the present child was born. The second way of responding to the sorts of issues raised in Williams' thought experiment that I shall consider involves drawing upon ethnographic studies relating to traditions and cultures in which beliefs in reincarnation or rebirth have a central place. Of particular significance for one of the key strands in Williams' argument is a belief – varieties of which occur among Amerindian, Inuit, African and other peoples – in a phenomenon that anthropologists have dubbed *multiple simultaneous rebirth*. Taking this latter form of belief seriously – that is, seeking to improve our understanding of it and acknowledging its role in certain people's lives – will, I propose, help to deepen philosophical inquiries into questions of rebirth and personhood.

My claim is that, in contrast to the rather attenuated appreciation shown by both Williams and Phillips of the possible senses that a belief in rebirth can have, each of the ways of responding to Williams' thought experiment that this chapter will explore has the potential to enrich our appreciation of those senses.

Allegedly Fatal Objections to a Belief in Rebirth

Early on in his little book *Death and Immortality*, D. Z. Phillips identifies what he considers to be 'some logical objections to various suggestions about the possibility of survival after death' (1970a: xi). According to Phillips, 'The notions of the survival of non-material bodies, disembodied spirits or new bodies, after death, all seem open to fatal logical objections' (ibid.). Among the notions that he takes to be (or to 'seem') open to such objections is that of reincarnation, the idea that 'the departed soul lives again in a new body' (11). Phillips' reason for holding that ideas of reincarnation are logically suspect is his acceptance of a central component of Bernard Williams' argument for bodily continuity's being essential for personal identity.

The relevant component of Williams' argument is a thought experiment that requires us to suppose that someone named Charles claims, upon awaking one day, 'to remember witnessing certain events and doing certain actions which earlier he did not claim to remember; and that under questioning he could not remember witnessing other events and doing other actions which earlier he did remember' (Williams 1973: 4). The question in which Williams is interested is whether this scenario would give us grounds for regarding the man who has woken up as a different person from the one who earlier went to sleep in the same bed. Williams goes on to elaborate the thought experiment by inviting us to suppose that, after investigating the events and actions that Charles is now claiming to remember, 'our enquiry has turned out in the most favourable possible way, and that all the events he claims to have witnessed and all the actions he claims to have done point unanimously to the life-history of some one person in the past – for instance, Guy Fawkes' (1973: 7). In such circumstances, Williams suggests, the temptation to say that Charles is now Fawkes is certainly 'very strong', and it 'is difficult to insist that we *couldn't* say that Charles (or sometime Charles) had become Guy Fawkes' (8).

Williams gives us a clue as to the force of '*couldn't*' in the sentence just quoted when he subsequently writes that declaring Charles to be Guy Fawkes 'is certainly what the newspapers would say if they heard of it' (8). It thus appears that he is suggesting that since some people (such as newspaper journalists) certainly *would* say that Charles is now Fawkes, it would be implausible to maintain that no one *could* say this.[1] But in view of where Williams' argument ends up, he would have to add

---

1. As we saw in Chapter 2, it is likely that some philosophers, such as Robert

that regardless of what some people *would* say, they would be wrong to say it, because it is logically confused.

To ward off the temptation to refer to Charles as Fawkes, Williams embellishes his thought experiment in a way that generates what he calls his 'reduplication argument' (1973: chs 2 and 5). This involves supposing that, simultaneous to the changes that Charles has undergone, someone else, such as his brother Robert, has undergone 'the same changes' (1973: 8). In this new scenario, Williams contends, it would be 'absurd' to maintain that Charles is Fawkes. It would be absurd because there is no more reason for regarding Charles as Fawkes than for regarding Robert as Fawkes; and it would be absurd to regard them *both* as Fawkes because, first, 'if they were, Guy Fawkes would be in two places at once, which is absurd'; and second, 'if they were both identical with Guy Fawkes, they would be identical with each other, which is also absurd' (8). From the absurdity of regarding either Charles or Robert as Fawkes when both Charles and Robert exist contemporaneously, it follows, according to Williams, that it would also be absurd to regard either of them as Fawkes even if only one of them existed at a particular time. This inference follows on the basis of a principle which Derek Parfit, in his interpretation of Williams' argument, states in the following terms: 'Whether a future person will be me must depend only on the *intrinsic* features of the relation between us. It cannot depend on what happens to *other* people' (Parfit 1984: 267).

In his précis of Williams' argument, Phillips expresses approval of the contention that the distinction between a relation of *identity* (if we want to call numerical identity a 'relation') and a relation of *exact similarity* can operate in the case only of bodies and not of memories. Williams maintains that, to say of Charles (or Robert) that he has memories that are identical with – that is, they are the very same memories as – those of Fawkes, in the absence of material continuity between the respective bodies of Fawkes and Charles (or Fawkes and Robert), fails to mark a contrast with saying that the memories are merely exactly similar. This is because the only means of distinguishing a relation of identity from one of exact similarity in the memory case is to trace a continuity of body between the person who claims to remember having done or experienced a given action or event and the person who actually did or experienced the action or event in question. This is equivalent to the point that we saw being made by Penelhum in Chapter 2 (p. 48 above).

Almeder, would gladly go along with the opinion of the newspapers on this matter.

Williams' particular way of making it is to observe that the problem with relying on memory claims as a criterion of personal identity is that someone's 'being disposed to make sincere memory claims which exactly fit the life of [some given individual]' is a 'many–one' and not a 'one–one' relation, 'and hence cannot possibly be adequate in logic to constitute a criterion of identity' (1973: 21). Summing up his agreement with Williams, Phillips writes: 'Thus, it seems, if a claim is to be borne out that so-and-so is so-and-so living again, it must be established that there is a one–one relation between the material bodies involved in the two spans of existence' (1970a: 12).

In a later book, Phillips makes a passing reference to reincarnation, and there states that he is 'not denying such beliefs' (2004a: 163 n. 10). There, and in other places, Phillips is keen to maintain a distinction between, on the one hand, religious beliefs as they function in the lives of actual religious believers, and on the other hand, the metaphysical constructions of philosophers which are liable to bear only a surface similarity to the religious beliefs in question. Phillips emphasizes this in, for example, his discussions of the term 'soul'. 'In philosophy of religion', he writes, 'we are often offered analyses which pay no attention to and, hence, fail to capture, the "soul" in the words of religious beliefs' (1995: 447). Phillips describes these failed analyses as involving 'a dislocation of language', by which he means that certain terms or phrases, which have a vivid life in the beliefs and practices of religious believers, are abstracted from their contexts by philosophers. By uprooting forms of language in this way, philosophers inevitably overlook the connections with lived human activities that enable us to see the meanings that the salient concepts have.

With regard to his treatment of the notion of reincarnation in *Death and Immortality*, a charitable reader might suppose that Phillips is taking Williams to have discredited only a philosopher's reconstruction of this notion, and not the belief in reincarnation or rebirth as it inheres in believers' lives. For to judge that Williams' reduplication argument has somehow shown that billions of believers have fallen prey to a logical absurdity – that what appears to be a profoundly meaningful aspect of their lives is, in reality, the product of confusion on their part – would hardly be in keeping with the kind of Wittgenstein-influenced approach to religious forms of life that Phillips espouses. Styling his (and Wittgenstein's) conception of philosophy as a 'contemplative' one, Phillips asserts in one of his last books that philosophy's disinterested 'contemplation of the world' does not seek to arbitrate 'between our beliefs and convictions in the name of rationality' (2004b: 55). Such arbitration is precluded, Phillips maintains, because the distinction between what is rational and what is irrational is not independent of the contexts in which beliefs and convictions arise. Whether it is rational for someone to hold a particular belief will show itself in the life of the individual, and in many cases the question of whether a belief is rational may be entirely out of place. It may be out of place because, for example, the belief goes too deep in someone's life to be intelligibly evaluated in terms of rationality: it forms part of the very framework within which assessments of what is or is not rational are made.[2] A consequence of this for Phillips is that the role of philosophy in its investigation of religious beliefs 'is not to justify, but to understand' (1970b: 7), and 'To understand what it is to embrace a religious truth is at an infinite distance from embracing it' (2004b: 89). So, too, is it an infinite distance from *rejecting* it. To engage in contemplative philosophical inquiry is to seek neither to validate nor to undermine the modes of human life that one is examining. A deeper understanding – clarity as an end in itself, as Wittgenstein might put it – is the exclusive purpose.[3] This is, to a large extent, the philosophical approach that I am pursuing in the present study.

A less charitable reader of *Death and Immortality*, however, might point out that in his remarks on reincarnation *there*, Phillips does not make any overt distinction between actual religious beliefs and mere philosophical constructions. He appears to toss the notion of reincarnation into the bag of 'suggestions about the possibility of survival after death' that 'seem open to fatal logical objections', without giving a second thought to the contexts in which beliefs in reincarnation have their home. This lack of contextualization – and hence, we might say, this dislocation of language – is a conspicuous weakness in the first chapter of *Death and Immortality*. And since Phillips never returned to reincarnation or rebirth in his writings, other than to make the passing reference to it in the note I have mentioned, we must look elsewhere for more considered approaches to the topic.

    2. On this point, Phillips concurs with Norman Malcolm, who writes that, 'Within the framework of each system there is criticism, explanation, justification. But we should not expect that there might be some sort of rational justification of the framework itself' (Malcolm 1977: 209); cf. Phillips (1988: ch. 9).

    3. 'For me ... clarity, transparency, is an end in itself' (Wittgenstein 1998: 9e).

The Ethical Significance of 'Same Person'

Apart from accepting Williams' conclusion, as Phillips does, there are other ways of responding to the contention that even when he is the exclusive candidate for being Fawkes, Charles *cannot* be Fawkes, because our regarding him as such is contingent upon there not being one or more equally credible candidates. The next section will consider a possible response that involves paying attention to actual rebirth beliefs, including the belief that someone can be reborn as more than one person at the same time. In this section, meanwhile, I shall discuss a response exemplified by David Cockburn, who questions the claim that, as he puts it, 'how an individual is to be thought of and treated cannot depend ... on what are not facts about *him*' (1991: 204).

What Cockburn is questioning is the move in Williams' argument that takes us from an acknowledgement that it cannot be the case that both Charles and Robert are Guy Fawkes, to the conclusion that in a case where only one candidate is present we still could not legitimately deem that candidate to be Fawkes. This move, it will be recalled, is thought by Williams to be licensed by the fact that even in the absence of a second candidate such as Robert, the relation in which the single candidate, Charles, stands to Fawkes remains, logically, a many–one relation; that is to say, even when it is not *in fact* the case that there are more than one individual displaying the apparent recollective capacities that Charles displays, it nevertheless *could* be the case, and it is this logical possibility that vitiates the propriety of regarding Charles as Fawkes reborn. It vitiates that propriety because it makes the plausibility of Charles being regarded as Fawkes dependent upon something extraneous to Charles' relation to Fawkes; more precisely, it makes it dependent on there *not* being a second candidate.

While admitting that the principle in question – of thinking of and treating an individual only on the basis of facts about the individual himself – 'sounds very plausible in the abstract', Cockburn submits that 'in practice we constantly violate it' (1991: 204). To illustrate this latter point, he cites the examples of (a) someone's being treated as the winner of a race depending 'not only on how fast he ran but on whether anyone else ran faster', (b) the severity of the punishment imposed on a drunk driver depending not only on whether it was he who knocked down a child but on whether the child dies as a result of her injuries and (c) someone's attitude towards his second wife changing as a consequence of discovering that, despite what he had previously believed, his first wife is not in fact dead (ibid.). Examples of this kind could, of course, be multiplied. Someone's voting for one politician, Bennett, may be largely dependent on the other candidates in the election having made appalling campaigning gaffes. In a case such as this, should we say that Bennett was voted for because she ran a better campaign than her rivals and that her having run such a campaign is, after all, a fact about *her*? That is certainly something we *could* say. But the credibility of that statement will nevertheless depend on facts about her rivals' campaigns.

A supporter of Williams' argument could respond to the examples just given by noting that none of them bears upon the *identity* of the person concerned. Whether, for instance, Brownlee is the winner of the race, and is to be treated as such, obviously depends on facts about other contestants as well as on facts about Brownlee. But whether Brownlee is, in fact, Brownlee – whether *this particular athlete* is the same one who, say, won the triathlon in the 2012 Olympic Games – cannot be dependent on facts about anyone other than Brownlee (on facts about his brother, for example). It is the significance of its being, specifically, a relation of numerical identity between a person at one time and a person (the same person) at an earlier or later time that Parfit is getting at when he formulates the relevant principle as the requirement that a future person's being *me* depends 'only on the *intrinsic* features of the relation between us' and not 'on what happens to *other* people'.

An aspect of Cockburn's strategy in his essay as a whole is to coax us away from the assumption that the notion of identity at issue in this debate can be straightforwardly understood. Williams is concerned exclusively with bodily continuity and memory, and with trying to nail down which, if any, of these two conditions is necessary, or sufficient, for its being logically correct to say of someone at one time that he is the same person as someone at an earlier time. Cockburn, meanwhile, is careful not to take it for granted that we know in abstraction from any particular context what it means to regard someone as the same person as someone at an earlier time: that this must amount to only one kind of thing (only one way of regarding someone) in all possible situations. One of the central points that Cockburn stresses is that in at least some cases, and almost certainly in the case of relating to people whom one loves, the factors that come into play in relating to someone *as that particular person* will include emotional and ethical ones. What Cockburn explores in interesting ways are the possible implications of this latter consideration for what might be said of cases in which one or both parents of a child have spoken of that child as the 'same person as' (or as 'the reincarnation of') a previously deceased person.

The sorts of cases that Cockburn has in mind are precisely those that have been documented by Ian Stevenson and his associates, especially the type in which the previous life that a child is allegedly remembering is that of a sibling who died before the present child was born.[4] Many people who reflect upon cases of this sort are liable to assume that *if* rebirth has genuinely occurred, what must have happened is that some immaterial component of a human being has 'transmigrated' from one physical body to another. Such people might also assume that, before any useful discussion can take place concerning the ethical implications of regarding the present child as a reincarnation of the other, we first have to determine to the best of our ability whether it is *really the case* that the two children are continuous in the way that the notion of rebirth or reincarnation implies. Cockburn does not deny the legitimacy of asking whether the living child is *really* (the same as) the one who died; rather, he aims to free us from the grip of 'a certain picture' that dominates our thought of what arriving at an answer to this question must involve, 'a picture which is modelled on our understanding of scientific enquiry' (1991: 205).

Imagining a scenario in which a married couple disagree over whether their new child is a reincarnation of a former one who died, Cockburn contemplates how ethical considerations might feature in their disagreement, not as *consequences* of the child's being regarded as (or not being regarded as) her sibling's reincarnation, but as *constitutive of what it means* to regard her as such. Cockburn's intriguing suggestion here is that the ethical disagreement over how the child is to be treated – over whether, for example, it would be failing to acknowledge the present child's uniqueness and individuality to speak of her as the previous child's reincarnation – could be the very deepest level of disagreement; there may be no level that is 'more basic' than this (ibid.). Although this way of thinking about persons has been articulated by Cockburn in other places,[5] those who are unfamiliar with it are apt to misunderstand his contention. They are apt to assume that he is somehow denying the importance of the 'factual' question – the question whether the child really is the reincarnation of her deceased sibling – and replacing it with questions concerning what is

---

4. Cockburn cites the case of Alexandrina Samona, as presented in Stevenson (1961: 20-1); see Cockburn (1991: 199–200). Similar cases include that of Susan Eastland, reported in Stevenson (2001: 79–83).

5. See, e.g., Cockburn (1990: 10): 'That a certain attitude is appropriate towards a person is central to our understanding of what a person *is*.'

best for the child and how she ought to be treated. To hear Cockburn's contention in this way is to miss its radical point. For the point is to raise doubts about what could be meant by 'the question whether the child really is the reincarnation of her deceased sibling' if this latter question is assumed to be amenable to being answered *prior to*, and hence independently of, questions concerning how she ought to be treated. 'For it seems that, in a straightforward sense', says Cockburn, 'all the facts might be in and yet there still be disagreement about whether this [child] is [the one who died]' (1991: 205).

If we review Williams' thought experiment in the light of these contentions from Cockburn, we begin to notice how little can be decided on the basis of such a thought experiment when it is sketched as thinly as Williams sketches it. Among the questions that need to be asked would be ones concerning how those who come into contact with Charles behave towards him and whether those ways of behaving are appropriate. Moreover, we should need to take seriously the thought that, when addressing the latter question, there might be no 'deeper', 'more basic', level of facts about Charles' true identity that can be appealed to than that at which the question of appropriateness itself resides. When faced with a question such as 'Should Charles be held morally, and perhaps legally, responsible for deeds committed by Guy Fawkes?', those who remain convinced that there is a deeper level of facts to be uncovered will want to say that this question cannot be satisfactorily answered until we have some reliable means of establishing whether Charles really is Fawkes. But what the line of thought pursued by Cockburn urges us to do is to at least entertain the idea that it is precisely how we respond to questions concerning moral and legal responsibility that is constitutive, or partially constitutive, of what we mean by declaring that someone is the same person as (or is relevantly continuous with) so-and-so.

Again, it would be easy to miss the important point here. What is being suggested is not that we *first* have to decide how to treat Charles and only then will we be in a position to address the question whether he really is Fawkes. The suggestion is, rather, that it is *through*, or *in the process of*, coming to some kind of recognition of how we ought to treat Charles that we shall come to see his identity in a particular light, a light which may present him to us as Guy Fawkes, or as connected with Fawkes in some way, or, alternatively, as having no strong connection with Fawkes at all. How we do, or would, come to see him cannot be answered on the basis of a thinly sketched thought experiment. A question of this sort could begin to be addressed only in relation to the kind of detailed depictions that one finds in works of literature or in relation to real-life cases with all their contingencies and messiness. Such contingencies and messiness, of which we saw some instances in the case studies outlined in Chapter 2, do not well serve the objectives of philosophers who want, once and for all, to settle the issue of what conditions have to be in place for *x* to be identical (or otherwise relevantly related) to *y*. But, as I have been arguing in this and the previous chapter, there may be good reason to suspect that settling this issue in abstraction from the contingencies and messiness of life is neither a realistic nor an especially illuminating objective to pursue.

Simultaneous Multiplicity

One of the crucial assumptions underlying the conclusion that Bernard Williams draws on the basis of his thought experiment concerning Charles and Robert is that it makes no sense to regard two simultaneously existing people as numerically identical to one another. Given this assumption, we can say that since it makes no sense to regard Charles and Robert as the same person, neither would it make sense to regard both of them as Guy Fawkes. This would make no sense because identity is transitive: if A is identical to B, and B is identical to C, then, necessarily, A is identical to C. Taken as an abstract logical principle, it is difficult to see how the transitivity of identity could reasonably be challenged. There remains, however, a question of whether, or to what extent, a logical principle such as this is applicable to actual beliefs in rebirth.

Part of Cockburn's response to Williams' argument is to prompt us to see that, in the context of our emotionally and ethically inflected relationships with other human beings, what it means to regard someone as 'the same person as' (or as 'a reincarnation of') a particular individual may not be well captured by abstract logical principles. This kind of response can be pursued further by attending to some specific forms that beliefs in rebirth have taken within various human societies. Especially pertinent to the sort of scenario imagined by Williams is what has been designated by some anthropologists and other researchers as the belief in *multiple simultaneous rebirth*. In an encyclopaedia entry under 'Rebirth, simultaneous', Norman McClelland writes:

> This is a belief found in Tibet and a few other places such as among the Inuit and Northwest Pacific Coastal American Indians. According to this belief it is possible for a soul to be reborn into two

or more entities at the same time. Another version of this simultaneous rebirth does not require that any double rebirth be at the same time; for example, a single soul may be shared by one person living from 1940–2015 and a second person living from 1955–2030. (2010: 230)[6]

Similarly, writing of the rebirth belief held by the Haida people of British Columbia, Margaret Blackman remarks that it 'does not require that one be born after the death of the reincarnate kin. Furthermore, an individual can be reincarnated into more than one person at a time' (1992: 145 n. 1).

Antonia Mills has observed that belief in multiple simultaneous (or temporally overlapping) rebirth within some Amerindian communities is connected with the prestige that attaches to having a highly esteemed chief be reincarnated in one's family. Among the Gitxsan (or Gitksan) people of Northwest coast America, for example, the 'cases of multiple simultaneous rebirths ... occurred when the previous personality was wished or willed in multiple families' (Mills 1988: 403).[7] One way of reading an account such as this would be to see it as offering a reductive psychological explanation of the belief in question – as suggesting, that is, that the underlying motivation for holding the belief is a wish or desire on the believers' part (mere 'wishful thinking') as opposed to the cognitive- or truth-value of the belief itself. In other writings, Mills makes it clear not only that she is not advocating a reductive explanation, but that she is open to the possibility that beliefs in rebirth could be true, or, at any rate, 'that some paranormal process cannot ... be ruled out' (1994a: 238). But the sorts of cases that have been referred to as involving multiple simultaneous rebirth remain highly complicated, to say the least.[8]

One of the complicating factors is the presence in many relevant communities of a belief that each of us comprises, or possesses, more than one 'soul'. In an extensive comparative study of numerous Native American and Inuit peoples, Åke Hultkrantz identifies various types of soul in which they appear to believe. A basic distinction that he

6. See also Beyer (1992: 378–9) and Mills (1994b: 28–9).
7. See also Mills (1994a: 234): 'Among the Gitksan, families practically vie to have it acknowledged that a well-beloved family member, especially a high chief, has been born among them.'
8. Mills acknowledges that these cases add 'complexity ... to the question of what an "individual" is, and what comes back and why' (2001: 318).

attributes to them is between the 'free-soul' and the 'body-soul' (1953: 51 *et passim*). The former is commonly associated with a person's dream-life, for it is sometimes said of someone who dreams of roaming widely through various scenes and landscapes that the soul has temporarily become freed from the body. The body-soul, meanwhile, is more closely associated with life and breath; its departure is the death of the body. As Hultkrantz's analysis deepens, however, he has to admit that the conceptual distinctions at work are far more intricate and variegated than the initial dualism between free- and body-soul would suggest. The conceptions of the soul that one is faced with are 'polymorphous' and 'diffuse', and hence the term 'soul' must itself be recognized 'as a covering name for a multifarious complex' (1953: 43, 56).[9] The description of these polymorphous conceptions in terms of multiple souls might generate an impression more exotic than is necessarily called for. In many instances what appears to be going on is the identification by the peoples concerned of a multiplicity of psychological capacities, personal characteristics and biological functions, some of which are more essential to a person's continuing life and identity than are others. Nevertheless, whether or not we refer to these factors as 'souls', the belief that there are many of them tends to go along with a belief that some but not all of them are reincarnated after a person's bodily death; and if there are more than one to be reincarnated, then the possibility for believing in multiple reincarnations is opened up.

Bernard Williams argues that a reincarnation case of the sort he invites us to entertain in his thought experiment is in fact 'logically impossible' and that it would therefore be 'absurd' to believe that such a phenomenon could occur. Especially pertinent to the belief in multiple simultaneous rebirth is Williams' insistence that,

> Granted that in a certain context the expressions 'the man who did A', 'the man who saw E', do effectively individuate, it is logically impossible that two different persons should (correctly) remember being the man who did A or saw E; but it is not logically impossible that two different persons should *claim* to remember being this man, and this is the most we can get. (1973: 8)

9. See also Gernet (1994: 41), who remarks upon the need that Hultkrantz discovered to apply 'finer divisions, definitions, and labels' to accommodate the '[s]ubtle conceptual nuances among certain groups'.

Is it 'logically impossible that two different persons should (correctly) remember being the man who did A or saw E'? In the light of the sorts of ethnographic studies to which I have referred, there would be some justification for replying that the answer depends on the conception of a person that is at issue. 'The logic the Gitksan use in no way makes it impossible for person A to "be" person B', writes Mills (1994a: 234). The scare quotes around 'be' could be taken to indicate some uncertainty on Mills' part over whether this is quite the right way of putting the point. Perhaps it is the case that there is *a* sense in which the logic that she is attributing to the Gitxsan allows for two people to be one and the same person but there is also a sense in which the two people remain ontologically distinct. With an eye on the sorts of case studies that Mills and others have adduced, we might imagine two Gitxsan families, each of which has a child who claims to remember being the same high chief. Are these families obliged by dint of the laws of logic to restrict themselves to speaking of the children only as *claiming* to remember being the high chief and not as really having been him? Williams' answer, I take it, would be 'yes'. But now suppose that the two families know each other, and hence know that there are at least two children who are claiming to have been the high chief. Are we forced to hold that, if they continue to speak of the children as really having been the high chief, they are irrational and are failing to see the logical error that they are, purportedly, making?

Part of the difficulty here is in the assumption that there is a straightforward distinction between '(merely) claiming' and 'really being'. Mills' scare quotes alert us to that difficulty by drawing to our attention the fact that there might be different senses in which person A *is* person B. I noted in passing in Chapter 2 that we should not assume that 'same person as' and 'reincarnation of' are universally interchangeable expressions. Neither should we assume that the differences between these expressions are fully determinate. It might well be the case that someone who believes she is the reincarnation of a particular individual is apt to speak of herself as *being* that individual (that is, as being *the same person as* that individual) while also acknowledging, either explicitly or tacitly, that she is not the same person as that individual in exactly the same sense that she is the same person as the one she was yesterday and will be tomorrow. She might, for example, regard herself as being morally and legally responsible for things she did yesterday in ways that differ from any sense in which she is responsible for things done by the person of whom she is a reincarnation.

In the absence of the assumption that expressions such as 'same person as' and 'different persons' – and, crucially, 'reincarnation of' – are logically fixed independently of the roles that these and similar expressions have within the communities that use them, it would be mistaken to suppose that any straightforward judgement can be made concerning whether the two Gitxsan families that we imagined above should be deemed to be irrational. If there is a universal logic, abstracted from human life and activities, that determines whether a given way of speaking makes sense, then it might be the case that people whose ways of speaking *appear* to have a sense within particular contexts are, in reality, merely confused. If, however, one takes it to be the very ways in which forms of language are used by human beings in the stream of their lives that imbue those forms of language with sense, then the contention that certain forms of language which play an active role in people's lives are 'in reality' senseless will itself fail to have a clear sense.[10]

None of this amounts to a refutation of Williams' point that there is an important difference between a one–one relation (that is, a 'relation' of numerical identity) and a many–one relation (that is, a relation in which there can be more than one thing that stand in the same relation of exact similarity to another thing). What it does is force us to pause before taking it for granted that any obvious conclusion follows concerning what ought to be said about beliefs in rebirth as they are found in, as it were, the real world rather than in the confines of a philosopher's thought experiment.

Rebirth and the Spirit World

Before concluding this chapter there is one further example that is worth mentioning due to its relevance to the idea of someone's having more than one existence, or more than one *kind* of existence, simultaneously. It was noted in Chapter 1 that a prevalent belief held by several African peoples is that a person can undergo rebirth on earth while nevertheless continuing to reside in a 'spirit world' or 'afterlife', and that various attempts have been made, both by anthropologists and by exponents from within the communities themselves, to offer an

---

10. Someone who accepts this latter view would be sympathetic to Peter Winch's contention 'that criteria of logic are not a direct gift of God, but arise out of, and are only intelligible in the context of, ways of living or modes of social life' (Winch 2008: 94).

account of how sense can be made of this apparently paradoxical belief. Different points would, no doubt, need to be made in relation to different groups. Writing with particular regard to the Nupe of Nigeria and Niger, E. Bọlaji Idowu observes that they deal with the problem by maintaining that everyone has two souls, one of which goes after death to dwell 'permanently with the Maker, while the other one reincarnates' (1973: 188).[11] Putting it in these terms makes the idea of two souls sound like an ad hoc remedy for an internally conflicted belief, and hardly begins to address the question of why one would want to hold the internally conflicted belief in the first place. Idowu goes on, however, to suggest 'an interpretation of this delicate topic' that may be instructive for our thinking about beliefs concerning death and rebirth more generally.

Idowu's proposal is that the conjoint belief in rebirth and in a spirit world expresses two significant lines of thought: first, 'that the genius of the family never dies [but] keeps manifesting itself in unbroken sequence in offspring'; and second, that 'the life of the ancestors in the after-life is a reality: it does not depend on the remembrance of them by those who are living on earth'. The ancestors, Idowu adds, 'have their own independent existence; and their being is in no way a fulfilment of the theory that "To live in hearts we leave behind is not to die"' (1973: 188).[12] This refusal on Idowu's part to accept a psychologically reductive account of the belief in a spirit world might equally be applied to the belief 'that the genius of the family never dies'. To regard oneself as reincarnating the spirit of one's ancestors, or of a particular ancestor, need not be reducible to the thought that one shares with them certain character traits, which have been passed on through the family line. It may bring with it a stronger identification, in which one's own biography is merged with theirs in such a way that one feels one's own life to be a continuation rather than a starting afresh.

To pick up the thought that we saw being pressed by David Cockburn earlier in this chapter, we might want to say that the direction in which to look if we are to see the meaning of a belief

---

11. S. F. Nadel similarly ascribes to the Nupe a belief in 'a double soul ("shadow-" and "life-soul")' (1952: 18), but in a more comprehensive study acknowledges that the Nupe really distinguish between three souls – 'life soul', 'shadow soul' and 'personal soul' – the third of which is reborn on earth after death (Nadel 1954: 21–3).

12. Idowu is here quoting from Thomas Campbell's 1825 poem, 'Hallowed Ground'.

such as that held by the Nupe is towards the ethical relations in which members of the community stand to their ancestors and to one another. As Alma Gottlieb has observed, an implication of belief in reincarnation that is common to many groups in West Africa is the attribution of 'deep spiritual activity to young children', who are revered as 'reincarnated ancestors with active memories of an afterlife' (2006: 160). There are resonances here also with certain manifestations of rebirth beliefs in South Asia, where the individuality of newborn children is held not to be exhaustively traceable to what they inherit directly from their parents, for there remains 'something the child brings with it from a pre-natal existence' (Yamunacharya 1967: 68). As Cockburn indicates, ideas such as these might generate worries for some people that the uniqueness of *this particular child* is being overlooked, that her identity is being conflated with that of others who have gone before. An alternative view would be that the idea of a child retaining elements of its personality from former lives does not detract from but rather emphasizes the child's uniqueness, adding extra layers to how it is conceptualized which go beyond genetic inheritance and environmental influence.

The ethical significance of believing a child to be a reincarnation is thus by no means obvious or inevitable; it is liable to take different forms amid different cultural surroundings. But that its significance will have an ethical dimension, and that there may be no more 'fundamental' level at which the belief can be understood than that at which its ethical significance resides, is the central point that we can take from Cockburn's discussion, and is one that will recur in Chapter 4.

Concluding Remarks

The essay by Cockburn to which I have been referring in this chapter ends with the following intriguing paragraph:

> Many are suspicious when a philosopher writing about reincarnation is clearly totally ignorant of the religious traditions in which a doctrine of reincarnation has a central place. The present paper is, no doubt, a case in point. My hope is that there is at least one thing that a philosopher suffering from such ignorance can usefully do. That is, try to show that the suspicion is well grounded. (1991: 207)

The sort of suspicion to which Cockburn here refers should, I think, be carried over into philosophical discussions of 'personal identity'. As has been highlighted both in this and in the previous chapter, the philosophical literature on personal identity is replete with wondrous thought experiments. I have not ventured into those that comprise speculations about whole-brain and brain-hemisphere transplants, amoebic fission of human beings, teleportation, and the like.[13] Though in certain respects no more 'bizarre' than many real-life rebirth-related beliefs – at least from the perspective of someone from a culture in which rebirth beliefs are generally not at home – these imagined puzzle cases are typically described only in enough detail for their respective philosophical inventors to derive the conclusion that they sought to derive. What tends to be lacking is any sustained attentiveness to the multiplicity of forms that conceptions of persons take in different cultural and religious traditions.

Pace Ayer (1963), any talk of *the* 'concept of a person' is something of which we ought to be suspicious, whether it comes from a philosopher or from any other theorist. Though social and cultural anthropologists are certainly not immune from such over-generalizations themselves, their detailed studies of the ways of life and forms of language engaged in by various cultural groups can serve the vital purpose of releasing us from the clutch of unwarranted assumptions, including assumptions concerning what inferences can or ought to be drawn on the basis of philosophical thought experiments.[14]

Like Cockburn's essay, this chapter has perhaps done little more than accentuate the well-founded nature of the suspicion at issue. Yet, as Cockburn points out, merely doing this can be to make a valuable contribution. It is when we overlook the broad repertoire of forms that human life and interactions with one another take that we, like D. Z. Phillips in his early work, become prone to jump to hasty conclusions concerning the intelligibility of certain kinds of belief or conception.

---

13. Discussions of this topic are legion. Most of the best-known thought experiments are concisely covered in Noonan (2003). See also Paul, Miller and Paul (2005), esp. the chapters by Feser and Belzer respectively. For criticisms of these kinds of approaches to the philosophy of personal identity, see Wilkes (1988: ch. 1).

14. In some instances anthropologists go further, and offer philosophically astute cross-cultural analyses both of different concepts of persons and of competing theoretical ways of accounting for those differences; see, e.g., Shweder and Bourne (1982).

Of course, if one is convinced that there is a single, correct understanding of what a person is, which is amenable to being defined in terms of individually necessary and jointly sufficient conditions for the application of 'the concept of a person', then one will remain unimpressed by the sorts of considerations with which this chapter has been concerned. If, however, one is open to the idea that conceptions of persons arise not within a vacuum, but within particular streams of life – confluences of belief and practice that mingle with many other modes of human and non-human activity while nevertheless retaining their own cultural inflections – then, regardless of whether one believes that we live multiple lives, one may come to see how someone could find meaning in this belief. And the view that it is a logically impossible absurdity may come to seem oddly parochial.

Chapter 4

INTEGRATING REBIRTH AND ETHICS

There are, as we saw in Chapter 1, different ways in which believers in rebirth have conceptualized the connection between the serial lives of a reincarnating individual. A central distinction is that between, on the one hand, conceptions of the connection that involve the idea of retributive consequences of one's actions, and on the other hand, non-retributive conceptions. Those of the former type are commonly associated primarily with traditions originating in South Asia, such as Hinduism, Buddhism, Jainism and Sikhism, and secondarily with certain other traditions, such as that exemplified by Pythagoreans and Platonists in ancient Greece. Non-retributive conceptions, meanwhile, are commonly associated with what used to be called 'primitive' societies. These days the vocabulary has changed – irredeemably pejorative terms such as 'primitive' and 'savage' have been replaced by 'indigenous', 'traditional' or 'small-scale' – but still the basic distinction remains in place.[1] In itself, there is nothing inherently suspect or fallacious about it. There are indeed some forms of belief that connect rebirth with retributive effects and other forms that do not, which is why I introduced this distinction in Chapter 1. The distinction can become misleading, however, when it is knitted together with two dubious assumptions.

The first of these dubious assumptions is that the retributive varieties of rebirth beliefs are at a 'higher' or more 'advanced' stage of development along an imagined continuum or evolutionary trajectory, with the non-retributive varieties having so far progressed only a relatively short distance from some primordial prototype. This assumption is typified by the idea that, 'When advanced religions adopted this theory [namely, the theory that souls transmigrate], they added a rider

---

1. It is difficult to find terminology that is not hotly contested. For cautionary remarks on the use of the term 'traditional' in relation to African societies, for example, see Spiegel and Boonzaier (1988).

thereto that the soul carries with it the results of the good or bad acts done by it' (Tatacharya 1967: 48). The second dubious assumption is that the retributive varieties are, whereas the non-retributive ones are not, properly 'ethical' in nature. Sometimes this latter assumption is expressed in terms of a distinction between philosophical and pre-philosophical versions of the belief. 'In its simplest form', writes G. R. S. Mead, 'the notion of the return of the soul to this earth is found far apart from all philosophical consideration or over-beliefs in widely scattered primitive tribes, and must, it is reasonable to conclude, be due to elementary experience of some sort' (1912: 170). This is deemed 'reasonable to conclude', it would seem, because such 'primitive tribes' could not possibly be capable of 'philosophical consideration'.

Aside from any stereotypical judgements that they may tend to reinforce concerning the ethical and intellectual sophistication of the respective peoples, the main problem with the assumptions just outlined is the over-simplifying and hence distorting effect that they have on our understanding of what I called in Chapter 1 the 'multiplex phenomenon' of rebirth beliefs. The continuum model implies a linear sequence of development from lower to increasingly elevated strata of cultivation, whereas what we see upon examining the phenomena themselves is a tangled skein of diverse beliefs, all with their own peculiarities: a fascinating multiplicity, sharing many connections and affinities, but nothing that suggests a straightforward path from the rudimentary to the refined. Furthermore, the assumption that what is being cultivated and refined along this imaginary continuum is some kind of ethical or philosophical sensibility risks obscuring from view the fact that rebirth beliefs in general, and not just those that involve ideas of retributive karma, tend to be infused with ethical dimensions. The doctrines and activities in which these dimensions manifest may be no less heterogeneous than other aspects of the cultures concerned, yet that hardly speaks against their being identifiably *ethical* dimensions nonetheless. So distinguishing between types of rebirth belief on the basis of whether they are 'ethical' or 'pre-ethical' (or 'non-ethical') is unlikely to produce an illuminating analysis. More informative would be a consideration of the *forms* that ethical values and responses take within and across rebirth-believing societies.

The anthropologist Gananath Obeyesekere has characterized the kind of rebirth belief that is present in Hinduism, Buddhism and Jainism (and also to some extent in ancient Greece) as 'ethicized', distinguishing this from the 'unethicized' or 'non-ethicized' kinds that occur in several Amerindian and Inuit cultures as well as in many other 'small-scale' societies (see Obeyesekere 1968; 1980; 1994; and esp. 2002: ch. 3). While acknowledging that societies of the latter sort are not devoid of ethical norms and practices, and that such societies' rebirth beliefs often have ethical ramifications, Obeyesekere persists in drawing the distinction between two broad categories of rebirth belief in terms of 'ethicization', this being the name that he gives to the process by which ethicized forms of the belief purportedly evolved from non-ethicized ones. Although there need be no specific value-judgement contained in this evolutionary model, it inevitably suggests the idea, which I outlined above, of small-scale societies' beliefs somehow residing at a stage of development earlier than that of ethicized forms. Moreover, notwithstanding Obeyesekere's caveats, the very terms 'ethicized' and 'non-ethicized' are prone to be construed as meaning that, in the case of 'non-ethicized' forms, there is an absence of connection between rebirth beliefs and ethics in general, rather than merely an absence of a specifically individualistic retributive conception of that connection.

Issues concerning the relations between what at first blush might be called, respectively, *ethical values* and *metaphysical beliefs* have far-reaching implications for the study of religions. They reverberate through debates between those who follow Clifford Geertz in regarding religions as 'synthesizing' a metaphysical worldview and an 'ethos' or 'style of life' (Geertz 1973: chs 4 and 5) and those who see such metaphysically imbued conceptions of religion as hangovers from outmoded Christian-dominated approaches (e.g., Asad 1983; 1993: ch. 1).[2] My aim in this chapter is not to try to settle such disputes but to contribute to them by exploring the specific issue of how rebirth beliefs and ethics come together. Part of this exploration will involve questioning whether 'coming together' is the right description here. To speak of a *connection between* or a *coming together of* ethics and a belief in rebirth implies the existence of two conceptually distinguishable phenomena: ethics on the one hand, comprising certain ethical commitments, judgements and practices, and on the other hand, a belief that all of us (or some of us) live successive lives. In Chapter 3 we saw this distinction being challenged by David Cockburn, who proposes that it may be misleading to regard questions of metaphysics (whether, for example, person A 'really is' a reincarnation of person B) as logically prior to questions of ethics (of how, for instance, persons A and B ought to be treated); this is because the attitudes one considers to be appropriate in relation to persons may

---

2. For a recent defence of Geertz, and for further references, see Schilbrack (2005).

be fundamental to what one understands a person to be, and this understanding will in turn be inseparable from whether one holds rebirth to fall within the range of human possibilities. One purpose of the present chapter is to extend that challenge further: to argue that there is no necessity to conceive of a belief in rebirth, and of the ethical values and practices that 'accompany' it, as being two separate things. Rather, in at least many cases, it is more plausible to see a belief in rebirth as partially constitutive of an outlook on the world that is not readily divisible into neatly partitioned doxastic and practical components.

Central to this chapter's argument will be a discussion of Obeyesekere's contrast between the respective beliefs of South Asian and 'small-scale' societies. In the penultimate section I shall adduce some examples to illustrate my contention that the conceptions of rebirth in societies of the latter kind are often best understood as permeated with ethical significance, thereby placing strain on the viability of designating these conceptions as 'non-ethicized'. First, however, in order to begin unsettling the distinction between metaphysical beliefs (or 'theories') and ethical values and practices, I shall critically examine a thesis put forward by Catherine Osborne regarding the origins of beliefs among some early Greek philosophers concerning the transmigration of souls.[3]

Transmigration and Moral Outlooks in Ancient Greece[4]

In Chapter 3 of her book *Dumb Beasts and Dead Philosophers* (2007), Osborne examines the respective conceptions of transmigration discernible in the philosophies of Pythagoras, Empedocles and Plato, giving particular attention to the relation between these conceptions and ethical attitudes towards animals. The thesis for which Osborne argues is that, contrary to a common presupposition, it is not the case

---

3. Since publishing the book that I shall be discussing, Osborne has reverted to using her maiden name, Catherine Rowett. To avoid confusion, I continue to refer to her as Osborne in this chapter.

4. Philosophers occasionally stipulate a technical distinction between ethics and morality (e.g., Williams 2011: 7 *et passim*; Habermas 1993: ch. 1). I shall not be assuming or making a distinction of this kind in this chapter or elsewhere in this book. For suspicions about the viability of such a distinction, see Canto-Sperber (2008: 17–23).

that the three philosophers in question first devised (or inherited from others) a theory of transmigration according to which human souls can be reborn in non-human animals and then, on that basis, developed a moral outlook that advocates vegetarianism and respectful treatment of animals.[5] Rather, Osborne contends,

> The claim that these beasts have human souls, and that they are related to us as close family members, is an *expression* of a distinctive outlook on the world, in which one can come to hold such creatures dear and find oneself as one of them (but temporarily in human form). The theory does not ground the moral advice; rather, the moral outlook generates the theoretical justification. (2007: 45)

Underlying Osborne's thesis is a more general contention concerning the asymmetrical relation between theories (whether scientific or philosophical) and evaluative judgements. According to Osborne, while any theory or body of information about the respective biological or psychological characteristics of humans and animals cannot avoid being guided by value judgements, the theory or body of information itself lacks any power to guide our evaluative perceptions and activities. So, for example, a taxonomy of animal species based on similarities and differences between them will inevitably be guided by judgements concerning which features of the respective species are important for the purposes of classification; yet once the taxonomy has been concocted, it in itself cannot usefully inform our judgements about how members of different species ought to be treated. 'There is', Osborne writes, 'no reason to suppose that the lines of division drawn up for a taxonomy of species include any differences that are morally relevant' (2007: 60).

5. Although Osborne does not explicitly identify authors who have asserted the view against which she is arguing, recent examples include Walters and Portmess (2001: 2), Kumar (2010: 192) and Newmyer (2011: 100). Colin Spencer maintains that belief in the transmigration of souls 'leads *logically* to vegetarianism' (1996: 74, my emphasis), a view against which there are many counter examples: e.g., the Kabbalists who believed 'a soul "exiled" into an animal body could be redeemed and liberated if the animal was ritually slaughtered and eaten, piously and with the appropriate mystical intentions, by the qabbalist saints' (Werblowsky 1987: 23; cf. Sears 2003: 289). I should also note here that, in the case of Plato, it remains an open question whether he was vegetarian himself (Dombrowski 1984a: 61–3; 1984b).

In the light of this underlying conception of the relation between theories and evaluative judgements, Osborne's thesis regarding Pythagoras, Empedocles and Plato can be read as the claim that, irrespective of what these philosophers *thought* they were doing, it cannot be the case that their dedication to animal welfare derived exclusively from cool value-neutral thinking about psychological similarities between humans and animals, with these similarities in turn being taken as indicative of cross-species transmigration. This cannot be the case because such thinking is invariably guided by certain evaluative commitments while being impotent to generate any such commitments itself.

Osborne's thesis is striking in the way that it seeks to undermine an apparently obvious assumption. It would be easy to assume that if someone's being vegetarian is linked with the belief that the souls of animals are likely to have formerly been those of human beings, then it is this belief in the cross-species transmigration of souls that precedes (logically and chronologically) the person's vegetarianism. What Osborne insists on is that the order of priority is – indeed, *must* be, if her underlying view about theories and values is right – the other way round. My two main worries about this thesis are: first, its reliance on an equivocation over notions such as 'values' and 'evaluation'; and second, its uncertainty about whether to merely reverse the standard order of priority between theory and moral outlook or instead to abandon the assumption that there need be any order of priority here at all. I shall elaborate each of these worries in turn.

While it is plainly true that a theory pertaining to the similarities and differences between various animal species, including humans, will be guided by evaluative judgements (either explicit or implicit) about which features of the species concerned need to be attended to, it by no means follows that these judgements are themselves *moral* in nature. By analogy, my decision to go shopping may depend on a logically prior evaluation that I need to restock my food cupboard, but this in itself does not entail that the evaluation that my food cupboard needs restocking is a moral one. So it thus sounds suspicious when Osborne moves from the non-contentious claim that 'How we classify the animals and plants that are the subject of biology will depend upon the needs that the system of classification is required to serve' (2007: 60) to the contentious proposal that, when Pythagoras, Empedocles and Plato emphasized the commonality of 'capacities and origins' between ourselves and other creatures, 'Their claims were based on a revised *moral* understanding of how the world is divided' (61, my emphasis).

Admittedly, there is an intermediate step in Osborne's argument. This involves citing a particular example of how, in offering 'a taxonomy according to the habitat that a creature occupies', Plato 'builds a set of value judgements into that classification by suggesting that one gets closer to the earth the more disabled one's intellectual powers' (Osborne 2007: 60).[6] Osborne submits that, rather than having first observed the respective intellectual powers of various creatures and then inferred the correlation between these powers and the proximity of creatures to the earth, Plato's deliberations were imbued from the outset with evaluative associations such as those of 'higher' and 'lower' (Osborne 2007: 60–1). Plato assigns to worms weaker intellects than to birds, for example, 'because he despises the weaker intellects, and because he thinks that worms are low on the *scala naturae*' (61). In other words, he has already made up his mind about which animals are least (morally) valuable before he contrives a system of classification that ranks them according to their alleged intellectual capacities and proximity to the earth.[7]

While the example just cited poignantly illustrates Osborne's thesis, the generality of the thesis nevertheless relies on the underlying contention that systems of classification are substantially influenced by value judgements and that these value judgements are themselves specifically moral. It still remains far from obvious that this is so, and even in the exemplary case of Plato the situation may be more complicated than Osborne makes out. Might he not have had other

6. Osborne makes reference here to Plato's *Timaeus* 40a and invites us to compare *Sophist* 220a. A more directly relevant passage would seem to be *Timaeus* 91d–92c, part of which Osborne refers us to subsequently (2007: 61 n.42).

7. Some commentators have supposed that the whole passage from *Timaeus* 91d–92a is largely intended to be humorous. According to A. E. Taylor, for example, Plato's 'lumping together' of various sea creatures into one category 'should show that we are dealing with humour, not with science' (1928: 644). Osborne would not deem Plato's taxonomy to be merely humorous, and I would agree. Part of what Plato is doing is 'persuad[ing] us to see those positions [of "higher" and "lower"] as evaluative' (Rowett [formerly Osborne], personal communication via email, 24 January 2012). Taylor's dichotomy between humour and science leaves out the live possibility that the taxonomy's significance is best characterized as something other than either humour *or* science: as something, for instance, that *combines* playfulness with other purposes, such as serious allegory or a kind of ontology that is not straightforwardly biological.

reasons for assigning weaker intellects to worms than to birds, over and above his ranking them lower in the scale of nature? One might, for example, consider the behaviour of birds to be more complex than that of worms and believe complexity of behaviour to be correlated with intellectual capacity. If someone such as Plato had taken this view, it might remain true that he despised weaker intellects, but it would become less credible that his judging worms to have weaker intellects than birds was *due to* (or at least partially due to) his underlying evaluation of worms as less morally worthy than birds. Whether this latter suggestion genuinely applies to Plato himself is probably not determinable, yet the fact that it *might* apply should make us wary of saying that his verdict on worm intellects must be a consequence of his moral attitude. Clearly, the conception of intellectual capacity is bound up, for Plato, with his understanding of moral worth, but it is the idea that one of these (either the conception of intellectual capacity or the understanding of moral worth) must precede and undergird the other that I am questioning.

Turning now to my second worry, this was that Osborne's thesis betrays uncertainty whether to merely reverse the standard order of priority between moral outlook and rebirth theory or instead to dispense with the idea of an order of priority between these things. For the most part Osborne seems to be saying that, in the case of the philosophers she discusses, instead of regarding their conception of rebirth as grounding their moral outlook we should see their moral outlook as grounding their conception of rebirth. She says, for example, that 'To change whom we see as kin, we must *first* change our moral outlook' (2007: 62, my emphasis). This implies that the moral outlook can be changed independently of changing whom we see as kin, but that whom we see as kin can change only as a consequence of changing our moral outlook. Osborne then goes on to say of Pythagoras, Empedocles and Plato that they 'give us a story to explain how souls can transmigrate and how we might all be kin, but the story is there to defend and promote a revisionary moral outlook' (62), thereby again implying that the moral outlook comes before the story of transmigration.

Earlier, however, in a passage that I have quoted already, Osborne asserts of the claim that animals 'have human souls, and ... are related to us as close family members' that this 'is an *expression* of a distinctive outlook on the world, in which one can come to hold such creatures dear and find oneself as one of them (but temporarily in human form)'.[8] Here, Osborne's emphasis on 'expression' suggests not that the 'distinctive outlook on the world' somehow pre-exists the conception of human-to-animal transmigration, but that the outlook on the world *takes the form of* or *is articulated in terms of* this conception. Under this description, we are not forced to say that if the conception of animal–human relations is to be changed 'we must first change our moral outlook', for there is a sense in which the conception or 'theory' *is* the moral outlook: there is no logical separation between them. We come to see what the conception of transmigration means – what it amounts to – *in* the forms of ethical judgement and action by which the moral outlook is constituted. For this reason it would make just as much sense to say that the moral outlook at issue expresses the claim that animals have human souls as it does to say that the claim that animals have human souls expresses the moral outlook. We could also say that both of these are expressions of one integrated picture.

If Osborne would agree with the points I have just made, then her real thesis could be formulated by saying that the transmigration theories of Pythagoras, Empedocles and Plato are suffused with moral value and commitment from the outset. It is not that the theory is logically and chronologically prior to the moral outlook, but neither need it be that 'the moral outlook generates the theoretical justification'. Rather, what we have is a unified way of being with, and responding to, animals in the world – an outlook that involves seeing animals and humans as a community of commonly 'ensouled' creatures.[9]

Wittgenstein, in his 'Remarks on Frazer's *Golden Bough*', affirms a point comparable to the one I have just been making. What Wittgenstein is objecting to is James Frazer's purported explanation of the ancient rite of succession at Nemi, in which the successor had to kill the incumbent priest-king. More precisely, Wittgenstein is not so much

8. There is an affinity between this statement of Osborne's and Cockburn's view that 'we must think of a metaphysical picture of persons as an *expression* of an ethical outlook' (1990: 206, original emphasis). What I am about to argue is that (to echo Gilbert Ryle from another context) there is no *must* about it; we can just as well think of the metaphysical and the ethical as two expressions of an integral whole.

9. Cf. Osborne's assertion that Empedocles, Plato and Pythagoreans conceive of animals not merely as ensouled (*empsucha*), but as possessing '*exactly the same* kind of souls as we have' (2007: 59, original emphasis). On the vexed issue of the relation between human and animal souls in ancient Greek thought, see Sorabji (1993).

criticizing the particular explanation that Frazer offers, but rather questioning Frazer's assumption that an explanation must take the form of disclosing a belief upon which the action is based. Wittgenstein writes of Frazer that,

> When, for example, he explains to us that the king must be killed in his prime, because the savages believe that otherwise his soul would not be kept fresh, all one can say is: where that practice and these views occur together, the practice does not spring from the view, but they are both just there. (1993: 119)

This remark was written in 1931 shortly after Wittgenstein's first acquaintance with Frazer's text.[10] In a later manuscript from 1945 Wittgenstein makes a similar point with reference to peoples who hold a belief which, when rendered into a European language, is expressed as the belief that they are descended from an animal (such as a snake). In response to those who would then look at various practices within the society concerned and describe them as 'based on this belief', Wittgenstein asks rhetorically: 'But why should we not say: these customs and laws are not *based* on that belief, but they show *to what extent*, in what sense, such a belief exists' (Wittgenstein 2000, MS 116: 283, my trans.).[11]

Although Wittgenstein is writing in highly condensed form, we can see that what he is resisting is the assumption that we must postulate an order of priority between belief and practice – an order in which the belief, or view, provides the *rationale* for the practice. Exactly how far Wittgenstein is going in the direction of a wholesale rejection of any attempt at explanation at all is a moot point.[12] For present purposes all that needs to be noted is that he is enjoining us to recognize that there is no necessity to suppose that the practice is based on a prior belief. Both the belief and the practice – or, better, the belief–practice nexus – may, to use Osborne's phrase, express 'a distinctive outlook on the world'. And it follows from this that neither are we forced simply to reverse the

---

10. See the editors' introduction in Wittgenstein (1993: 115).

11. A similar translation, along with some of the surrounding text, is provided in Rhees (1997: 88).

12. For a thorough treatment of what Wittgenstein is up to in his remarks on Frazer, see Clack (1999: esp. chs 4 and 5). See also Needham (1985: ch. 7) and my own discussion in Burley (2012a: ch. 1).

direction of influence and say that the belief is based on the practice or moral outlook.

There are undoubtedly dangers associated with using the term 'expression' in these contexts; for when Osborne says that the transmigration-claims of Pythagoras and others are 'an *expression* of a distinctive outlook on the world', there are liable to be critics who will hear this as a denial that these philosophers 'really' believed in transmigration at all. It will be assumed that what is being asserted is that the philosophers merely found talk of transmigration congenial for voicing certain ethical commitments that they held independently of the vocabulary used to express them. In short, such critics will assume that Osborne is offering a reductive, non-realist, non-cognitivist analysis of the philosophers' transmigration-talk: non-realist in the sense that the talk does not entail belief in the reality of transmigration, and non-cognitivist in the sense that it does not aim to articulate knowledge about the world but merely to express value judgements. It is thus reductive inasmuch as it is eliminating any cognitive or truth-apt content from the transmigration-related statements of the philosophers and is reducing those statements to 'mere' expressions. Although I very much doubt that Osborne would look favourably upon this construal of her thesis, her claim that 'the moral outlook *generates* the theoretical justification' (my emphasis) may unwittingly encourage it.

One way of reclaiming Osborne's thesis from the reductive reading would involve rejecting the dualistic conception of facts and values upon which that reading depends. To interpret in non-realist or non-cognitivist terms the assertion that transmigration-claims express moral values, one would have to assume that moral values are incapable of connecting with reality in ways that are true or knowledge-bearing. Relinquishing *this* assumption opens up the possibility of conceiving of transmigration-claims as true, without necessarily affirming that the criteria for their being true must be identical to those that apply to, say, statements of empirical science. We might, for example, want to say that they could be *morally* true or *metaphysically* true without thereby committing ourselves to the supposition that transmigration beliefs are empirically testable.[13]

13. A related way of resisting the reductive reading of Osborne's thesis would be to reject the Cartesian metaphysical assumption that states of mind (including beliefs and value-commitments) are logically independent of and prior to the actions and responses that they are supposed to causally initiate. If, as argued by Wittgenstein (2009a and elsewhere) and by Ryle (2009), it is

These latter thoughts, however, are taking us further than my immediate purposes require. My principal reason for discussing Osborne's proposal was to indicate how a certain presupposition might be brought into question, the presupposition being that the relation between a theory of rebirth or transmigration and a moral outlook must be one of logical and historical priority, with the theory holding the prior position. Osborne displaces this presupposition by, apparently, switching the order of priority. What I have argued is that even this switching presupposes a dichotomy between 'theory' and 'outlook' or 'belief' and 'practice', which need not be present. At the very least, we should question the viability of this postulated dichotomy rather than simply assuming that it is there. In the next section I shall turn to the thesis proposed by Obeyesekere, that in the South Asian context rebirth theories did indeed precede the forms of ethical evaluation that came to be associated with them, and that the process of their acquiring those ethical associations can usefully be termed *ethicization*.

Eschatologies and 'Ethicization'

The difference between Obeyesekere's viewpoint and that of Osborne can be seen immediately by noting what Obeyesekere says about the Pythagorean commitment to vegetarianism. Osborne, as we have seen, argues that the latter commitment, along with the general ethical outlook towards animals of which it is part, gave rise to a conception of human-to-animal transmigration. Obeyesekere, meanwhile, maintains that it is the fact that the Pythagoreans' 'rebirth eschatology entailed animal rebirths' that 'explains the strong injunction against consuming flesh' (2002: 191).

Similarly, with regard to the South Asian traditions of Hinduism, Buddhism and Jainism, Obeyesekere presents a speculative narrative in which a conception of rebirth – including rebirth from one species to another – was formulated prior to the particular forms of ethical

---

in our actions and responses that our beliefs and values are characteristically seen, then the picture of an expression of a belief or value being logically (conceptually) detachable from the belief or value itself loses its grip. See, e.g., Ryle (2009: 116–18) and, for discussion of Wittgenstein, Churchill (1984). For a recent account of the relevance of these ways of thinking to the study of religion, see Springs (2008).

injunction and practice that came to characterize those traditions. Obeyesekere focuses especially on what he terms a transformation from 'rebirth eschatology' to 'karmic eschatology', and it is this transformation that he refers to as 'ethicization'. He articulates the thesis in bold terms, contending that the process he is describing (albeit speculatively and schematically rather than on the basis of clear historical evidence) has the force of logical necessity: 'When ethicization is systematically introduced into any rebirth eschatology, that rebirth eschatology must logically transform itself into a karmic eschatology' (2002: 78; cf. 1980: 147).[14]

Obeyesekere uses the term 'eschatology' not in the strict sense of a conception of the final destination or goal of humankind and of the world in general, but rather to denote any conception of what will happen to a person beyond death. Had he been aware of it, he could have borrowed from John Hick the term 'pareschatology', which Hick attributes to the scholar of biblical studies Michael Goulder (Hick 1976: 34 n. 2). 'Whereas eschatology is the doctrine of the *eschata* or last things, and thus of the ultimate state of man', writes Hick, 'pareschatology is, by anology, the doctrine of the *para-eschata*, or next-to-last things, and thus of the human future between the present life and man's ultimate state' (1976: 22). In Obeyesekere's terms, however, a rebirth eschatology is any belief or system of beliefs that comprises the view that at least some people, and perhaps some animals as well, will be reborn in a new form after their present life. This construal, in itself, says nothing about the ethical content of the outlook at issue, but when Obeyesekere is drawing a contrast between 'rebirth eschatologies' and 'karmic eschatologies' the difference that he means to highlight is a specifically ethical one. While a karmic eschatology remains a form of rebirth eschatology, it is one that has been 'ethicized'. This means that the conception of rebirth that has developed is one in which one's experiences beyond death – in the 'other world' – and also the nature of one's next rebirth (and perhaps rebirths posterior to that as well) are held to be conditioned by, determined by or dependent upon the moral quality of one's actions in the present life (2002: 79–80, 247).

The narrative of conceptual evolution that Obeyesekere presents involves two main steps, which successively effect the transformation from a simple rebirth eschatology to a specifically ethicized karmic

14. See also Obeyesekere (1968: 17): 'When any preliterate reincarnation religion is ethicized, a different set of eschatological consequences logically follows.'

eschatology. The first step is for the belief to be formed that a person's entry into an after-death world is conditional, not on exclusively religious actions (such as correct performance of funeral rites for the one who has died), but upon 'the ethical nature of one's this-worldly actions' (2002: 79). A further component of this first step is that the 'other world' is conceived as a location, or suite of locations, conducive to the appropriate reward or punishment of the deceased individual: 'Heavens and hells have to be invented in any ethicized eschatology' (79). The second step consists in the formation of the belief that, beyond one's sojourn in the 'other world', one's future earthly rebirths will also be 'ethically conditioned', taking a form consistent with and at least partially determined by the quality of one's moral behaviour in a previous life or lives (80). According to Obeyesekere's model, once the two steps of this conceptual shift have been taken, and the cycle of rebirth has been conceptualized as an ongoing series of ethically conditioned lifetimes separated by temporary intervals in the 'other world', 'a concomitant epistemological shift takes place', which involves viewing rebirth not as '*a thing in itself*' but as '*a product of the ethical nature of one's actions*'. From this new perspective, 'Rebirth cannot be divorced from ethics; it looks as if it is generated *from* ethics' (82, original emphasis).

When Obeyesekere says that from the point of view of a fully ethicized karmic eschatology rebirth appears to be generated from ethics, he is clearly not claiming that what appears to be the case from that point of view is that the sort of thesis presented by Catherine Osborne is true. Osborne's proposal – that with regard to the rebirth theories of Pythagoras, Empedocles and Plato 'the moral outlook generates the theoretical justification' – seems best understood as the claim that, whatever course these philosophers assumed their reasoning to be taking, they were in fact basing their rebirth theory on their moral outlook. What Obeyesekere is claiming in connection with South Asian karmic eschatologies is quite different. He is claiming that a constitutive element of those eschatologies is that, to the believers themselves, it appears that an individual's ethical actions produce (or condition, or determine) his or her 'future-life fate' (2002: 132). His suggestion is not that there is anything wrong or mistaken about this belief on the part of the believers; he is merely pointing it out as a feature of karmic eschatologies. Neither is he straightforwardly arguing that the ethical norms and commitments exhibited by adherents of karmic eschatologies are, in reality, generated out of their rebirth beliefs. Rather, what Obeyesekere is doing is presenting an idealized narrative – or, as he puts it, an 'imaginary experiment' – of the development of South Asian conceptions of rebirth, in which a particular kind of ethical picture is gradually incorporated into or superimposed upon a pre-existing mode of rebirth belief.[15]

A similarity between what Obeyesekere is claiming about South Asian rebirth beliefs and what Osborne claims about ancient Greek theories is that each of these claims relies on a conceptual dichotomy between rebirth beliefs on the one hand and the ethical values and practices of believers in rebirth on the other. Osborne's thought is that the ethical values and practices – or 'moral outlook' – can pre-exist a conception of rebirth that later comes to be used to justify the moral outlook. Obeyesekere's thought is that a conception of rebirth can pre-exist a set of ethical values and practices that later transform that conception. In contemplating each of these contentions – Obeyesekere's no less than Osborne's – we should do well to bear in mind Wittgenstein's remark that, as far as 'explaining' the phenomenon in question goes, 'all one can say is: where that practice and these views occur together, the practice does not spring from the view, but they are both just there'. Perhaps Wittgenstein goes too far in saying that the practice *does* not spring from the view. It would be more prudent, and more in keeping with Wittgenstein's own general reluctance to make categorical pronouncements, to say that the practice *may* not, or *need* not, spring from the view. But, either way, we are usefully cautioned against assuming that there must be an order of logical and historical priority between the practical and doxastic dimensions of a mode of human life. In the absence of such caution, we are prone to misunderstand the phenomenon under investigation by superimposing upon it conceptual dichotomies that might well be out of place.

I referred earlier to Obeyesekere's use of expressions such as 'must logically'. This requires closer attention, as it is indicative of a possible confusion on Obeyesekere's part about what sort of account he is providing. He presents his imaginative model, with its two main steps

---

15. For his use of 'imaginary experiment', see Obeyesekere (2002: 18, and esp. ch. 3). 'Imaginary experiment' is among the expressions that Obeyesekere inherits from Max Weber. For discussion of the latter's use of it, see Swedberg and Agevall (2005: 46). Obeyesekere (2002: 365 n. 27) himself cites an essay of Weber's first published in 1905 (see Weber 1949: 174–5), in which 'imagination' is said to be capable of applying knowledge derived from experience to our 'knowledge of certain "facts"' in order to arrive at a historical claim that is 'objectively possible'.

and their respective ramifications, as though he were offering a speculative historical reconstruction of how karma-imbued conceptions of rebirth emerged in South Asia around the middle centuries of the first millennium BCE.[16] Yet it is far from clear why such a speculative reconstruction should be held to carry the force of logical necessity which is implied by terms such as 'must logically'. By using this vocabulary, Obeyesekere blurs the distinction between an account of the *historical development* of particular beliefs and practices and an account of the logical relations, *at a given time*, between different conceptual features of those beliefs and practices. An account of the former kind concerns matters of diachronic change, whereas one of the latter kind concerns matters of synchronic relationship.

What Obeyesekere says about a karmic eschatology's being one that has become ethicized in the way he describes makes most sense, I propose, when read as an analytic description of what a particular conception of rebirth *is*; as an analysis, that is, of the strands of interconnected thought and practice that constitute the religious and cultural phenomenon that Obeyesekere terms 'karmic eschatology'. When viewed in these terms, Obeyesekere's analysis is plausible and illuminating. It provides what some philosophers, influenced by Wittgenstein or Ryle, have called a conceptual 'map', or what others have termed 'connective analysis'.[17] As characterized by Peter Hacker, the latter kind of analysis 'is concerned with describing and clarifying the concepts we employ in discourse about ourselves and about the world, and in elucidating their relationships – their forms of relative priority, dependency, and interdependency' (2004: 352).[18] Admittedly,

---

16. Obeyesekere follows Jaspers (2010) in regarding the 'Axial Age' (beginning in the sixth century BCE) as the critical period in the development of the 'historical religions', including Hinduism, Buddhism and Jainism (Obeyesekere 2002: 75). For more on the notion of an axial age, see Arnason et al. (2005).

17. The expression 'connective analysis' derives from Strawson (1985: 25); see also Strawson (1992: ch. 2). For discussion of the notion of a conceptual 'map' or 'the metaphor of logical or conceptual geography', see Baker and Hacker (2005: 284); cf. Tanney (2013b).

18. Examples of such an approach in the study of religions can be found in the work of D. Z. Phillips and some other Wittgenstein-influenced philosophers, although they are unlikely to use the particular term 'connective analysis'. One way of viewing the Wittgensteinian task in this area is as bringing out the '"internal" (or conceptual) connections between the various dimensions of

the concepts that Obeyesekere is endeavouring to describe and clarify, being specifically those of believers in rebirth, might not be ones that *we* (collectively) employ, since many of his readers will not be believers in rebirth themselves. But if 'we' in the passage from Hacker is expanded to encompass any given human community, then Hacker's sketch of connective analysis seems to fit what Obeyesekere is up to fairly well.

Even when considered under the aspect of conceptual connective analysis, Obeyesekere's use of the logical 'must' is still likely to sound too categorical to the ears of many philosophical readers. This is because he implies that, irrespective of the finer details and nuances of any particular cultural milieu, if certain basic conceptual factors are in place then certain other factors will necessarily also be there. The approach displays what Wittgenstein (1969: 17–18) would call a 'craving for generality' modelled on the explanatory methods of natural science. It carries with it the danger of neglecting what is important in particular cases. In other words, the search for commonalities across a range of phenomena risks obscuring what is peculiar to each of them. Nevertheless, Obeyesekere manages to avoid an exclusive preoccupation with schematic generalizations by also devoting sustained attention to specific textual sources such as the Upaniṣads, and to religio-cultural traditions such as Buddhism and the Ājīvika sect.[19] When examining these sources and traditions there is no problem with presenting one's account as containing a historical aspect, since relevant historical sources of evidence are available. The problem with Obeyesekere's treatment of rebirth on which I have been focusing is his insistence that a speculative historical account – an 'imaginary experiment' – has the force of logical necessity.

A further problem with Obeyesekere's thesis derives from his use of the terms 'ethicized' and 'non-ethicized'. Notwithstanding the care that he takes, advising his readers that by referring to certain rebirth eschatologies as 'non-ethicized' he does not mean to imply that there is an

religious belief ... and religious practice' (Wynn 1995: 423; cf. Phillips 1986: 10). Phillips sees a close similarity between his own approach and the interpretive anthropology of Geertz (Phillips 2001: 6–7), and Geertz himself acknowledges a significant debt to Wittgenstein (Geertz 2000: xi–xiii; cf. Geertz 1983: ch. 4).

19. The Ājīvikas were a non-Brahmanical religious group that is thought to have existed from at least as early as the sixth century BCE through to around the eighth century CE. See Obeyesekere (2002: 102–8) and, for further exposition, Basham (1981).

absence of ethics in the societies concerned, his use of these terms can hardly fail to be misleading. As Antonia Mills has pointed out (1994b: 17), the problem here is that Obeyesekere's distinction 'masks the fact that tribal eschatologies [such as those of many Amerindian and Inuit peoples] also contain ethical premises', even if they are different from those of supposedly 'ethicized' religions such as Hinduism and Buddhism. These ethical premises – values, judgements, practices and so forth – do not float free of the respective societies' rebirth beliefs, but are in many cases thoroughly integrated with them. Having already seen some indications of such integration in examples adduced in earlier chapters (notably in the discussions of consanguineous rebirth and attitudes towards ancestors in the penultimate sections of Chapters 1 and 3) let us, in the next section, consider some further cases.

Instances of Non-Karmic Ethical Integration

In the passage from Mills to which I referred above, she goes on to remark of the 'ethics of people with [what Obeyesekere calls] "unethicized eschatologies"' that these 'are based on the premise of the equality of human consciousness with that of other species of animals, fish, and fowl' (1994b: 17). By 'equality of ... consciousness', Mills here seems to mean that members of non-human species are held to have spirits which ought to be respected in ways that accord them equal value to the spirits of human beings. Elsewhere, when writing specifically about the Wet'suwet'en, Gitxsan and Beaver peoples of British Columbia, Mills observes that they

> believe that each species of animal and plant is endowed with an intelligence, comparable to human intelligence, which is fully aware of the actions and intentions of humans and that only when humans honor the spirits of the species will the game and fish and fowl leave their spirit homes and reincarnate so as to be taken by humans. (1988: 388–9)

Here we see how a belief in rebirth can be intimately bound up with profound ethical attitudes; in this instance, specifically attitudes towards animals. Yet, if we accept Obeyesekere's narrow conception of ethicization, this would have to count as a 'non-ethicized' form of rebirth belief.

The respect for animals exhibited by Amerindian peoples is also documented by Franz Boas (1896) in one of his many reports on the Kwakwaka'wakw people, again of British Columbia.[20] 'When a wolf has been killed', writes Boas, 'it is placed on a blanket. Its heart is taken out, and all those who have assisted in killing it must take four morsels of the heart.' A phrase that Boas translates as 'Woe! our great friend' is wailed over the wolf's body, which is then 'covered with a blanket and buried'. Boas adds that the weapon used to kill a wolf is considered unlucky and hence is given away by the owner, and that the killing of a wolf is held to produce 'scarcity of game' (1896: 579). This treatment of wolves is of a piece with the Kwakwaka'wakw belief that hunters who hunt on the land will be reborn as wolves, and those who hunt at sea will be reborn as killer whales (ibid.).[21]

If we were to adhere in this case to the line of thought that Osborne applies to ancient Greek philosophers, we might say that the belief that hunters are reborn as wolves is generated by the moral outlook of which respect for wolves is an integral part. But we are not forced to say this, any more than we are forced to say that the moral attitude towards wolves is generated by the belief in interspecies rebirth. The two things go together, but there is no necessity to give logical priority to one or the other. We see the sense that the rebirth belief has *in* the attitude of respect that is displayed towards wolves, and the attitude is expressed *in terms of* rebirth (or at least partly in those terms). This is not to deny that there could be forms of belief in rebirth that are not accompanied by a respectful attitude towards wolves. On the contrary, in a passage that I cited in Chapter 1 (p. 33) from the Brahmanical Hindu law book, the *Mānava Dharmaśāstra* (12.67), we see the view expressed that people who steal deer or elephants will be reborn as wolves, and in Plato's *Phaedo* (82a) Socrates declares that lovers of injustice, tyranny and robbery 'will join the tribes of wolves and hawks and kites'. These are not expressions of respect, and it is difficult to imagine a community for whom wolves are associated with theft or injustice honouring a wolf in the way that was typical of the Kwakwaka'wakw people described by Boas. What we have in these respective cases are examples of distinct kinds of rebirth belief, each infused with ethical significance, but not

20. Boas refers to them as the 'Kwakiutl', but 'Kwakwaka'wakw' is the preferred term among anthropologists these days (see Wurm et al. 1996: 1145).
21. See also Mills (1994b: 33); and for a useful summary of how both wolves and killer whales feature in the art and mythology of Northwest Coast Amerindians, see Shearar (2000: 115–16).

of the same sort. While any inquiry into these cases would need to recognize the important ethical discrepancies between them, it seems decidedly unhelpful to place the Hindu and Platonic examples in the category of 'ethicized' belief and that of the Kwakwaka'wakw hunters in the 'non-ethicized' category.

To further illustrate how the rebirth beliefs of small-scale societies can resound with deep ethical meaning, I shall here mention a few examples of ways in which the treatment of children is implicated in such beliefs. Among many of the Amerindian and Inuit peoples studied by Mills and others, belief in consanguineous rebirth is often tied to traditions of inheritance, according to which someone's right to inherit the title and land of an ancestor goes along with that person's being regarded as the ancestor reincarnated. As Mills indicates, a practice such as that 'of taking one's nephew and heir to one's title out to one's territory takes on new meaning when we recognize that this nephew is commonly presumed to be the reincarnation of a former holder of the land and title, as well as the mother's brother's heir' (1988: 402). In many instances the child will be given the same name as the person of whom he or she is deemed to be the reincarnation. Unsurprisingly, such practices can significantly affect the forms that intergenerational relationships take, and this becomes especially poignant in cases where the child identifies strongly with the ancestor in question.

Mills relates the case of a young man named Jeffrey who, at around the age of five, had announced to his grandmother, Louise, that he was in fact a son of hers, named Will, who had previously died. Even though Jeffrey's biological parents were still alive, he went to live with his grandparents, referring to Louise as 'Mother' instead of 'Grandma' (Mills 1988: 394). In another case, a member of the Haida people of British Columbia named Florence Edenshaw Davidson recalls in her memoir how, as a child, one of the reasons why she was favoured over her siblings by her father was that she was believed to be the reincarnation of his own mother: '"*Hada ding awu di ijing*," ["Dad, I'm your mother"] I kept saying. Those were my first words' (Blackman 1992: 78).

Although this strength of personal identification with one's previous incarnation is not typical among Amerindian peoples, cases such as these do illustrate the potentially radical significance of rebirth beliefs upon kinship relations in societies where such beliefs are commonplace. The precise form of the ethical implications is by no means easily describable, yet it would be implausible to suppose that the acceptance of a child's life as in some sense a continuation of that of its deceased uncle or grandmother would not bring with it major ethical repercussions. What Akhil Gupta has referred to as the 'narratives of reincarnation' within certain communities is indicative of conceptions of childhood that differ from those of communities in which belief in rebirth is, at most, only marginal. Children at the centre of such narratives are, Gupta suggests, 'inhabited by their (adult) thoughts and gestures, and clearly have to be conceptualized as more complex beings than is allowed by the standard narrative of childhood [within western, liberal and largely secular societies] which posits a new being who slowly finds his or her way in the world' (2002: 36). Part of this conceptualization is apt to involve alternative configurations of the emotional and ethical relations within families and wider kinship networks.

Another example of the bearing that particular forms of rebirth belief have upon the conceptualization of children, and upon ethical behaviour towards them, derives from a study of the Papel community of Guinea-Bissau on the west coast of Africa. Jónína Einarsdóttir observes that among the Papel, who believe in rebirth, 'mothers view their newborns as human at birth, each one having a particular personality' (2004: 103). She contrasts this with the attitude of the Alto people of Brazil, who do not have a rebirth belief and who regard 'infants as not yet fully human', lacking 'an individual personality' (103).[22] Comparing the infant care practices of these two communities, Einarsdóttir notes that 'holding, co-sleeping, rapid response to crying, and devoted care' are prevalent among the Papel, whereas Alto mothers often leave small children alone at home and 'have little physical contact with their infants, who sleep in their own cot' (103).

Without proposing a simplistic deterministic relation between belief in rebirth and childcare practices, Einarsdóttir plausibly underlines the relevance of this belief to Papel conceptions of infanthood. She also points out, however, that an aspect of Papel belief is that some children are 'born without human souls and [are] unable to get one'. In these cases, it is deemed that the children 'should be killed in order to prevent them from causing damage to their mother's lineage' (166). Thus, the ethical ramifications of Papel rebirth beliefs are complex, being associated both with diligent attentiveness to infants' needs when the neonates are regarded as reincarnate human souls, and with instances of infanticide when they are not.

22. Einarsdóttir is here drawing on the study of the Alto in Scheper-Hughes (1992).

Concluding Remarks

Expanding ideas intimated in previous chapters, the present chapter has explored the integrated nature of beliefs in rebirth and their associated ethical values and practices, placing in question the common presupposition that there must be an order of logical and temporal priority between them. Catherine Osborne cogently disrupts the assumption that this order of priority must be one in which it is the rebirth belief, or 'theory', that gives rise to certain ethical practices (such as respecting non-human animals and abstaining from eating them). Although Osborne is concerned specifically with the theories and practices of particular Greek philosophers, her discussion has far-reaching implications. Without directly contradicting Osborne's thesis, I have argued that the way in which it is presented gives the impression that the order of priority between rebirth theory and moral outlook has simply been reversed, when in fact there is no good reason for assuming that there has to be any order of priority at all. It could be the case that the belief in rebirth and the practices associated with respect for animals evolved together from the outset and are mutually constitutive of the same overall 'outlook on the world' – a 'fusion of the existential and the normative', to invoke a phrase from Geertz (1973: 127). Certainly, if we are to properly understand that outlook, it will be wise to seek the sense that 'rebirth' or 'transmigration' has for the ancient Greeks *in* the moral attitudes and practices that they exhibit, and to observe how these attitudes and practices are expressed and advocated *through* the vocabulary of rebirth.

This same point applies to Obeyesekere's 'imaginary experiment' concerning the development of karmic eschatologies in South Asia. *Pace* Obeyesekere, there is no compelling reason to suppose that the conceptions of rebirth which comprise, in part, a sophisticated doctrine of the post-mortem consequences of action (*karma*) for individual agents must have evolved from pre-karmic rebirth eschatologies. Indeed, there is scope in this context for an Osborne-style Copernican reversal, in which the kinds of rebirth beliefs typified by Hinduism, Buddhism and Jainism are seen as emerging out of a moral outlook that involves an understanding of individual culpability for one's actions. The conjecture has, on occasions, been made that the doctrine of karma developed from an instinctive 'tendency to retaliation', which was gradually refined into the idea of reformation and justice (Dasgupta 1965: 213); it has then been added that, since it is obvious that neither retributive justice nor reformation manifest consistently in a single lifetime, the belief in rebirth (or 'theory of transmigration') comes about as a 'necessary corollary to the doctrine of karma' (Hiriyanna 1949: 47).[23] Rather than advocating such a reversal, however, my purpose has again been to question the underlying presupposition that there must be an order of priority between rebirth beliefs and the ethical values and practices with which those beliefs are so intimately associated. When what is at issue are contingent historical processes for which clear, let alone decisive, evidence is lacking, talk of logical necessities or necessary corollaries is ill-advised.

The latter portion of the chapter has also challenged the appropriateness of speaking of the development of karmic conceptions of rebirth in terms of a transition from a non-ethicized to an ethicized mode of religion. There are undoubtedly many important differences to be observed between forms of belief in rebirth that involve notions of karmic retribution and other forms that do not, some of which I highlighted in Chapter 1. Obeyesekere's own work goes a long way towards bringing to the fore a number of these differences as well as important similarities across various rebirth beliefs. Yet the model of cultural evolutionary development that Obeyesekere offers risks, first, seriously underplaying the ineluctably ethical nature of the supposedly pre-ethicized beliefs of many small-scale societies, and second, misrepresenting these beliefs by implying that they are situated at an earlier stage of development along a continuum that culminates in the full-blown karmic eschatologies of South Asia.[24]

Finally, I want to re-emphasize the multiplicity of forms that beliefs in rebirth can and do take. No doubt some of these forms could be legitimately designated as rebirth beliefs without thereby entailing that any significant ethical dimension pertains to them; meanwhile, there are also many forms that are so thoroughly intermingled with ethics that the ethical dimension can hardly be detached from any adequate description of the belief. Wittgenstein occasionally suggested that to imagine a 'use of language' is to imagine a culture (Wittgenstein 1969:

---

23. See also Humphreys (1983: 27): '[T]he doctrine of Rebirth is a necessary corollary of Karma, for the longest life on earth will not suffice to restore the harmony disturbed by a daily round of self-regarding actions.'

24. Though present in Obeyesekere (2002), this risk is even more pronounced in his 1980 essay, where terms such as 'primitive' and 'preliterate' are used to characterize the societies that he later came to refer to by the less pejorative-sounding term 'small-scale'.

134; 1970: 202),[25] and this certainly applies to the imagining of uses of language that instantiate talk of rebirth. Whether it be a South Asian, Amerindian, West African or any other cultural context in which rebirth beliefs have a place, the beliefs are prone to be misunderstood if they are abstracted from the broader culture, for it is in that broader milieu that they have their life and meaning. What I have argued in this chapter is that one way of misunderstanding such beliefs is to assume that the belief in rebirth is one thing and the ethical values and practices with which it is associated are another. At least in many instances it will be inapt to say either that the practices spring from the belief or that the belief springs from the practices, or even simply that 'they are both just there'. Rather, it will be more apt to say that, in those places where talk of rebirth obtains, we find a cultural and religious mode in which belief and practice, 'theory' and 'moral outlook', are mutually integral to a cohesive form of life.

25. Cf. Geertz (1983: 73), where Geertz borrows Wittgenstein's analogy between language and an old city and extends it to include culture.

Chapter 5

DEMYTHOLOGIZING REBIRTH?

Religious beliefs, like many other beliefs, are not static. Not only do they come in numerous culturally inflected varieties in the first place, but each of those varieties is subject to processes of ongoing interpretation and reinterpretation. Sometimes an interpretation that appears to some as a return to the authentic doctrine will strike others as a radical innovation, subversive and revisionary of earlier forms. In the middle decades of the twentieth century, the term 'demythologizing' gained currency as the name of a particular approach to Christian biblical hermeneutics, an approach closely associated with the German theologian Rudolf Bultmann. From the 1970s onwards the term was picked up by scholars of other religious traditions to designate reinterpretations of those traditions that appeared to have something in common with Bultmann's approach to the New Testament. The common feature was, in many instances, an urge to strip away a tradition's mythological 'accretions' in order to disclose the spiritual message that had purportedly been submerged or distorted.

The notion of demythologizing has acquired salience in debates concerning the interpretation of rebirth and karma, especially in studies of Buddhism. Though the term is rarely used explicitly by members of the traditions themselves, 'demythologizing' has become a convenient label in academic discourse, used sometimes to denote interpretations devised by other scholars and sometimes to denote reformulations of teachings that are internal to a given tradition. On occasions, it can have both these applications at once, for the distinction between a scholarly and an 'internal' perspective is a fluid one, not least because scholars can be practitioners and practitioners can be scholars.

In accordance with the present study's overall aim of elucidating possibilities of sense embedded in rebirth beliefs of diverse kinds, this chapter investigates the phenomenon of so-called demythologized conceptions of rebirth by examining some representative examples. Three in particular will be given closest attention: first, the work of the scholar of English and South Asian literature, J. G. Jennings (1866–1941), who claimed to have excavated the 'original core' of the Buddha's teaching (1947: xxii); second, the interpretive approach of the Thai philosopher-monk Buddhadāsa Bhikkhu (1906–93), which involves deciphering what he considers to be the spiritual depth of Buddhist doctrines beneath the 'everyday language' in which they are commonly articulated; and third, the more recent work of Roderick Bucknell and Martin Stuart-Fox, who see Buddhadāsa's approach as being continuous with an ancient lineage of 'esoteric' Buddhism that they seek to expound. In addition to comparing and contrasting these respective interpretations, I shall critically evaluate their viability in the light of actual and possible objections. These objections typically amount to some version of the charge of reductionism; that is, the charge that demythologized accounts of rebirth illegitimately reduce a doctrine with major cosmological resonance to one that concerns merely psychological or ethical matters. I shall explore ways in which such a charge can be resisted while also asking whether some of these ways end up, in effect, retreating from a thoroughgoing demythologizing position.

Before turning to the main examples upon which my discussion will focus, it will be useful to begin with some more general remarks on the notion of demythologizing and its place in theological and academic discourse.

'Demythologizing' in Theology and the Study of Religions

The German term *Entmythologisierung*, which generally gets translated into English as 'demythologizing', was first coined by the philosopher Hans Jonas in a monograph on Augustine (Jonas 1930, 1965).[26] It was then taken up and popularized by Bultmann in his 1941 essay, 'New Testament and Mythology' (1972a). There, and in subsequent work, Bultmann advocates the need for Christians to replace a 'cosmological' reading of the New Testament with an 'existential' reading. By this, he means that ideas such as that of a 'three-storied' universe, with heaven above, earth in the centre and hell below, have become redundant mythological pictures in the light of modern scientific knowledge; they

---

26. Jonas' contribution is acknowledged in Bultmann (1972a: 12 n.1); see also Johnson (1974: 3 n.4).

should be jettisoned in favour of a firmer emphasis on Christ's message or proclamation (*kerygma*), which must be heard as the challenge for Christians to make 'a genuine existential decision', a decision about how to live (1972a: 16). This shift, or refocusing, of attention brings with it the eschatological implication that the final end of human existence is not to be conceived as chronologically later than our present life; rather, 'In every moment slumbers the possibility of being the eschatological moment.' The task is to 'awaken it' (Bultmann 1957: 155).

Through its appropriation by academic commentators and its application to non-Christian religious ideas, the concept of demythologizing has acquired a life and resonance that far exceed the context of Bultmann's project. In recent decades nineteenth-century Hindu social and religious reformers such as Rammohan Roy and Swami Dayananda Saraswati, and twentieth-century philosophers such as Sarvepalli Radhakrishnan, have been described as demythologizers, even though this was not an epithet they explicitly assigned to themselves.[27] Similarly, it has been pointed out that certain 'features of Buddhist modernism ... include the attempt to reinterpret or demythologize traditional cosmology in order to align the Buddhist world view with the modern scientific one' (McMahan 2012: 160), central among the identified Buddhist modernizers being figures such as Walpola Rahula and David Kalupahana.[28] Rahula's widely read book *What the Buddha Taught* (1959) has been described as exhibiting 'a rationalized, demythologized version of Buddhism devoid of reference to aspects of popular Buddhist beliefs and practices such as the Buddha cult or merit-making rituals' (Swearer 2010: 198), and it has been said of Kalupahana, who has published extensively on Buddhist philosophy and its history, that '[h]is highly selective use of texts and strained explanations ... suggests a strategy of implicit demythologization' (McMahan 2004: 92).

The first to apply the term 'demythologizing' to modern interpretations of Buddhism was probably John Hick in his introductory book *Philosophy of Religion*. From its second edition (1973) onwards this book included a chapter entitled 'Human Destiny: Karma and Reincarnation', the final section of which concisely discusses 'A Demythologized Interpretation', which Hick attributes to J. G. Jennings

---

27. For instances of such descriptions, see Williams (2008: 10), Clarke (2006b: 244) and Klostermaier (2007: 99).

28. The term 'Buddhist modernism' derives from Bechert (1966); cf. Gombrich (1971: 56 n.43, 284).

(Hick 1973: 116–17).[29] Hick's *Death and Eternal Life*, published a few years later, again devotes space to ways of 'demythologizing the doctrine of rebirth' (1976: 359), this time making reference to Buddhadāsa in addition to Jennings. Though Hick's examples are well chosen for illustrating some central features of modern reconceptualizations of rebirth within a Buddhist milieu, Hick says relatively little about them. Part of my purpose in this chapter is to offer a more detailed exegesis and analysis.

Karma and Rebirth without Personal Continuation

A reason commonly given by scholars and practitioners of Buddhism for seeking a revised interpretation of karma and rebirth is the difficulty of making standard interpretations compatible with the Buddhist denial of a permanent self. The doctrine of 'not self' or 'non-self' (*anattā* in Pāli, *anātman* in Sanskrit) is viewed by many exponents as Buddhism's most distinctive feature, a conception of human beings and of living beings more generally that, according to one commentator, 'separates Buddhism from all other religions, creeds, and systems of philosophy and which makes it unique in the world's history' (Malalasekera 1957: 33).[30] Although debates have persisted between different schools of Buddhism over precisely what the denial of self amounts to, the claim that it is this denial that constitutes Buddhism's most defining characteristic has been an enduring motif in Buddhist traditions.[31] One finds it, for example, in the insistence of Śāntarakṣita (eighth century CE) that knowledge of our being 'without self (*nairātmyaṃ*)

---

29. Jennings' initials are incorrectly given as 'J. C.' in the 1973 edition of Hick's book, an error that was corrected in later editions. The inclusion of the chapter in question has gained Hick praise for being a 'laudable exception' to the 'parochial' tendencies of analytic philosophers of religion, who generally give little attention to ideas from Indian religions (Perrett 1987: 173).

30. See also Rahula (1959: 51) and, for a more circumspect treatment of the topic, Collins (1982: 4).

31. Even the Buddhist defenders of *pudgalavāda* – the view that the 'person' (*pudgala*) is not simply reducible to the collection of factors upon which its existence depends – insisted that their position was opposed to that of 'eternalists' (the non-Buddhist schools that affirmed the existence of an eternal self). For discussion, see Priestley (1999) and Carpenter (2015).

... is the unique gateway to the highest good', and has been lost to all philosophers except those instructed by the Buddha (*Tattvasaṃgraha* 3321–4).[32] Even if, as Steven Collins notes (1982: 94), the not-self doctrine has had relatively little impact upon the practical lives of most lay followers, Buddhist intellectuals have singled it out as a means of distinguishing Buddhism from religious and philosophical rivals, most notably the various schools of Hindu and Jain thought, and more recently Christianity and Islam.

This emphasis on the absence of self has engendered explanatory problems for exponents of karma and rebirth, for it prompts the question how any sense can be made of moral responsibility persisting from one lifetime to another if there is nothing that could, even in principle, be identified as the permanent essence of an enduring individual (cf. Kern 1898: 49). Traditional sources have tended to rely heavily on analogies, such as that of a new candle being lit by the flame of a dying one,[33] or milk turning into curd which in turn becomes butter and ghee, thereby exhibiting continuity but not identity.[34] These analogies have placed in question the idea that there must be an all-or-nothing solution to the question whether the person who suffers the consequences of karma is identical to the one who initiated the karma in a former life. Famously, in the *Milindapañha* (first century BCE), when King Milinda asks the monk Nāgasena whether the one who is born is the same as or different from the one who died, Nāgasena replies: 'Neither the same nor another [*na ca so na ca añño*]' (§40, trans. Rhys Davids 1890: 63).[35] Buddhist philosophers have augmented and developed this contention in more or less innovative ways over the centuries.[36]

One means of developing the above lines of thought would be to devise a metaphysical theory of personhood according to which moral responsibility is retained over the successive lifetimes of an individual despite that individual's possessing no persisting essence. Alternatively,

32. I have slightly amended the translation in Jha (1939: 1468–70) and have followed the line numbering in Shastri (1968 II: 1048–9). Śāntarakṣita's attack is targeted especially at Jainism in this passage.

33. *Visuddhimagga* 19.22 (Buddhaghosa 2010: 628), Buswell and Lopez (2014: 708–9).

34. *Milindapañha* 40–1 (Rhys Davids 1890: 64–5).

35. For the Pāli text, see Trenckner (1880: 40).

36. See Collins (1982: ch. 6) and, for recent comparative analysis, Siderits (2003: esp. ch. 4).

one could take the more radical step of denying that the doctrine of karma and rebirth requires belief in successive lifetimes at all. Jennings exemplifies this radical interpretive approach in his book *The Vedāntic Buddhism of the Buddha* (1947).[37] He argues that the Buddhist notion of *ponobbhavikā*, commonly translated as 'rebirth', is best thought of as denoting the tendency of *taṇhā* ('thirst, desire, selfishness') 'to arise again, repeating itself, recurring ... causing the rebirth of itself, not of the individual' (1947: xxxvii). 'Rebirth' is thus understood as the recurrence of desires or cravings within a single lifetime, and hence the problem of having to explain how, in the absence of a persisting source of identity, we can be said to be reborn after our deaths is avoided. The doctrine of karma, meanwhile, is reinterpreted to mean, not that one's morally relevant actions generate consequences for oneself in a future life, but rather that they have consequences *for others* that extend beyond one's present lifespan. Jennings describes this as 'a doctrine of altruistic responsibility or collective Karma, according to which every action, word, and thought of the individual, transient though he be, brings forth inevitable consequences to be suffered or enjoyed by others in endless succeeding generations' (xxxvii). A roughly equivalent conception of karma has been espoused more recently by Stephen Batchelor, who writes that,

> Regardless of what we believe, our actions will reverberate beyond our deaths. Irrespective of our personal survival, the legacy of our thoughts, words, and deeds will continue through the impressions we leave behind in the lives of those we have influenced or touched in any way. (1998: 38)

Faced with the fact that numerous Buddhist sources, including early canonical ones, are replete with mythologically exuberant depictions of different 'realms of existence' in which one might be reborn, Jennings' strategy is to propose that the passages containing these depictions are probably later 'accretions', appended to the original teachings sometime after the time of Emperor Aśoka, who reigned over much of the Indian subcontinent from 268 to 231 BCE.[38] Thus, although it

---

37. The book was published posthumously, Jennings having died in 1941. For a concise summary of Jennings' thesis concerning the relation between early Buddhism and Vedānta, see Thomas (1947).

38. See Jennings (1947: xxvii). For the dates of Aśoka's reign, see Asher (2006: 51).

is generally accepted that 'Buddhist literature from its very earliest is brimming with [such things as] heavens and hells, miracles, and supernatural beings' (McMahan 2004: 92), Jennings would maintain that these features are 'Hinduizations' that have been superimposed upon 'the original core' of the Buddha's essentially ethical 'doctrine of pure altruism' (1947: xxii, lviii–lxxiii).[39]

A somewhat different hermeneutical strategy is deployed by Buddhadāsa Bhikkhu, the Thai social and religious reformer. Although he does, like Jennings, distinguish between core Buddhist sources and those that are 'superfluous' or 'inaccurate',[40] Buddhadāsa's main emphasis is on a distinction between two levels of meaning, which he names 'everyday language' (*phasa khon* in Thai) and 'Dhamma language' (*phasa tham*) respectively (see, e.g., Buddhadāsa 1971: ch. 3; 1974). Roughly speaking, to understand a Buddhist text at the level of everyday language is to read it literally, whereas to understand it at the level of Dhamma language is to read it as a figurative articulation of the *dhamma* (Pāli) or *dharma* (Sanskrit), this being both the underlying law that gives physical and moral order to the universe and the embodiment of that law in the teachings of the Buddha. 'Everyday language is worldly language', writes Buddhadāsa, 'the language of people who do not know Dhamma. Dhamma language is the language spoken by people who have gained a deep insight into the truth, Dhamma' (1974: 1). The hermeneutical task is to penetrate through the everyday level of meaning in Buddhist teachings in order to discern the deeper insight.

Buddhadāsa's distinction between everyday and Dhamma language can usefully be compared with Wittgenstein's distinction between 'surface grammar' and 'depth grammar'. The surface grammar of a word or phrase is '[w]hat immediately impresses itself upon us'; it is 'the part of its use ... that can be taken in by the ear' (Wittgenstein 2009a: §664). The depth grammar, meanwhile, concerns the connections between the word or phrase and the broader linguistic and behavioural surroundings that enable it to have the sense that it does.[41] Competent users of a term will typically not need to pause to

---

39. The view that Hinduism had a contaminating influence on Buddhist teachings extends at least as far back as the pioneering French scholar of Buddhism Eugène Burnouf (1801–52), who, as Lopez observes, held that 'the original teachings of the Buddha ... were eventually polluted with the most primitive elements of Hinduism' (Lopez 2008: 171).

40. See Jackson (2003: 101–19) and Odin (2011: 223–4).

41. Glock explains the surface–depth distinction as involving a contrast

consider its depth grammar unless they are engaged in philosophical contemplation. When we encounter forms of words that are unfamiliar to us, however, our comprehension may be obstructed by an unduly superficial appreciation of the operative grammar. Wittgenstein cites instances both of religious and of scientific modes of expression to illustrate cases in which 'there is a picture in the foreground, but the sense lies far in the background; that is, the application of the picture is not easy to survey' (2009a: §422). In Buddhadāsa's terms, it is the 'everyday language' that constitutes the foreground picture or surface grammar, and 'Dhamma language' that constitutes the depth grammar or background meaning. To discern the latter, one must be prepared to set aside first impressions and look for a deeper sense engendered by the particular context of Buddhist ethical and soteriological instruction.

A case in point is the term 'birth'. 'In everyday language', Buddhadāsa observes, 'the word "birth" refers to the physical entrance into the world from the mother's womb' (1971: 67). 'In Dhamma language', meanwhile, 'the word refers to the birth of the idea of "I" and "me" anytime it arises in the mind' (68). What Buddhadāsa claims to mean by 'the idea of "I" and "me"' is 'a mental event arising out of ignorance, craving, and clinging' (n.d.: 1). Such a 'mental event' is an instance of self-serving desire or 'self-centredness' (n.d.: 17). Thus, although expressed in somewhat different terms, the contention here is close to what we saw in Jennings' interpretation: 'rebirth' designates the recurrence of selfish cravings or desires. The soteriological goal of Buddhism accordingly becomes the eradication of egocentric motivations for action alongside the heightening of one's 'awareness' of whatever one is doing.[42]

'between the local surroundings which can be taken in at a glance, and the overall geography, that is, use of an expression' (1996: 155). The terms 'surface grammar' and 'depth grammar' in relation to Wittgenstein's work should not be confused with the use to which these and similar terms (most notably 'surface structure' and 'deep structure') are put in the linguistic theory of Noam Chomsky (e.g., Chomsky 1972). For discussion of differences between Wittgenstein and Chomsky, see Robinson (1975: esp. ch. 7).

42. 'The Buddha's goal was a life of awareness' (Buddhadāsa n.d.: 28). See also Swearer's description of a modernized conception of Buddhist teachings as one that 'demythologizes the tradition in the service of ethical and psychological values. Nibbana, for example, tends to be interpreted primarily as a nonattached way of being in the world' (2010: 198).

In traditional Buddhist cosmology there are six (or sometimes five) 'destinations' (*gatis*) into which sentient beings can be reborn.[43] In Buddhadāsa's model, these are reconceptualized as emotional states, moods or forms of behaviour that anyone may experience or display at different times. Hell is construed as 'anxiety'; the animal realm becomes a state of delusion or 'stupidity'; birth as a 'hungry ghost' (*peta*) is the state of 'extreme mental hunger'; to be a 'demigod' (*asura*) is to experience fear or timidity; to live as a human being is to undergo 'a condition of habitual fatigue'; and birth among the gods in heaven is to enjoy 'freedom from fatigue' and either abundant sensual pleasure or, in the higher heavens of Brahmaloka, 'freedom from sensuality' (1971: 70–4; n.d.: 21–4). These psychological interpretations are by no means original to Buddhadāsa; precursors of them are present in Buddhist scholastic sources from around the fifth century CE.[44] In more recent times they have been popularized by figures such as Chögyam Trungpa (2002: 31–53) and are commonplace within modernizing Buddhist movements in the West.[45] Traditionalists have been known to express the concern that an overemphasis on these psychological levels of interpretation risks deflating Buddhist teachings, reducing them 'to little more than a sophisticated ancient system of humanistic psychotherapy' (Bodhi 2010), and such charges of reductionism will receive further attention later in this chapter.

A key difference between Jennings and Buddhadāsa worth noting here is that, while the latter places considerable weight on the distinction between an 'everyday' or exoteric level of meaning and a 'Dhammic' or esoteric level, Jennings denies the need for such a distinction and maintains that the Buddha himself denied it as well. In support of this view, Jennings points to a passage in the *Mahāparinibbāna Sutta* in which the Buddha, who is approaching death, assures his disciple Ānanda that he has 'set forth the Dhamma without making any distinction of esoteric and exoteric doctrine' and has held nothing back with a 'closed fist' (DN II: 100, trans. Vajira and Story 1998: 29; cf. Jennings 1947: xxxviii).[46] For Jennings, the ethical sense of the Buddha's teachings does not lie behind a foregrounded pictorial form of words;

---

43. For a summary of traditional sources on the *gatis*, see La Vallée Poussin's note in Vasubandhu (1991 II: 500 n. 26).
44. See esp. *Abhidhammāvatāra* 182–289 (Buddhadatta 1980 I: 36–42); cf. Gethin (1998: 122, 289 n. 14).
45. See, e.g., Nagapriya (2004: 97–101) and Triratna NYC (2010).
46. See also Walshe (1995: 245, 568–9 n. 388) and Story (2000: 63).

in order to see it one simply has to pay attention to those passages in the Buddhist scriptures that emphasize the absence of a permanent self and to disregard those that show signs of having been influenced by Brahmanical Hindu ideas.

Buddhadāsa's distinction between two levels of meaning is defended by Bucknell and Stuart-Fox, who argue for the existence of an 'esoteric transmission' of Buddhist teachings stretching all the way back to the Buddha and typically articulated by means of a 'twilight language' (saṃdhyābhāṣā), 'a purposely created mode of communication having a concealed meaning' (Bucknell and Stuart-Fox 1986: 10, 12).[47] Whether 'twilight language' is the correct term for the linguistic phenomenon in question, or whether it should instead be 'intentional language' (saṃdhābhāṣā), remains disputed.[48] The case that Bucknell and Stuart-Fox make, however, does not hinge on resolving this terminological issue; it hinges primarily on the viability of deriving a cogent account of meditative techniques from passages in Buddhist texts that appear to be discussing other things. Central to their case is the claim that canonical reports of three kinds of knowledge, which the Buddha allegedly acquired on the night of his spiritual awakening, can best be interpreted as descriptions of meditative practices rather than as the supposedly cognitive products thereof.

As I noted briefly in Chapter 2, canonical accounts of the first kind of knowledge describe the Buddha's recollection of thousands upon thousands of his former lives.[49] In each case, the Buddha recalls such details as what his name was, the clan and caste to which he belonged, his diet, the good and bad experiences he underwent and the extent of his life (DN I: 81; MN I: 22; SN II: 231). Accounts of the second kind of knowledge describe the Buddha's seeing with his 'divine eye' or 'godlike vision' (Gethin 2008: 34) the fortunes of beings that follow from their past actions. Those who acted badly in body, speech or thought, 'with the break up of the body, after death, have been reborn in a state of misery', whereas those who acted well 'have been reborn in a good destination' (SN II: 214, trans. Bodhi 2000: 674).[50] The third kind of knowledge relates to 'the destruction of the taints' (Gethin

47. See also Davidson (2002: ch. 6).
48. See, e.g., Bharati (1965: ch. 6), Wayman (1968) and Broido (1982).
49. The operative Pāli term is *pubbenivāsa*, which is translated variously as 'previous existences' (Walshe 1995: 106), 'past abodes' (Bodhi 2000: 673–4), 'previous lives' (Gethin 2008: 33) and 'former dwelling(s)' (Collins 2009).
50. See also DN I: 82; MN I: 22–3.

2008: 35) or 'destruction of the corruptions' (Walshe 1995: 107); that is, the knowledge of how one's thoughts become tainted with selfish desires, ignorance and so forth, and of how to free oneself therefrom (DN I: 83-4; MN I: 23; SN II: 214).

On the face of it, the first two kinds of knowledge attributed to the Buddha appear to conflict with the respective ethical or psychological accounts of rebirth propounded by Buddhadāsa and Jennings. If it were merely the recurrence of self-serving desires and attitudes that was denoted by 'rebirth', then what sense would there be in the Buddha's identifying distinct names and biographical information pertaining to each of his former lives? Jennings omits the passages in question from his selection of excerpts from the Pāli Canon;[51] Bucknell and Stuart-Fox, on the other hand, reinterpret them in psychological terms. 'The death of a being', they propose, 'is the ceasing of [an] image' (1986: 88); and by 'image' they mean 'not only visual images but also their counterparts in the other modalities', including 'mental verbalizing' (159). 'Rebirth', meanwhile, 'is the arising of the next image; and the *karma* which determines that birth is the previous emotional involvement which determines the course of the linking process' (88). In the light of this analysis, the Buddha's recollection of his previous lives is understood as a 'retracing' of the sequence of images or thoughts further and further back into his early life, but not (or at any rate not explicitly in the account provided by Bucknell and Stuart-Fox) into any life that chronologically preceded his current one; and his perception of the karmic relations between previous actions and present circumstances is construed as his insight into the emotionally influenced process of one image or thought giving rise to the next in an ongoing sequence (Bucknell and Stuart-Fox 1983; 1986: 51-60). The destruction of the taints is the cessation of, first, the failure to observe the images and the connections between them, and second, 'emotional involvement in sense objects and images' (1986: 89).

Unlike Jennings, both Buddhadāsa and Bucknell and Stuart-Fox are careful not to claim that a psychological conception of rebirth is the only one that could have been intended by the Buddha. Buddhadāsa allows that rebirth after death occurs, but considers the question of what form it will take to be a 'trivial' one, given that as long as 'the "I" and the "mine"' continue to arise, any future life will be pervaded by suffering. The essential task remains that of eliminating self-serving impulses (Buddhadāsa n.d.: 18-19). Bucknell and Stuart-Fox,

51. See Jennings (1947: 27 n. 14, 33 n. 2).

meanwhile, distinguish between 'physical' (or 'macrocosmic') and 'mental' (or 'microcosmic') phenomena, proposing that many terms central to Buddhist thought have a 'double reference'. For instance, they suggest that the term *saṃsāra* refers both to an ongoing series of ('physical') lifetimes, each connected by relations of karmic consequence, *and* to 'the stream of thought' that is patterned by relations of 'emotional involvement' (1986: 93–4).

In view of these latter considerations it becomes evident that, in the context of interpretations of Buddhism, there are two quite distinct demythologizing strategies in play. On the one hand are those typified by Buddhadāsa and Bucknell and Stuart-Fox, which contend that there is a systematic ambiguity between two levels of meaning in the teachings traditionally attributed to the Buddha; these interpreters emphasize the soteriological importance of one of the levels (the psychological, meditative, ethical level) while downplaying the importance of the other (the level according to which there is some form of individual continuation after biological death). On the other hand is the interpretation typified by Jennings, which maintains that the ambiguity is merely apparent; when the Buddha's teachings are correctly understood, and disentangled from the corrupt doctrines that have become intermixed with them, we see that he did not affirm the continuation of the individual after death at all, but professed a purely ethical message of selfless altruism and the recognition that the consequences of our actions extend far beyond our individual lives.

Critical Discussion

As with other areas of religious hermeneutics, how we respond to the demythologizing interpretations of karma and rebirth that I have summarized will depend in large part on what we understand those interpretations to be aiming to do. Bultmann, in his work on the New Testament, distinguishes between *elimination* and *interpretation*: '[W]hereas the older liberals used criticism to *eliminate* the mythology of the New Testament', he writes, 'our task to-day is to use criticism to *interpret* it' (1972a: 12). This distinction is pertinent for the discussion of reformulations of karma and rebirth in Buddhism, though whether a given reformulation is to be regarded as eliminative or interpretive may in many instances be a matter of degree. Unabashedly eliminative is recent work by Owen Flanagan, whose aim is to eradicate all the 'nonnatural, supernatural' or 'metaphysically extravagant' baggage from traditional Buddhism in order to leave a 'naturalized' residue of metaphysical, epistemological and ethical teachings that are philosophically 'interesting and defensible' (2011: 3, 4). Flanagan does not pause to try to interpret the doctrine of karma and rebirth: he dismisses it along with other instances of 'incredible superstition and magical thinking' (3). The respective approaches that we have seen in this chapter are more interpretive than eliminative in comparison with that of Flanagan, though Jennings' interpretation has more eliminative elements than those of Buddhadāsa and Bucknell and Stuart-Fox.

The principal charge typically laid at the door of demythologizing interpretations is that they are *reductive*. By this it is implied that something important, even essential, has been lost or distorted. The comparison with Bultmann can again be instructive, for he has often been accused of reducing theology to anthropology, of treating indicative statements about God as though they were nothing more than imperative statements concerning human action. By manipulating theological language, it is alleged, Bultmann turns into an allegory about how we ought to live what is really factual assertion about divine reality. Such allegorizing, Klaus Bockmuehl protests, 'opens the door to arbitrary exposition and the dominion of man over the message' (1988: 32). Other critics, too, presume that what is going on in Bultmann's writings is the reduction of factual descriptions to evaluative expressions; Bultmann is thus blamed for subscribing to an outmoded 'dualism of fact and value' (Thiselton 2002: 42). A strong case could be made for regarding these criticisms as having overlooked some central features of Bultmann's approach, notably his emphatic retention of a close connection between the imperative and the indicative, maintaining that they are 'inseparable' in the theological statements with which he is working (Bultmann 1972a: 22, 32). My interest here, however, is not in defending Bultmann; rather, it is in the charge of reductionism itself and in whether similar objections could be raised against demythologizers of karma and rebirth.

Bockmuehl's worry about opening the way 'to arbitrary exposition' is echoed in a remark from Donald Lopez, that 'once the process of demythologizing begins, once the process of deciding between the essential and the inessential is underway, it is often difficult to know where to stop' (2008: 72). Those who set off down the road of demythologizing would, no doubt, concur that there must be some constraints on their procedure and that arbitrariness would be a disastrous exegetical result. They would also contend, however, that allegorizing cannot be off limits, not least because the textual traditions with which they are concerned patently contain allegorical material; just as the parables of the Christian Gospels constitute forms of allegory, so the textual sources of Buddhism are saturated with allegorical motifs and narratives. As Keown observes, we see in the Pāli Canon, for example, that 'the Buddha excelled as a skillful teacher, elucidating his doctrines using anecdotes, parables, metaphor, imagery and symbolism, or as the texts have it teaching "in many a way and in many a figure"' (1998: 201).[52] So avoiding the interpretation of certain texts or portions of texts as allegorical, analogical or symbolic is not a viable option; the question is, as Lopez indicates, that of 'where to stop'.[53]

A supporter of Jennings' interpretation could reiterate the centrality in Buddhism of the doctrine of not-self. In the light of this doctrine, it might be argued, any interpretation of karma and rebirth that presupposes continued individual existence beyond death would generate an inconsistency, and therefore the only cogent interpretive strategy is one that treats these notions as figurative articulations of exclusively ethical and psychological ideas. What tends to weaken the credibility of Jennings' approach, however, is the sheer quantity of canonical material that he is obliged to reject as having purportedly been infected with more literalistic (or 'Hinduized') connotations. Since the criterion for the excisions is inconsistency with a presumed 'fundamental doctrine' (1947: xxvi), and this doctrine is deemed to be fundamental because it is propounded in the 'core' sources, the justification for rejecting certain texts becomes, in effect, circular: they should not be regarded as essential because they are contaminated, and we know they are contaminated because they are incompatible with what is essential.[54] Though a defender of Jennings' expurgatory method could invoke the principle of hermeneutical charity in order to insist that the excisions are necessary, other interpreters are likely to remain unconvinced, their verdict being that when 'charity' demands a decimation of the

52. See also Gombrich (2006: 75): '[M]uch of the narrative telling what the Buddha did in the days and weeks following his Enlightenment is allegorical in origin.'

53. Canonical Buddhism itself evinces a distinction between discourses of the Buddha 'whose meaning is explicit' and those 'whose meaning requires interpretation' (AN I: 60, trans. Bodhi 2012: 151). 'Unfortunately', as Amber Carpenter remarks, 'there is no authoritative *sūtra* indicating which sayings fall into which category' (2015: 31 n. 7).

54. For the complaint that Jennings has given insufficient grounds for his excisions, see Burrow (1949: 201) and Jayatilleke (1963: 270–1).

source materials, it may be more reasonable to conclude that the source materials do contain some internal tensions after all.

What interpretations such as those of Buddhadāsa and Bucknell and Stuart-Fox appear to offer is a way of adhering to the principle of charity by providing a coherent reading of the sources while avoiding the eliminative tendency exhibited by Jennings. There are, however, further objections that could be raised against their interpretations, two of which I shall focus on in this discussion. One of these is what we might call the *vapidity objection*, that the interpretations in question sacrifice substance for coherence and thus end up being unpalatably vapid. The other could be designated the *double incoherence objection*, for it consists in the claim that by allowing that rebirth can be understood in both cosmological and psychological terms, incoherence has not in fact been alleviated; if anything, it has been doubled. I shall discuss each of these objections in turn.

A version of the vapidity objection was exemplified above in the quotation from Bhikkhu Bodhi, in which the concern is expressed that an overemphasis on the capacity of Buddhist methods to improve mental composure in one's present life can have unduly reductive implications. Bodhi is perturbed that a narrow focus on Buddhism's psychotherapeutic value tends to go along with a downplaying of the doctrine of rebirth, thereby divesting 'the Dhamma of [the] wider perspectives from which it derives its full breadth and profundity' (Bodhi 2010). Although Bodhi's target is not specifically either Buddhadāsa or Bucknell and Stuart-Fox, it is not hard to see how someone might find the accounts offered by these interpreters lacking in the cosmological and eschatological pertinence with which traditional Buddhism has generally been associated. When Bodhi speaks of the 'full breadth and profundity' of the Buddhist teachings, one of the things he has in mind is the central soteriological motivation that drives them. As both he and other authors have noted, it is the fact that not even bodily death can be relied on to permanently terminate our suffering that supplies the stimulus for following the Buddhist path; in the absence of the idea of successive lives, the depth and significance of liberation dissolves, given that nirvāṇa is to a large extent defined in terms of the cessation of rebirth (Bodhi 2010; Williams, Tribe and Wynne 2012: 204 n. 20).[55]

A variant of the vapidity objection is raised by Hick, who, having drawn a broad distinction between 'factual' conceptions of rebirth

---

55. Cf. Dumont (1970: 49): '[W]ithout transmigration the liberation or extinction (*nirvāṇa*) which [the Buddha] recommends would lose all meaning.'

on the one hand and 'mythic' conceptions on the other, argues that it is only conceptions of the former type that 'could be of any practical interest to anyone' (1976: 356). Hick's argument is complicated, but I shall draw out its main elements here.[56] It begins by assuming that for any conception of rebirth to be one that genuinely involves the continuation of a person from one life to the next, there must be some criterion of identity or continuity across lives. Since bodily continuity is precluded *ex hypothesi* by the traditions themselves, the criterion must be a 'mental' one; that is, there must be something mental that persists from life to life (Hick 1976: 304–5). Two such candidates are considered by Hick, namely: (a) 'the psychological continuity of a pattern of mental dispositions' (1976: 307; 1990: 134), which Hick refers to in later work as a 'dispositional (or karmic) structure' (2010: 11); and (b) 'a link of memory' (1976: 364). The tenability of the first of these candidates is deemed by Hick to be undermined by the fact that similar dispositions can, and do, manifest in more than one person at the same time; their manifestation can thus provide no basis on which to infer a metaphysical connection between a now living person and someone who died some time ago, for to draw such an inference in any one case would be arbitrary, given the possibility of other equally viable cases (1976: 307–8). This part of Hick's argument is structurally equivalent to Bernard Williams' reduplication argument, which I discussed in Chapter 3. It differs from Williams' argument only inasmuch as it focuses on the possibility of exactly similar dispositions or character traits, as opposed to exactly similar apparent memories, being simultaneously possessed by different individuals.

When it comes to discussing the tenability of a 'memory link' as the criterion of rebirth, Hick does not deploy the sort of Williams-style reduplication argument that he does in the case of dispositions. Instead, he initially admits that, in view of the rarity of even remotely plausible cases of past-life recollection, the existence of such cases fails, on its own, to establish memory as a criterion of rebirth; it fails in this regard because rebirth is generally considered by believers to be a universal phenomenon rather than one restricted to only a small minority of people (Hick 1976: 304–5). Later on, however, Hick cites the sorts of claims concerning past-life recall among spiritually enlightened individuals, most famously the Buddha, to which I drew attention both earlier in this chapter and in Chapter 2. In view of this purported potentiality for 'a total retrospective awareness' of all one's past lives

---

56. For a more detailed discussion, see Burley (2014b).

(1976: 388), Hick maintains that a viable account of the continuity between successive rebirths has been provided. Even though the disposition to have these memories will be 'actualised [only] at the end of a long journey through many lives' (Hick 2006: 196) it is nevertheless sufficient, in Hick's opinion, to constitute the sought-after criterion.

What these considerations of Hick's have to do with the vapidity objection to demythologized accounts of rebirth is as follows. Hick maintains that what it is for a belief or theory to be 'factual' is for its truth or falsity to make an actual, or at least a possible, 'experiential difference' (1976: 356). In the light of the criterion that he takes himself to have discovered, he thinks that the belief in rebirth can count as a factual belief, for even if a believer does not presently recall any past lives, he or she may legitimately expect to do so eventually – in the final stages of spiritual enlightenment – and recalling one's past lives is indeed something that would make a difference to one's experience.[57] When the link of memory is omitted, however, 'we have nothing left which there could be any reason to assert or which could be of any practical interest to anyone'. Furthermore, 'It is only when we add memory – even if this should only become conscious at the end of the series of lives – that we have either the buddhist, the hindu, or the popular conception of reincarnation or rebirth' (1976: 356).[58] Since what Hick means by 'the series of lives' here is a succession of biologically discrete lifetimes connected by a common thread of memory, this pronouncement leaves little room for the demythologized construals of rebirth that we have been considering in this chapter.

What Bodhi's and Hick's respective versions of the vapidity objection have in common is a concern that allegorical or demythologized accounts of rebirth cannot plausibly elucidate the importance that is accorded by Buddhism (and by other relevant traditions) to the goal of spiritual awakening that constitutes the culmination of soteriological striving. As Bodhi sees it, in the absence of a multiple-lives perspective the idea of nirvāṇa as the permanent cessation of an otherwise ineluctable cycle of suffering is lost, to be replaced by a relatively facile notion of psychological well-being. For Hick, the only thing that can give 'factual content' to the doctrine of rebirth is the 'total retrospective

---

57. Hick is not as clear as he might have been concerning what he means by an 'experiential difference'. The summary that I am providing is based on what I take to be the most coherent reading of his argument.

58. The lower-case initials for 'buddhist' and 'hindu' are in Hick's original text.

awareness' of one's former lives that a tradition such as Buddhism promises as one of the cognitive achievements of the process of spiritual liberation. How might the interpretations of Buddhadāsa and Bucknell and Stuart-Fox be defended against objections of this sort?

A way of responding to a worry such as the one expressed by Bodhi would be to emphasize that Buddhist practice has always been principally directed towards increasing mental stability, concentration and awareness. Even when the soteriological goal has been assumed to involve the cessation of any further rebirths after death, the means to fulfilling that goal has been understood in terms of cultivating moral virtues and progressively deepened levels of meditative insight in one's present life (see, e.g., Harvey 2013b: ch. 11). What the analyses of Buddhadāsa and Bucknell and Stuart-Fox provide, it could be argued, are accounts of how traditional Buddhist teachings relate directly and systematically to these ethical and meditative practices: not reducing them to secular modes of psychotherapy, but rather bringing out their life-transforming capacity. Moreover, the redescriptions of 'realms of existence' as affective states that one might undergo from moment to moment need not be viewed simply as reducing cosmology to psychology, for the redescriptions serve to expand and enrich the practitioner's understanding of the affective states themselves. By describing states of anxiety figuratively as hell realms, for example, aspects of these states may be elucidated that could not be adequately expressed in more literal terms. As Max Black has pointed out with regard to metaphors more generally, a literal paraphrase is often inadequate not merely because it is 'tiresomely prolix or boringly explicit (or deficient in qualities of style)', but 'because it fails to give the insight that the metaphor did' (1962: 46). A metaphorical or allegorical reading may disclose additional layers of meaning in a doctrine that a more literalistic reading leaves obscure.

Buddhadāsa's contention, that when the notion of rebirth is conceived in 'Dhammic' as opposed to 'everyday' terms it relates to the recurrence of egocentric thoughts and desires, is supportable by again accentuating the centrality of deconstructive accounts of selfhood in Buddhist traditions. If, as Buddhist philosophies generally maintain, the phenomenon of personhood or continuity of self is analysable into a constantly changing assemblage of physical and psychological processes (Collins 1994: 64–5; Harvey 2013b: 57), then the claim that what is 'reborn' is a type of psychological or conative impulse is fully congruent with Buddhist teachings. The exposition offered by Bucknell and Stuart-Fox of the retrospective 'retracing' of the series of fleeting thoughts and images embellishes this conception of the self as 'process' rather than 'substance', showing how meditative practice informs Buddhist ontology.[59] By contrast, a more literalistic interpretation of the Buddha's looking back over his innumerable former lives could easily be taken to presuppose some essential constituent of personhood that remains constant throughout the rebirth sequence, a presupposition that runs counter to the doctrines of impermanence and not-self.

Emphasizing the latter point would be one way of beginning a response to Hick's concerns. It could then be added that the demythologizing approach does not abandon the 'link of memory', which Hick considers to be so indispensable; it merely reframes the context in which that link is understood, viewing it as a gradually acquired product of meditative discipline rather than as an exotic 'special power' that mysteriously emerges only in the final stages of spiritual fulfilment.[60] In response to Hick's insistence that a belief can be 'factual' only if its truth or falsity makes an 'experiential difference', it could be noted that the sorts of ethical and meditative achievements described by Buddhadāsa and Bucknell and Stuart-Fox, and indeed by Jennings, do make very real experiential differences. In the case of Jennings' demythologized conception of karma, for instance, the contention that the consequences of one's present actions unavoidably ripple out across the world and go on to affect future generations might not appear especially profound or surprising in itself; indeed, when put in these terms it is apt to come across as banal. But when accompanied by the demand that this simple truth be repeatedly contemplated in relation to all one's actions, its implications become considerably more significant.

A useful analogy could again be drawn with Bultmann in this connection. In reply to critics who accuse him of reducing indicative claims about God and the world to imperative claims about a change in

59. For discussion of the distinction between 'substance-selves' and 'process-selves', see esp. Gowans (2003: Part 2).

60. Indeed, the idea that one's recollection of the chain of preceding moments in one's life can be incrementally enhanced by means of a regular meditative procedure is affirmed in certain traditional sources such as *Visuddhimagga* 13.22–71 (Buddhaghosa 2010: 408–18) and *Abhidharmakośa Bhāṣya* (commentary following 7.43d, in Vasubandhu 1991 IV: 1159–60). Admittedly, however, in each case the capacity to recall earlier experiences in one's present life is described as merely preliminary to recalling lives *prior* to this one.

self-understanding, Bultmann maintains that the accusation is premised on a false dichotomy. He makes the point that coming to understand differently one's own relation to others involves both a change in self-understanding *and* a change in how one understands realities beyond oneself. Seeing oneself in the light of another's love, for example, is to 'understand the other in such a way that the whole world appears in a new light, which means that it has in fact become an entirely different world' (1972b: 203). Analogously, an advocate of Jennings' construal of karma could argue that the construal has not reduced cosmology to ethics; it has, rather, brought out the cosmological ramifications that ethical transformation carries with it: insofar as one's ethical attitude towards others is changed, so thereby is a change engendered in the moral universe (and the moral universe is not a different place from the universe per se). Though one might, in this case, want to deny that the effected change means that the world has become 'entirely different', the response does at least begin to dissolve the sort of binary opposition that Hick seems to presuppose between the 'factual' or 'experiential' on the one hand and an ethicized or psychologized 'myth' on the other. Similar points could be made in connection with the meditation-related interpretations of rebirth and karma suggested by Buddhadāsa and more comprehensively worked out by Bucknell and Stuart-Fox: though these interpretations are indeed concerned with a shift in self-understanding, this very shift is such 'that the whole world appears in a new light'.

If a critic were to persist in pressing the charge that demythologized readings of karma and rebirth lack the 'breadth and profundity' (Bodhi) or 'practical interest' (Hick) of a more explicitly cosmological reading, those demythologizers who adopt the approach of Buddhadāsa and Bucknell and Stuart-Fox could, as we have seen, admit that they are not really seeking to replace the cosmological reading; they are merely highlighting an additional level at which the doctrine can be understood. This response might be seen as being susceptible to the second of the two objections that I noted above, namely the 'double incoherence' objection. This is because it is not immediately obvious how the discourse concerning karma and rebirth could be both cosmological and psychological at the same time, unless this is to be understood as meaning that it contains a pervasive equivocation or conceptual confusion. It should be noted, however, that the idea that certain Buddhist doctrines, including the doctrine of karma and rebirth, are imbued with two levels of meaning is far from being unique to the interpreters I have been discussing. Indeed, it has been endorsed by several leading commentators.

Rupert Gethin, for instance, speaks of 'the principle of *the equivalence of cosmology and psychology*' in Buddhist philosophy (1998: 119, original emphasis; cf. 1997: 189, 211), and among the examples he adduces to illustrate this principle is the experiencing of 'unpleasant mental states, such as aversion, hatred, or depression'. These experiences can be described in terms of a person's temporarily visiting one or other of the hell realms; and if the unpleasant states become habitual and deeply ingrained, then it can be said that one is liable to be reborn in a hell realm after death (1998: 122–3). Formulations of this kind accommodate the two levels of meaning by distinguishing between a state of mind into which one is figuratively 'born' in one's present life and a state of being, pervasively characterized by that state of mind, into which one is born in a more concrete and tangible sense in a succeeding life. Conceptual space is thus made for the psychological significance of the notion of rebirth while retaining the overarching mythological framework comprising multiple cosmological 'realms of existence' – a framework which, of course, readers such as Jennings would see as an unacceptable accretion.

It seems then that if, as Bultmann maintains, demythologizing consists in recovering the truth of a religious doctrine for those 'who do not think in mythological terms' (1972a: 15), interpreters of Buddhism such as Buddhadāsa and Bucknell and Stuart-Fox have in the end pulled back from offering a fully demythologized vision. What these interpreters have provided, however, are valuable reminders of how the mythic vocabulary so pervasive in traditional Buddhist sources expresses a level of truth with direct application to everyday life and experience.

Concluding Remarks

This chapter can be read as an extension of Chapter 1 insofar as it has been dealing with further ways of conceptualizing rebirth. These ways, while taking seriously the forms of language in which belief in rebirth has been expressed in traditional textual sources, endeavour to go beyond a superficial reading of those forms in order to draw out their implications for ethics and meditative practice. Speaking of them in terms of demythologization is helpful to the extent that it alerts us to instructive affinities between these expositions of rebirth and karma on the one hand and certain hermeneutical tendencies within other areas of theology and the study of religions on the other; but it could easily become unhelpful if it were to conceal the idiosyncrasies of particular cases.

Of the interpreters of Buddhism that I have discussed in detail, Jennings evidently pursues the most aggressively demythologizing approach. Treating the not-self doctrine, according to which there is no enduring essence of personhood, as itself the very essence of the Buddha's teachings, he uses this doctrine as a barometer against which to test the authenticity of all other elements in the early Buddhist canon. In doing so, Jennings injects vitality into the ethic of altruism with which he connects the denial of enduring selfhood, showing how this ethic is articulable through talk of karma and rebirth; 'karma' is understood as denoting the responsibility that we have for the effects of our actions upon a collective whole, comprising both present and future generations, and 'rebirth' is taken to stand for the recurrence of selfish desires that we must strive to terminate. Regarded as a personal commendation of this moral message, Jennings' highly selective interpretation embodies a humanitarian outlook with considerable appeal for many contemporary votaries of Buddhism, especially in western countries. Regarded as a scholarly account of the 'original core' of the Buddha's teaching, however, it may prompt us to wonder how conceptual justice can be done to that core when it has been denuded of so much of the scriptural material in which it has traditionally been embedded.

As for the respective interpretations of Buddhadāsa and Bucknell and Stuart-Fox, these, as we have seen, elude charges of over-selectivity or reductionism by retaining a dual-aspect or twofold character. The question of exactly how the two aspects – the cosmological and the psychological – relate to one another remains philosophically troublesome, calling for a more sustained examination than I can offer here.[61] The contention that we have seen from Gethin is that the two aspects can be reconciled by our regarding the psychological as characterizing a mode of experience that is a temporary precursor of a more enduring, though still impermanent, state of being that can be expected after death. Assuming that Buddhadāsa would accept this account does not in itself explain why he regards as 'trivial' the question of what form a future life will take; what appears to be his motivation, however, is ensuring that due attention is given to transforming one's ethical life here and now rather than putting it off until some future rebirth. This motivation chimes well with the attitude of the Buddha typified in

---

61. I have discussed it at greater length in Burley (2014a).

parables such as that of the poisoned arrow, according to which, against a physician's advice, a man who has been shot with an arrow refuses to have it removed until he is given the answers to numerous questions concerning who fired it, the type of bow with which it was fired and so on (MN I: 429–30). The implication of the parable is that, given our existential predicament, it is irrational to fritter away our time by ruminating on matters that have no direct bearing upon the relief of our suffering. Buddhadāsa, it could be said, is epitomizing this spirit of exigency when he privileges the significance of 'rebirth' within life as opposed to after death.

A comparable reconciliation seems feasible in the case of the analysis of meditative discipline proposed by Bucknell and Stuart-Fox as an explication of what it meant for the Buddha to remember his own previous lives and to perceive the karmic connections between a current life and its forerunners. The practice of 'retracing' that they describe enacts at the microcosmic or intrapsychic level the process of recollecting prior mental states that, in moments of heightened lucidity, is succeeded by a macrocosmic awareness that reaches back to before one's own current life and also encompasses knowledge of the multiple lives of others. As I noted above, to countenance this latter level of significance involves retreating from a demythologized interpretation; yet by elaborating how the cosmic cognition of the enlightened sage is prefigured in a method of meditative discipline, the interpretation nevertheless lends additional continuity to Buddhist narratives of spiritual awakening, narratives that are articulated through the everyday lives and discourse of Buddhist practitioners.

Chapter 6

KARMA AND EVIL

Karma rushes like a cataract. Things float on it, hither and thither following the movements of the current.

(Meenakshisundaram 1967: 28)

[T]he way of *karma* is complex and strange ... and difficult to discern.

(*Yoga Bhāṣya* 2.13 [*c*. fifth–sixth century CE], trans. Bhāratī 2001: 145)

Central to the major rebirth traditions deriving from South Asia is the doctrine of karma, and hence it is hardly surprising that this has been a recurring theme throughout the present book. In Chapter 1 for instance, when mentioning the Weberian distinction between 'religious virtuosos' and the large majority of lay religious practitioners, I noted Melford Spiro's observation that, for many lay Buddhists, the goal of life is conceived in terms of improving one's position within the ongoing stream of life (*saṃsāra*) by performing correct actions (*karman, kamma*). For the monastic virtuosos, too, right action – good karma – is essential to the spiritual path, even if their goal is more readily conceived as a final cessation of suffering and of the stream of life altogether. This essential role for karma is equally prevalent in Hindu, Jain and Sikh traditions, as is the idea that one's morally significant actions generate a retributive effect that returns to haunt the agent with a high degree of inevitability. It is this mechanism, according to which, in its simplest terms, we 'get what we deserve' (Nayak 1993: 59) or 'reap what we sow' (Radhakrishnan 2008 I: 200), that has come to be known as the *law* of karma (*karma niyama*) (Keyes 1983a: 2; Lopez 2012: 55–6).

This doctrine of a universal law of reward and retribution has, however, long been controversial, attracting vigorous criticism from both 'outsiders' and 'insiders' to the traditions concerned. Some of this criticism has been targeted at what is perceived as the sheer implausibility of such a presumed law, but much of it has had a more explicitly moral emphasis. Thus, while advocates of and sympathizers with the doctrine of karma portray it as a source both of hope and comfort and of intellectual satisfaction in the face of apparent evil and suffering,[1] critics condemn it as a source of profound evil in itself. According to some, it is 'a philosophy of despair' owing to its purportedly fatalistic implications (Kuppuswamy 1977: 46).[2] It is deemed to promote complacency and a sense that attempting to alleviate hardship or socio-economic disparities is futile, for it supposes these to have been set in place by a just law of cosmic proportions; it is thus decried as 'a convenient tool for explaining away the perceived inequality in human society' (Ramendra 2011: 56), a tranquillizer for just indignation (Garrett 2005: 201) and the apotheosis of 'blaming the victims' (Edwards 1996: 46; cf. Kaufman 2007: 559).

This chapter will critically examine the debate over the morality of the doctrine of retributive karma. In order to orient the discussion I shall concentrate on three especially striking charges, all of which have received recent articulations or reiterations in the philosophical literature. The first of these is that, despite the claims of its proponents to the contrary, the doctrine 'is completely vacuous as a principle of moral guidance' (Edwards 1996: 42). The second is that the very concept of retributive karma involves a kind of incoherence owing to its both requiring the reality of free moral agency and, simultaneously, precluding its possibility. The third is that giving credence to the doctrine of karma entails, as noted above, a flagrant and pernicious mode of blaming victims for the evils they suffer. Possible responses to these accusations will be considered along the way and attention given both to the depth of disagreement that often divides opponents in these debates and to the existence of alternative ways in which belief in karma manifests in people's lives. With reference to a variety of examples, I shall argue that although it is difficult to see how the deep disagreements at the heart of this issue can be resolved, there exists within the doctrine of karma considerable room for interpretation; this ought to give pause to those who are tempted to emit either wholesale condemnations or unqualified endorsements.

---

1. Wadia (1965: 147–8), Rao (1967: 141), Yamunacharya (1967: 72).
2. See also Keith (1925: 596), Kane (1977: 1566), Bhattacharji (1982).

Karma as a Principle of Moral Guidance

It is often assumed that believing in karma brings with it certain determinate normative implications for how one ought to act. On some accounts these implications are laudable: the belief gives one a reason to behave virtuously, knowing that immoral behaviour leads to future suffering for oneself. Others declare the implications to be baleful: belief in karma gives one a reason to neglect the misfortunes of others, presuming them to be the natural consequences of past sins on the sufferer's part. This latter view is part of a common moral objection to the karma doctrine. A somewhat different objection is that the doctrine provides no guidance for action whatsoever. According to Paul Edwards' version of this objection, although the doctrine does have ramifications for the believer's *attitude* towards victims of suffering (ramifications that will be discussed later in this chapter), it lacks any practical action-guiding significance because, due to a certain essential feature of the doctrine, it turns out that absolutely anything one does must be presumed to be the 'right thing' to do (Edwards 1996: 42–3).[3]

The essential feature in question is the belief in an unmediated mechanism of natural justice – the idea that, notwithstanding any appearances to the contrary, the world is in the final analysis a perfectly just place. As Paul Larson puts it, 'Karma ... represents the idea of universal justice; the belief that in the end, good will be rewarded and wrong-doing punished' (2010: 499); the universe is thus regarded as being 'so constructed as to sustain moral values and uphold them' (Rao 1967: 139–40). Such an idea is commonly associated with the term *dharma* or, at any rate, with one of the many meanings of this polysemic term. For many Hindus in particular, dharma is a principle of 'universal order' that is 'eternally there' (Koller 1972: 139), an eternal law underlying all laws, both natural and normative (Pappu 1987c: 303).[4] From the perspective of those who hold this conception of the universe non-negotiably or categorically, it follows, Edwards maintains,

---

3. A similar criticism has been made by Paul Griffiths (1982: 290), who argues that the karma doctrine avoids being demonstrably false only by being 'sufficiently vague to be compatible with any state of affairs whatever'.

4. We should note, however, a cautionary historical observation by Alf Hiltebeitel (2011: 7) that claims made by modern-day Hindus and Buddhists concerning an 'eternal' dharma often have more to do with current conceptions of the universe and of the past than with careful description of early

that regardless of what eventuates, and hence regardless of whether we assist those who are in need (or whether our efforts to do so are successful), 'the ultimate outcome will be just, in the sense that every human being will be getting exactly – no more and no less – what he deserves' (1996: 43).

To delineate the problem signalled by Edwards, I shall here adapt a scenario from the classic Hindu text, the *Bhagavad Gītā* (*c*. first century CE). In its opening chapter the warrior-prince Arjuna stands in his chariot surveying the battlefield of Kurukṣetra, upon which are ranged two armies ready to violently settle a feud between cousins over who should inherit the kingdom (Edgerton 1944 I: 2–12). Arjuna becomes perplexed about whether to take part in the battle: should he participate, and thus run the risk of having his kinsmen's blood on his hands, or should he refrain, thereby foregoing his duty as a born warrior? If one assumes that a law of universal justice obtains, then it hardly seems to matter what he does. If he slaughters his cousins, it must be the case that they 'deserved' to die. If, on the other hand, he lays down his weapon and is himself slain, this must be what justice demands. Necessarily, whatever happens, it cannot be wrong; for, to borrow a phrase from Alexander Pope's *Essay on Man*, 'One truth is clear, Whatever is, is right' (Epistle 1, line 294). And hence, it seems, the decision is arbitrary. Morality is abolished.

Many would call the view just expressed *fatalism*. Edwards is willing to concede to the believer in universal justice that it need not be fatalistic (1996: 42–3), because Edwards has a rather stringent conception of what fatalism is, according to which a fatalistic view is one that entirely precludes human freedom. With reference to the example outlined above, to say that Arjuna has no choice in the matter would, on Edwards' account, be fatalistic. But, he would admit, the believer in a supremely just world need not go that far. Instead, such a believer can grant that Arjuna has a genuine choice, that whether he charges into battle or retreats to the sidelines is, in some meaningful sense, *up to him*;[5] it is merely that whichever decision he makes will turn out to be in perfect accordance with justice. Some would argue that

textual sources. For discussion of representations of dharma as a normative legal concept and of the limitations of those representations, see Rocher (1978).

5. Speaking of genuine choices, or free decisions, as involving something's being 'up to him' (or 'up to her', 'up to us', etc.) is typical in the literature surrounding free will and moral responsibility; see, e.g., Frankfurt (1969: 836), Kane (1996: esp. ch. 3), Lehrer (2004).

the doctrine of karma could in fact be construed as entailing the kind of freedomless, deterministic picture that Edwards is identifying as fatalism, and this is certainly an issue that warrants closer attention.[6] In order to take the discussion further, let us consider another illustration of the sort of problem that Edwards is exercised about.

Francis Story offers an instructive real-life example. He cites the case of a medical doctor who specializes in pulmonary diseases and is also a Buddhist. While acknowledging the carcinogenic effects of smoking cigarettes, the doctor himself continues to smoke fairly heavily, remarking that even if cancer's 'physical causes' are all present, the disease will develop only if the individual's karma is 'also a predisposing factor' (Story 2000: 45). Is this a fatalistic attitude, in Edwards' strong sense of holding that there is no room for free will in the matter? Although Story leaves many details unclear, there is nothing in what he tells us that should lead us to suppose that the doctor considers himself to be without free will. His motivation for continuing to smoke is not that he is straightforwardly addicted or in some more mysterious way impelled by his karmic inheritance to pursue this habit; it seems that he would admit that he could give it up if he wanted to. Moreover, his talk of 'predispositions' and 'physical causes' implies that karma is not perceived as fully determining whether one contracts cancer; and yet the doctor's sanguinity about his own situation implies the assumption that karma plays the *major* role. The case is complicated, and we should not of course rule out the possibility of some degree of confusion or self-deception on the doctor's part. Yet the complicatedness should alert us to the danger of making premature pronouncements either about whether the doctrine of karma is fatalistic or about whether it is capable of offering moral guidance.

A believer with a strongly deterministic conception of karma's operations might admit that, were the doctor in Story's example to develop cancer, it is his heavy smoking that would be the primary causal factor, while adding that it is the doctor's karma that is responsible for his smoking in the first place; that is, were it not for certain nefarious deeds done by him in the past (perhaps in a previous life), the doctor would not have suffered the misfortune of taking up the habit. Such a view ascribes to the law of karma a far more universally

6. There also remain fraught interpretive questions concerning whether the *Bhagavad Gītā* itself allows for any free choice on Arjuna's part (Sharma 1979; Johnson 1997). But my purpose in borrowing the example of Arjuna's predicament was not to enter into exegetical issues pertaining to this particular text.

determining role, as it implies that it is not only the *outcomes* of our decisions for which our karma is responsible, but also the decisions themselves. Paradoxically, then, if the emphasis on personal responsibility for our circumstances that lies at the heart of the karma doctrine is taken to an extreme, we are robbed of even the possibility of such responsibility. For if the circumstances for which past karma is responsible include such things as the family and social environment into which one is born, and the type of physical attributes with which one is endowed, then why, one might ask, should they not also include one's character, one's psychological make-up and one's very competence for moral decision-making? In short, why should we not hold, 'not merely that I am circumstanced as I am but that I am what I am, because of my prior karma' (Sastri 1961: 234)?[7] This contention is indeed paradoxical; it risks exposing the karma doctrine as being not only devoid of any capacity to guide moral action, but conceptually incoherent to boot. I shall pursue these considerations further in the next section.

Is the Doctrine of Karma Incoherent?

Proponents of the karma doctrine are generally keen to emphasize the vital role for free action that it not merely leaves room for, but positively requires. The doctrine requires an affirmation of free will because of the importance it attaches to moral responsibility. As Wadia puts it (speaking from a largely Hindu perspective), 'Morality to be morality implies responsibility, and responsibility implies free will.' From this point of view, if sense is to be made of the idea of karma generating consequences for which the agent is responsible, it must be the case that while '*karma* determines the field of life', there remains 'within that field' scope for us to develop ourselves and cultivate 'new *karma*' (Wadia 1965: 151). With regard to Buddhism, meanwhile, the question of whether Buddhist psychology has conceptual space for free will has been a bone of contention in recent discussions;[8] nevertheless, one prominent view is that, owing to (among other things) the central place given in Buddhist ethics to 'intention' or 'volition' (*cetanā*), we can safely attribute to the Buddha the view that 'We have free will and are wholly

---

7. It should be noted that Sastri is here mentioning rather than endorsing this view.

8. Goodman (2002), Federman (2010), Wallace (2011).

responsible for ourselves' (Gombrich 2013: 13). Moreover, Gombrich adds, 'this responsibility extends far beyond this present life. So we are entirely responsible for our moral condition and what we make of it.' A great deal hinges, however, on what counts as (to use Wadia's phrase) the 'field of life' or (to use Gombrich's) 'our moral condition'; for if what these phrases denote includes certain features of our psychological constitution as well as more obviously 'external' circumstances, then it begins to look as though our being 'responsible for ourselves' entails the paradox outlined in the previous section, in which case an incoherence is exposed in the very concept of retributive karma.

A variant of this charge of incoherence has been presented by Whitley Kaufman in the form of a dilemma concerning what he sees as an irresolvable tension between the principle of universal justice on the one hand and free will on the other. If one believes in the former, then one holds that everything that happens (or, we might say, everything that happens which has any moral significance) is morally just; in effect, there is no evil, because any putative 'victims' of apparently evil acts or events must have received only what they deserved ('no more and no less', as Edwards puts it). In the case of apparently evil acts, the ostensible agent cannot be blameworthy: she is an instrument of karmic law, like 'the executioner who delivers the lethal injection' (Kaufman 2005: 25) – or, if we take the image of an 'instrument' more literally, like the syringe through which the lethal injection is administered. And yet the very idea of *desert* presupposes the possibility of free agency. Without it, moral responsibility would be eliminated, and then no one would be deserving of praise or blame: judgements that appear to be moral would have been denuded of moral purport. So belief in the principle of universal justice – and hence also in the law of karma (given a certain rather exacting rendition of it) – seems both to require belief in free moral agency and to obviate it.

Whichever way of spelling out the above incoherence charge one opts for, what it comes down to is the claim that any fully consistent world-picture in which the law of karma guarantees perfect justice ends up making this impersonal law the sole protagonist: karma becomes both cause and effect in an ongoing cycle, leaving no room for personal agency, and it is precisely this personal agency that is internally related to concepts such as *responsibility*, *desert* and *retribution*. There are, no doubt, ways of responding to this charge that would involve trying to draw sharper distinctions between the relevant concepts than my account has offered. Whether, for instance, an internal relation obtains between the concepts of free will and moral responsibility has been challenged in recent literature (Waller 2011). This would not, however, be my approach. Rather, I should want to scrutinize a basic assumption underlying the sorts of criticisms we have been considering from Edwards and Kaufman, namely the assumption that to hold a belief in the law of karma is to subscribe to a theory of how the world operates that is closely analogous to a scientific theory and is to be critically evaluated as such.

It cannot reasonably be denied that some advocates of the doctrine of karma do portray it as though it constituted a theory with a scientific status that distinguishes it from what they perceive as mere religious dogmas such as the idea of God's providential will. 'The theory of Reincarnation is logical and satisfactory', declares Swami Abhedananda in a lecture delivered at the end of the nineteenth century. It 'solves all the problems of life and explains scientifically all the questions and doubts that arise in the human mind' (1957: 83). Abhedananda is among those enthusiasts for the doctrine who regard rebirth and karma as being capable of improving Darwin's theory of evolution, supplementing its biological explanations with an account of the 'psychical, moral and ethical laws' governing 'inner' or 'spiritual' development (1957: 66, 79 et passim). Close analogies between Darwinian theory and conceptions of karma and rebirth have also been commended both by certain scholars of Buddhism and by the biologist Thomas Huxley.[9]

More recently, the eminent Indologist Karl Potter has claimed 'that karma and rebirth are treated in Indian thought in the manner of scientific theories' (1987: 162). By 'Indian thought', Potter here means specifically 'the classical treatises which it has become habitual to call "philosophical"' (139). He then proceeds to admit, however, that arguments defending the purported 'theory' of karma and rebirth are very thin on the ground in the classical treatises. He puts this down to the fact that schools of Indian philosophy have tended to be predominantly either 'realist' or 'superskeptical'. While schools

---

9. 'Like the doctrine of evolution itself, that of transmigration has its roots in the world of reality; and it may claim such support as the great argument from analogy is capable of supplying' (Huxley 1947 [1893]: 69). See also Rhys Davids (1881: 94): 'And the more thorough-going the Evolutionist, the more clear his vision of the long perspective of history, the greater will be his appreciation of the strangeness of the fact that a theory [i.e., the Buddhist theory of karma] so far consistent with what he holds to be true should have been possible at all in so remote a past.' For discussion, see Lopez (2008: 146; 2012: ch. 3).

of the former type simply take the reality of karma and rebirth for granted and then move swiftly on to try to demonstrate the superiority of their own ontological system over others, the supersceptics regard karma and rebirth as mere 'conventional truths', all of which 'are ultimately indefensible' (161). Though doubtful that such a broad-brushed characterization of the Indian philosophical milieu is helpful,[10] I concur that karma and rebirth are, at least for some schools, accepted as basic presuppositions rather than being seen as conjectures that stand in need of argumentative or evidential support. This, however, is precisely why it is misleading to suppose that ideas of karma and rebirth are in general treated 'in the manner of scientific theories'; this is misleading because scientific theories are exactly the sorts of things for which argumentative or evidential support *is* required.

Although it is unhelpful and indeed anachronistic to attribute a specifically scientific outlook to schools of classical Indian philosophy, it would be true to say that the period since the nineteenth century has seen a growing number of philosophers – many of them based in South or Southeast Asia – arguing for the scientific credibility of karma and rebirth. So too is it the case that some of these philosophers have given karma a central place in their attempts to formulate systematic explanations of, or justifications for, the existence and prevalence of evil. It is this trend that Kaufman is picking up on when he sets himself the task of critically examining 'this modern development of karma as systematic theodicy' (2005: 18). 'Theodicy' is here used in a broad sense to mean not exclusively an argument seeking 'to show that God is righteous or just despite the presence of evil in the world' (Davis 2001: xi), but rather any attempt to provide a systematic account of how the universe can be considered just in the face of evil, regardless of whether God features in the account. Among the theorists who have encouraged this broader usage is Max Weber, who praised the karma doctrine as 'the most consistent theodicy ever produced' (1958: 121).[11] Other commentators, feeling the sense of 'theodicy' to be somewhat strained in this context, have proposed alternative terms such as 'Cosmodicy' (Huxley 1947: 68), 'anthropodicy' (Larson 2003: 254–5)

---

10. Equally unhelpful is Potter's claim that Wittgenstein advocated a form of 'superskepticism' analogous to that of the Buddhist philosopher Nāgārjuna (Potter 1987: 160). For far more illuminating comparisons between Wittgenstein and Buddhism, see Gudmunsen (1977).

11. See also Weber (1963: 145) and Berger (1967: 65–7).

and 'karmadicy' (Herman 1987), but none of these has gained any popularity. Notwithstanding these terminological reservations, recent decades have witnessed fresh contributions to debates over what, if anything, karma can bring to attempts at resolving one or another version of the 'problem of evil'.[12]

When treated as a systematic attempt to confront the question of why evil exists in the world, it is difficult to see how the doctrine of karma can be adequately defended against the sorts of objections raised by Edwards and Kaufman. It is important to recognize, however, that the role of the doctrine in the lives of its non-academic adherents is rarely such a systematically theoretical one. Attending to the lives of believers in karma reveals a frequent intermingling of other beliefs: beliefs, for example, in the efficacy of magical spells or amulets,[13] or in the capacity of gods and spirits to intervene on one's behalf when propitiated, to unleash their ire when angered and to affect the course of one's life by their capricious and mischievous games.[14] Such attention also reveals multiple more or less significant variations in the belief across different cultural and religious groups, many of whom place a strong emphasis on retributive consequences, but others of whom highlight the educative or rehabilitative benefits of karmic effects.[15] This diversity and lack of systemization will not, of course, impress those seeking a philosophically or scientifically rigorous theory; indeed, these factors are liable to be seen as indicative of inconsistency, superstition and woolly-mindedness on the part of many believers in karma. In response, however, one might regard such a verdict as itself indicative of unrealistic expectations about what sort of thing a belief in karma generally is, and hence also about the kinds of criteria by which it ought to be judged.

Whatever we think about the critical reach of the attacks on karma considered so far, however, there remains a further grievance that is commonly raised, one which is even more vehemently moral in tone and which surely does find purchase against the doctrine in some of its everyday varieties as well as in its more academic reformulations.

12. Aside from Kaufman's essays (2005, 2007), these contributions include Reichenbach (1990: ch. 5), Herman (1993), Nayak (1993), Chadha and Trakakis (2007), Sharma (2008). For related discussions, see Filice (2006) and Goldschmidt and Seacord (2013).
13. Spiro (1982: ch. 6), Tambiah (1984: Part 3).
14. Daniel (1983), Hiebert (1983), Goldman (1985: 420).
15. Meenakshisundaram (1967: 30), Miles (2002: 67).

The grievance is that the doctrine of karma, at least in its explicitly retributive varieties, embodies an odious form of 'blaming the victim'. It is to this charge that we now turn.

The Problem of 'Blaming the Victim'

Ancient or traditional expositions of the doctrine of karma often come across to modern audiences as harsh and insensitive. For example, the *Chāndogya Upaniṣad* (*c*. eighth to fifth centuries BCE) declares that, while people of good behaviour are apt to be reborn among one of the highest three classes of society, those 'of foul behavior can expect to enter a foul womb, like that of a dog, a pig, or an outcaste woman' (5.10.7, trans. Olivelle 1998: 237). Among those whose past deeds have led to their being reborn in a condition 'despised by good people', the *Mānava Dharmaśāstra* includes people who are blind, deaf or mute as well as those with other physical or mental impairments (11.53, trans. Olivelle 2005: 217). Similarly, numerous Buddhist texts attribute responsibility both for supposedly negative qualities (short life, poor health, ugliness, lack of influence, poverty, low social status, meagre intelligence and so forth), and for their opposites, to the character of a person's actions in previous lives.[16]

Yet it is not only in traditional sources that people affected by such things as illness, disability or destitution are proclaimed to be suffering the inevitable outcomes of their own former sins; such assertions are also heard in the contemporary world, much to the consternation of campaigners against social discrimination who perceive them as throwbacks to a 'pre-modern' or 'medieval' era.[17] Christmas Humphreys, for instance, affirms that it is we who bring evil upon ourselves and that those born blind, deaf, of short stature or with bodily impairments 'are the products of their own past actions' (1983: 55); and Joseph Prabhu is willing to uphold as 'plausible and coherent' the idea that children or infants might be 'stricken with illnesses or handicaps' as 'the consequence of some crime committed in a previous life' (1989: 65, 73).

---

16. See esp. *Cūḷakammavibhaṅga Sutta* (MN III: 202–6), but also AN II: 203–5; SN I: 93–6; Śāntideva (1922: 73–4).

17. For critical reactions of this kind, see Anne Rae (quoted in Sharma 1999) and Shakespeare (2007: 421). For discussion, see Burley (2013).

For those in whom the belief in karma and rebirth is deeply ingrained, the view that suffering is the result of earlier wrongdoings is apt to be regarded as the expression of a basic truth or brute fact rather than as a judgement that might itself be open to moral or political objections. It goes too deep to be aptly described as anything like a scientific theory, for it is not based on empirical evidence and neither is there any such evidence that could dislodge it. It is, rather, constitutive of a way of seeing the world and, in particular, of a way of seeing suffering and distress, whether it be one's own or that of others. This is not to say that the belief is immune from change; it can of course evolve, just as it could be weakened or lost altogether. But the process by which such changes occur is unlikely to bear much resemblance to seeing the soundness of a line of reasoning or recognizing a new piece of evidence as decisive; it is more likely to be the result of underlying transformations in the cultural group with which one identifies, or of something like a religious conversion – a complex shift in one's worldview and form of life. Acknowledging these points will not, however, prevent explicit articulations of the belief in karma and rebirth from often striking unsympathetic non-believers as morally deplorable; and it is perhaps this difference – the difference between, on the one hand, regarding a statement as the expression of a simple fact without intrinsically moral evaluative content, and on the other hand, regarding it as imbued with egregious moral sentiments – that constitutes the major divide between firm believers in retributive karma and many of those for whom there is no place for that belief in their lives.[18] This issue can be explored in greater depth in relation to a further example.

In 1986, during a visit to Toronto, Lati Rimpoche was interviewed for a Buddhist periodical by a professor of Buddhist studies named Richard Hayes. Lati Rimpoche (1922–2010) was a *tülku* in the Geluk order of Tibetan Buddhism, a tülku being a high-ranking preceptor or lama who has been officially recognized as the reincarnation of a previous master within his religious lineage.[19] During the interview, Hayes puts to the Rimpoche the awkward question of how, from his

---

18. The point I am noting here has an affinity with Peter Winch's observation of something 'which brings great difficulty into moral philosophy', namely 'that people, besides disagreeing on the rights and wrongs of particular moral issues agreed to be such, may *also*, and perhaps more fundamentally, disagree on what is to be counted as a moral issue at all' (Winch 1972: 4).

19. For more detailed exposition of the relevant Tibetan terms, see Powers and Templeman (2012: 31, 199–201, 393–4, 658–9) and Wylie (1977).

Buddhist perspective, he would account for the trauma undergone by so many Jewish children under Nazi persecution in the 1930s and 1940s (Hayes 1998: 76). Confronted with a question of this kind, some might have expected (or perhaps hoped) that the only honest answer would be that there is simply no way of accounting for such horrors. As I noted in Chapter 2 (p. 55), the Buddha himself is purported to have said that the precise working out of the results of karma is among the 'inconceivable matters', conjecturing about which 'would reap either madness or frustration' (AN II: 80, trans. Bodhi 2012: 463).

Lati Rimpoche, however, does not forego conjecturing. Almost as though offering the official party line on the matter, he replies (via an interpreter):

> The proper Buddhist answer to such a question is that the victims were experiencing the consequences of their actions performed in previous lives. The individual victims must have done something very bad in earlier lives that led to their being treated in this way. Also there is such a thing as collective karma. (Quoted in Hayes 1998: 76)[20]

Hayes, pressing him on this reference to 'collective karma', asks whether individuals can do anything to change the karma of the group to which they belong. The Rimpoche's answer is that all karma can be changed by means of practice; individuals 'can persuade the group to adopt pure attitudes and to develop pure practices' (77). Again Hayes pursues the point, enquiring whether the suggestion being made is that the humiliations suffered by the Jews were consequent upon their having fallen short of Jewish purity laws or, alternatively, whether it was Buddhist standards that they failed to meet. 'There are attitudes that all peoples regard as pure', replies the Rimpoche, such as '[b]eing kind to other

---

20. Lati Rimpoche is not alone in having made a claim of this sort about victims of the holocaust. Air Chief Marshal Hugh Dowding (later Baron Dowding) is purported to have said in a speech to the Theosophical Society in London in November 1945 that the victims of concentration camps such as Belsen and Buchenwald were reincarnations of those who had themselves been persecutors of heretics during the Inquisition (Fisher 2001: 283). See also the politically incendiary remarks of the ultra-Orthodox Rabbi Ovadia Yosef reported in Katzenell (2000).

people'. He adds, though, that he does not 'know specifically about the history of the Jews' (77).

The people of Lati Rimpoche's own country, Tibet, have of course suffered grievously since the Chinese invasion of 1950. Hayes proceeds to ask the Rimpoche whether he believes these circumstances to be due to 'impurity of practice within Tibetan culture as a whole' (77). Once again the response given by Lati Rimpoche, who successfully escaped from his occupied homeland in 1964, will strike many non-believers in karma as stark:

> I'm sure that those Tibetans who were left behind to suffer great hardships under the Chinese Communists must have done something very bad in previous lives to deserve such consequences. It could be that in former lives they tortured other people or were responsible for injustice. As a result they must now live under an unjust system. (Quoted in Hayes 1998: 77)

Though a natural way of hearing an assertion that someone 'must have done something very bad' is as a moral indictment or rebuke, there is no discernible criticism or disapproval expressed in the Rimpoche's words; his confidence that this must have been the case stems from the internal logic of the doctrine of karma to which he is adhering.

Nor is Lati Rimpoche alone among Tibetans in taking this view of the situation. Similar statements have been made by other esteemed lamas. Samdhong Rinpoche, for example, speaks of the 'collective karmic force' of the Tibetan people, maintaining that an accumulation of 'positive collective karmic force' is needed if change is to be effected in Tibet (2006: 139–41). His account is complicated, for he combines analysis of what he sees as the Tibetan leadership's political failings in the period preceding the Chinese invasion with claims that 'the majority of the Tibetan people could have a purer mind and power of love, and reduce the hatred and anger towards the Chinese rulers' (140). By holding corruption in Tibetan governmental and monastic institutions, along with a more general 'weakness of the positive karmic stance', to be responsible for Tibet's predicament, he blends political, moral and spiritual elements together in his diagnosis. The one thing he does not do is blame the Chinese invaders. Critics would thus see his portrayal of events as an instance of blaming the victims, even though his being implicated among the supposedly blameworthy victims inevitably changes the moral character of this charge.

Aside from the difficulties involved in making sense of the notion of collective or group karma,[21] a dimension of the problem that some have highlighted with retributive karma more generally is the issue of proportionality. Believers in karma such as the Tibetan lamas referred to above exhibit no doubts about the correlation between the amount and intensity of suffering in the world on the one hand and the seriousness of the transgressions committed by those who endure it on the other; but many who do not share their conviction will wonder how the worst of torments could be remotely proportionate to any transgressions, even if the cumulative aggregation of sins over numerous lifetimes is taken into account. Warren Steinkraus voices this concern by asking whether 'the defender of *Karma* [can] admit that some suffering is outrageously severe' or whether, in the end, the defender must 'say that all suffering is *a priori* just and necessarily deserved merely because it occurs' (1965: 151). In view of the high degree of variability between different conceptions of karma, an honest answer would be that the defender of karma could go either way, depending on which version of the doctrine is subscribed to. In responding to a similar worry from Kaufman, however, Monima Chadha and Nick Trakakis have proposed that doubts concerning proportionality are apt to dissolve when one contemplates 'the brutality and ruthlessness' of which human beings are capable (2007: 538).[22] Their point could be elaborated by noting that anthropogenic atrocities such as the Nazi holocaust and the Chinese abuses in Tibet themselves epitomize the depths of evil to which humans can sink, thereby supplying examples of precisely the sorts of behaviour for which horrendous suffering would constitute just punishment. For those willing to take this position, there cease to be any forms of suffering so severe that they could not, in principle, be 'explained' by reference to the sufferers' past-life sins.

Replying to Chadha and Trakakis, Kaufman somewhat surprisingly turns the problem into one of numbers: 'it is simply implausible that so many people could have been so evil' (2007: 557). By putting it in these terms, Kaufman implies that a world containing fewer instances

21. The idea of collective karma invoked by Lati Rimpoche, for example, is of an entirely different sort from J. G. Jennings' notion of 'a doctrine of altruistic responsibility', which we saw in Chapter 5 (p. 110 above). For discussion of the concept of group or collective karma, see McDermott (1976) and Pappu (1987c).

22. For the particular argument to which they are responding, see Kaufman (2005: 21–2).

of suffering than ours would be one in which it were easier to accept that, even in its most extreme forms, suffering is invariably deserved. An alternative response, which is already suggested in Kaufman's initial essay, would be to question how certain modes of suffering could figure in any system of justice whatsoever, whether human, divine or cosmic.[23] A response of this latter kind would be indicative of a deep disagreement between the participants in the dispute, a disagreement that, as I suggested above, goes beyond the question of which moral attitude is the right one to take in responding to suffering; it carries over into the question of what counts as a moral attitude in the first place. The capacity to see the condition of someone who has been crushed by intolerable afflictions as justified retribution for something she 'must' have done in a previous life is not only a mode of perception that many others will not share; it is one that some will regard as morally reprehensible. This deep level of disagreement will be given closer consideration below.

A Deep Disagreement

Apologists for an emphatically retributive conception of karma are often willing to 'bite the bullet' with respect to the charge that this conception involves blaming victims for the misfortunes they experience. The doctrine *does* blame the victims, they admit, but it does not do so unfairly, for the 'victims' are themselves the guilty ones: 'Our misery and happiness are in exact proportion to our wickedness and virtue' (Nayak 1993: 59). The doctrine is saved from fatalism and cruelty, it will be added, by its ardent rejection of passivity in the face of affliction. As Humphreys puts it, 'even if all deserve their suffering, in that they have caused it, there is no excuse for callous indifference to their suffering by those more "fortunate"' (1983: 38–9). While critics may see callousness in the very tendency to regard suffering as deserved, defenders seek to shift the focus of attention towards the doctrine's implications for remedial action.

---

23. See, e.g., Kaufman's remark that 'It is certainly hard to stomach the notion that the inmates of Auschwitz and Buchenwald did something so evil in the past that they merely got what was coming to them – but the rebirth theory is committed to just this position' (2005: 21). I take it that the difficulty of stomaching such an idea is not due entirely to the *numbers* of inmates involved.

Looking back to the early teachings of Buddhism, Bhikkhu Bodhi reports that, without claiming belief in karma and rebirth to be the foundation of ethics, the Buddha had nevertheless emphasized its role as 'a strong inducement to moral behavior' (2005: 3). Spelling out what he means, Bodhi observes that recognizing the potential of 'our good and bad actions' to 'rebound upon ourselves, determining our future lives and bringing us happiness or suffering, ... gives us a decisive reason to avoid unwholesome conduct and to diligently pursue the good' (ibid.).[24] Again, from an alternative moral perspective, one might feel perturbed that this purportedly 'decisive reason', far from encouraging moral behaviour, is itself decidedly unwholesome, replacing, as it does, genuinely altruistic motivation with coarse self-interest. That the desire to receive reward and escape punishment in an afterlife can have a corrupting rather than edifying effect has long been a complaint made against certain eschatological visions. Why, it has been asked, should we not regard virtuous behaviour as *intrinsically* good, irrespective of its potential to bring happiness to the agent?[25] Bruce Reichenbach puts the central question succinctly when he asks whether we should 'do the right because it is right, or ... because it is in our best interests and to our benefit' (1990: 137). Taking the latter option, he submits, 'is to falsify the character of morality' (138).[26]

Though it is difficult to see how philosophical analysis alone could resolve a dispute such as this, one thing that philosophy can usefully do is to signal what kind of dispute it is. Believers in retributive karma often assume that what is at issue is a basic question of fact that could in principle be settled independently of any further differences over ethical matters, the basic question being that of whether our condition in this life is indeed determined (to a greater or lesser extent) by the moral quality of actions we performed in previous lives. Given this

24. See also Chakravarthi (1967: 62): 'Belief in this doctrine is sure to serve as a perpetual incentive to right conduct.' C. D. Broad, too, commends the doctrine of reincarnation as 'furnishing a reasonable motive for right action' (1938: 639).

25. For an example of this question being asked in the context of Christian theology, see Jantzen (1984: 37).

26. Reichenbach's point is connected with the idea of virtue for virtue's sake, which receives its classic formulation in Stoic philosophy. See, e.g., Seneca, *De Beneficiis* 4.1.3: "'And what shall I gain,' you ask, "if I do this bravely, if I do it gladly?" Only the gain of having done it ... . The reward of virtuous acts lies in the acts themselves.'

assumption, disbelievers are seen as having no reason to take offence at the doctrine of karma, since believing in it does not preclude benevolent modes of action towards disadvantaged people: it merely precludes one's regarding those disadvantaged people as innocent. But this way of representing the debate underplays the conceptual gap – the divergence in perspectives on the world – that separates the two parties. To develop a more accurate representation, we might usefully adduce a distinction that Wittgenstein makes between different levels of agreement: 'What is true or false is what human beings *say*', he remarks, 'and it is in their *language* that human beings agree. This is agreement not in opinions, but rather in form of life' (2009a: §241). One of the points for which I have been arguing in this chapter is that in the dispute over retributive karma we encounter a disagreement that would be poorly described as a disagreement in opinions; it is a disagreement that can be resolved not by rational deliberation alone but only by one or other party in the dispute undergoing a change of perspective so transformative that it would amount to a change in form of life.

But since 'form of life' is not a technical term for Wittgenstein, and lacks any strict definition,[27] we might wonder whether anything has really been illuminated by invoking it. What may help is an example that I take to be illustrative of the kind of thing Wittgenstein has in mind when he speaks of agreement, or disagreement, in form of life as opposed to agreement, or disagreement, in opinions. In one of his 'Lectures on Religious Belief' Wittgenstein is reported to have said the following:

> Suppose someone is ill and he says: "This is a punishment," and I say: "If I'm ill, I don't think of punishment at all." If you say: "Do you believe the opposite?"—you can call it believing the opposite, but it is entirely different from what we would normally call believing the opposite. I think differently, in a different way. I say different things to myself. I have different pictures. It is this way: if someone said: "Wittgenstein, you don't take illness as punishment, so what do you believe?"—I'd say: "I don't have any thoughts of punishment." (1966: 55, line breaks omitted)[28]

27. Cf. Ross (2009: 20): '"form of life" should not be seen as a theoretical or technical term but should be looked at as simply descriptive of the way language operates: it is interwoven with our lives.'

28. I am not the first to have noticed the relevance of this passage to

In a case such as this it is entirely possible to imagine the two individuals concerned getting along fairly well together. The one who thinks of his illness as a punishment might even be a patient being treated by the other, who is his doctor. The fact that the patient thinks as he does need not interfere with the doctor's ability to treat him, but it does mean that, at a certain level, they do not understand each other. It is not just that they conceive of illness differently: it is that their different ways of conceiving of illness are liable to be ramifications of their conceptions of life more broadly. The patient sees his own experiences as having a dimension of significance that is absent from the doctor's conception of life. He finds moral and spiritual meaning in occurrences that, for the doctor, appear lacking in such meaning. This is why the difference between them goes too deep to be veraciously described as a difference of opinion.

The doctor and one of her colleagues might have a difference of opinion with respect to how the patient's illness should best be treated; they might disagree over the correct diagnosis of the condition (is it glandular fever or merely a severe case of flu?) or about the most effective medication to prescribe (should it be steroids or antivirals?). Disagreements of these kinds occur within a view of the situation – a form of life – that is for the most part shared. But the difference between someone who thinks of illness as a punishment and someone who has no such thoughts is of a different order. The disagreement over diagnosis and medication could, at least in principle, be resolved by carrying out further tests on the patient and by appealing to past experience of which treatments have been most effective. But how could a disagreement over whether illness is a *punishment* be resolved? How this question is to be answered would depend on many details about the particular case, but, as a general point, it is far from clear how it could be resolved by appealing to evidence that both parties already agree to constitute evidence of a relevant type. The kind of disagreement at issue is a difference of moral and religious outlook. None of this entails that a disagreement in form of life, or the particular type of such a disagreement to which I have just been referring, is necessarily irresolvable. There are, no doubt, pathways along which the conversation could continue. But it should make us wary of presuming that it could be resolved without a significant change in worldview on the part of at least one of the two parties.

One implication of these considerations is that we should not expect

considerations of karma and rebirth; see Purton (1992).

the debate over whether a belief in retributive karma constitutes a morally unacceptable form of blaming the victim to be resolvable by appeal to commonly agreed criteria of evidence or logical inference. There will not be any knockdown argument to persuade one side that the other is right, for the starting assumptions are too disparate. For one party it just *is* the case that suffering, misfortune and various types of disadvantage are consequences of sins committed in previous lives. For the other party, suffering, misfortune and disadvantage are simply not understood in that way: different things are thought and said, different pictures are applied.

Alternative Aspects of Karma

Before concluding this chapter, I want to cite a further example that brings out different aspects of a belief in karma from those which have predominated in the foregoing discussion. When the emphasis is placed on particular people or groups who are undergoing persecution or distress, and we are told that they deserve their lot because even if we have no idea what they did to deserve it they must have done *something*, it is easy to see how critics will seize upon such claims and denounce them as 'unbearably cruel' and perhaps even arrogant (Edwards 1996: 14, 46). But just as, throughout this book, I have highlighted variations in rebirth beliefs that should give us pause before assuming what such beliefs 'must' amount to, so too in this chapter I have endeavoured to indicate that belief in karma is a multiform phenomenon as well. Among the features of this belief that are frequently underplayed in critical treatments are the intimate connections that it often has with impulses towards self-purification and compassion – especially, though by no means exclusively, in Buddhist traditions. I shall here discuss some poignant illustrations of these connections that occur in the memoir of a Tibetan 'warrior nun' named Ani Pachen.[29]

Lemdha Pachen Dolma was born in the eastern Tibetan province of Kham in 1933. Her father was a regional clan chieftain who commanded a resistance army against the invading Chinese troops

---

29. In addition to the memoir itself (Pachen and Donnelley 2001), sources of information for the following discussion include two obituaries (Martin 2002; Canada Tibet Committee 2002).

in the 1950s. Having joined a monastery of her own accord at the age of seventeen, and taken on the title *Ani* ('nun'), Pachen was called home by her father in 1954. When her father died four years later, Ani Pachen inherited the role of chieftain and, with some reluctance, led a guerrilla brigade in the struggle to regain Tibet's independence from Chinese occupation. She was captured in 1960 and held in Chinese prisons within Tibet for the next twenty-one years, often under conditions of extreme brutality. After eventually being released in 1981, Pachen initially remained in Tibet, involving herself again in the resistance campaign. Under threat of being rearrested, in 1988 she escaped across the border to Nepal and then to Dharamsala in northern India, home of the Tibetan government-in-exile, where her dream of meeting Tenzin Gyatso the Fourteenth Dalai Lama was fulfilled. She died in 2002, two years after the first publication of the memoir that she wrote with the assistance of an English-speaking translator, Adelaide Donnelley.

In one of several instances of torture that she describes, Pachen was subjected under interrogation to a merciless whipping with wet willow sticks. She recounts how she could feel 'the drops of water flicking off the sticks' as the guards approached her:

> Then they were on me. They lashed my face, my hands, my back, my feet, my head. *Om Mani Peme Hum*, I whispered under my breath. *Guru Rinpoche*. ... My ears were beginning to ring, and my face was burning. My previous karma, I thought. The pain will eliminate my sins. (Pachen and Donnelley 2001: 217)

This harrowing passage typifies the insight that Pachen's memoir affords us into the religious sensibility that informs her perspective on life and the world. In these circumstances of intense physical and psychological abuse, the thoughts that come to her mind are not coloured by hatred or resentment. The mantra she recites is in veneration of the 'jewel lotus' (*maṇi-padme*) traditionally associated with Avalokiteśvara, the bodhisattva of compassion (cf. Lopez 1988: 7; 1998: ch. 4). She also invokes Guru Rinpoche ('Precious Master'), the common Tibetan name for Padmasambhava, who is popularly revered for having converted Tibet 'into a realm of Dharma' (Lin 2003: 150).[30] But there is no sign of self-pity in Pachen's account; though taking

---

30. Padmasambhava is estimated to have lived in the eighth century CE (Gyatso 1996: 150). For more about his legend, see Dalton (2004).

responsibility for her situation by referring to her past karma, she views the trauma that she is undergoing as a kind of purification.[31]

Elsewhere Pachen prays that her own tribulations may relieve those of others (2001: 243). Praying also for her persecutors, including Chairman Mao Zedong himself, that their sins be 'cleared', she attributes their lamentable behaviour to their own former karma (256).[32] The relationship is complex between these different strands of belief – the belief, for example, that both the suffering of the persecuted and the inhumanity of the persecutor are in some way consequent upon the respective individuals' past-life actions. When abstracted from the life in which they are expressed, these strands may appear incongruous; yet when seen in the context of the life as a whole, they coherently mesh together.

The idea of suffering as a purifying process is, of course, far from uniquely Buddhist; it is associated also with certain other religious traditions, including forms of Christianity in which suffering becomes 'a welcome friend of the soul, not an enemy to be resisted' (Scheler 1992: 111). The Buddhist perspective represented by Pachen differs from that of Christianity, however, in that one's present life is comprehended as part of a series of innumerable lifetimes stretching back indefinitely far into the past and forward into the future. The suffering that one endures in this life is conceived as being beneficial in the longer run, not merely because it balances out the misdeeds of one's former lives but also because that balancing out is, in itself, a form of spiritual progress. Resonances with Christian ethics recur, though, when we notice that spiritual progress is here measured in terms of an increased decentring of concern, a looking outwards to the needs of others and a corresponding relinquishing of self-interest (cf. Eckel 1997: 341–2; King 1962: esp. ch. 6).

On one occasion, after having been hung up by her arms so painfully that she wished the prison guards would kill her rather than continue the torture, Pachen overcomes her despondency with the thought that death at this point would result only in her being 'reborn

---

31. 'I thought of the terrible karma I must have had in a previous life to be beaten like that, and prayed that the pain I was feeling would eliminate all sins that had been built up' (Pachen and Donnelley 2001: 219).

32. See also Martin (2002), reporting excerpts from statements by Pachen: '"I felt terrible for those who imprisoned me," she said, and also expressed sorrow for the captors who tortured her, saying she held the Buddhist belief that their cruelties resulted from their past lives.'

with the same sins in front of me'; it is thus 'better to suffer and hope for a higher rebirth' (2001: 219). There is here a notion of conquering one's own pain in which some may hear an echo of the maxim that Nietzsche attributes to the 'Military School of Life': 'Whatever does not kill me makes me stronger' (Nietzsche 1998b: ch. 1, §8). But in Pachen's case, the thought is that the catharsis of suffering will diminish her selfish motivations and enhance her compassionate nature, whereas for Nietzsche strength is more likely to be evaluated in terms of one's capacity to *surmount* feelings of compassion in the struggle for the victory of one's will over others (Nietzsche 1998a: §225; 2007: ch. 1, §4).[33] Moreover, for Pachen there is a sense in which even that which kills one could ultimately make one stronger, inasmuch as one's dying without fear or resentment contributes to a spiritually elevated rebirth. What she acknowledges in this particular instance, however, is the error of perceiving death as a *release* from suffering; given a worldview in which rebirth is presupposed, to die before suffering's absolving effects reach completion is merely to postpone the process until the next life. Thus we witness in Pachen's response to persistent torture both tremendous forbearance and a resignation to what, in view of her past karma, she regards as inescapable affliction.

Amid all the adversity and death that surround her, Pachen recalls the injunction of one of her spiritual teachers, Gyalsay Rinpoche: 'At the moment of death, the only protection is the force of one's own goodness' (quoted in Pachen and Donnelley 2001: 239). This is redolent of the tenet ascribed by Plato to the unrepentant Socrates in the *Apology*, 'that a good man cannot be harmed either in life or in death' (*Apology* 41d). Though elsewhere in Plato's works Socrates apparently espouses the idea of rebirth,[34] this idea is not evident in the *Apology* (cf. Ehnmark 1957: 2-3). Thus it is not a purified future life on earth to which Socrates is looking forward when he affirms that a good person cannot be harmed. Rather, his contention seems to be that a virtuous life has an integrity that cannot be diminished no matter what afflictions the world throws at it; whatever succeeds death, whether it be annihilation or an everlasting existence in Hades among the previously departed, the goodness of one's life remains intact. In the *Gorgias* this theme of

---

33. For relevant discussion of Nietzsche, see Panaïoti (2013: esp. ch 5).

34. See esp. *Meno* 81b-d; *Phaedo* 70c-82b; *Phaedrus* 248c-249c; *Timaeus* 42b-d, 90e; and most famously the 'Myth of Er' in *Republic* 614b-621d. Though not attributed to Socrates, relevant remarks also occur in Plato's *Laws* 903d-905b.

unassailable moral integrity is linked with that of genuine fulfilment or happiness (*eudaimonia*): the happy life is that of the person of integrity, regardless of whether he or she *feels* happy. Socrates, in effect, defines happiness as a state of moral goodness, and misery as a state of moral turpitude, irrespective of what any given individual's psychological or emotional disposition happens to be (*Gorgias* 470d–471a).[35] In the light of the doctrine of karma and rebirth professed by Pachen, meanwhile, the idea of one's own goodness serving a protecting role takes on a different significance. What is being protected against in this case is the suffering that one would be destined to undergo in a future life were one's current life to lack moral goodness. Although, on this account, acts of benevolence are seen as good in themselves and as typifying one's cultivation of selfless compassion, they also serve to secure for the agent a more auspicious rebirth, which in turn contributes towards an eventual liberation from suffering.

Comparison with Socrates' ethics in the *Gorgias* can also illuminate the compassion that Pachen directs at her tormentors. Writing of Mao Zedong, she remarks upon the 'huge karmic sin he gathered to act as he did'. While visualizing him in meditation, she prays for his burden of sin to be relieved (Pachen and Donnelley 2001: 256). What Pachen recognizes could be expressed by quoting Socrates' avowal that it is worse to commit injustice than to suffer it and that the one who puts someone to death unjustly is more deserving of pity than the one unjustly put to death, 'because doing what's unjust is actually the worst thing there is' (*Gorgias* 469b). However, while Socrates comes across as somewhat brash and sanguine about this ethical insight, Pachen more readily acknowledges the recalcitrant emotional obstacles associated with putting it into practice. Such are the injustices that she and her family and the Tibetan people more generally have been forced to endure, she cannot avoid the repeated resurgence of depression and anger. Pachen struggles to let go of these feelings by means of her religious practices (2001: 256).

The respective passages that I have considered in this chapter from Lati Rimpoche and Ani Pachen exemplify two ways of inheriting and articulating the doctrine of karma as it obtains within Asian rebirth traditions and especially within Tibetan Buddhism. There is on the face of it no contradiction between them; both the Rimpoche and Ani Pachen give voice to the idea that those who undergo oppression do so as a result of their past actions. Nevertheless, there is at the very least

---

35. For thoughtful reflection on this topic, see Duff (1976: esp. 297).

a marked difference of emphasis, and we see in that difference two distinct aspects of a belief in karma. Lati Rimpoche affirms, almost as though it were a statement of policy ('The proper Buddhist answer'), that victims – even child victims of genocide – 'must have done something very bad in earlier lives that led to their being treated in this way'. Pachen's words, meanwhile, convey a self-effacing goodwill towards her fellow sufferers along with an awareness that committing evil is itself a kind of misfortune, the most serious misfortune of all. One way of capturing this difference would be to say that while the mode of expression exemplified by Lati Rimpoche exhibits a cold detachment, that exemplified by Pachen wears compassion on its face.

Concluding Remarks

David Toolan has noted, in an essay discussing the apparently growing popularity of rebirth beliefs in western countries, that like the doctrine of original sin, the notions of reincarnation and karma belong 'in the arsenal of those who take the mystery of evil seriously' (1993: 44). They belong in that arsenal because, among other things, they constitute a response to what might otherwise be regarded as mere contingencies and vicissitudes of life; they acknowledge our inheritance of a mind and character as well as a body that are profoundly rooted in things and events which, though antedating our present existence on earth, nevertheless shape the trajectories of our respective lives, often in ways that involve suffering and dissatisfaction both for ourselves and for others. Although the analogy with original sin ought not to be pushed too far, we might observe that the doctrine of karma similarly represents human beings as having been 'born into sin' and yet as also being responsible for their sinfulness, individually and collectively. This chapter has explored some of the doctrine's facets along with some of the most acute moral objections that have been raised against it.

The three main criticisms of the karma doctrine that I have considered could also be said to 'take the mystery of evil seriously', for each of them is bound up with a concern that the doctrine, at best, only befuddles our thinking about evil and, at worst, exacerbates the problem by pointing the finger at those who are themselves in need of help. My discussion of these criticisms has registered their incisiveness against attempts to formulate the doctrine as a systematic theoretical solution to the 'problem of evil', but it has also highlighted how the complexities of the doctrine's manifestations in ordinary believers' lives conspire to deflect the criticisms' force. The charge that the karma doctrine offers no practical moral guidance, for example, carries considerable weight against any formulation that treats the doctrine as though it offered something comparable to a normative ethical theory. That weight is severely diminished, however, when the doctrine is recognized as being just one among a number of cultural and religious elements constitutive of a rich conceptual palette, upon which believers draw in order to articulate their responses to an unpredictable and ostensibly hostile world.

It has been said of the belief in karma that it is 'pure dogmatism' (Edwards 1996: 39) or 'pure apriorism' (Steinkraus 1965: 151).[36] Such characterizations are of course typically intended as criticisms. Yet there is a real sense in which, in at least many cases, belief in karma is indeed both dogmatic and *a priori*, without this necessarily counting against it. It is dogmatic in the sense that it involves holding fast to a religious principle, and *a priori* in the sense that the principle at issue is not founded upon experience; rather, as I have noted already, karma contributes to a *way* of experiencing and of thinking about the world. That way of experiencing and thinking about things – about suffering and evil in particular – is one that, as we have seen, many people find intensely troubling but which others find ethically and spiritually profound. The point of this chapter has been to make some inroads into clarifying why such attitudes run so deep.

---

36. See also Kaufman's complaint that 'an *a priori* conviction that karma is true can lead one into a distorted conception of reality' (2007: 557).

Chapter 7

CONCLUSIONS

In a poignant embellishment of Wittgenstein's image of the stream of life as the medium in which our expressions (verbal and otherwise) acquire their meanings, the anthropologist Rodney Needham remarks upon the difficulties encountered in trying to understand the expressions of others, especially those of people whose forms of life diverge very far from our own. Charting 'the stream of human life' is no easy matter, Needham observes, for 'it meanders, changes course, erodes its banks, exposes hidden strata, submerges what had seemed safe elevations, and in every conceivable characteristic it exhibits a perpetual inconstancy' (1972: 244–5). With reference to the present study, we can see that difficulties of these kinds inevitably arise when we seek to deepen our understanding of the expressions and forms of life pertaining to beliefs in rebirth, and the task hardly becomes less hazardous when we bring in a comparative component by selecting examples from diverse cultural sources. Although a broad diet of examples is necessary if a lopsided view of the concepts at issue is to be avoided, the risk is that by increasing the number of examples one ends up not doing full justice to any of them. This risk is, however, worth taking, for it is in the interplay between the examples – the interplay of perpetual inconstancies – that particularities are able to emerge and possibilities of sense are brought to the surface that would otherwise have remained undisclosed.

In another of Needham's works he speaks of his anthropological method as comprising a series of 'reconnaissances', each of which identifies certain characteristics of the landscape while leaving others for future 'full-scale expeditions' (1980: 3). This again furnishes a suggestive metaphor for the approach I have deployed in this study, provided we think of the reconnaissances not as attempts to register only 'main features and the general lie of the land' (ibid.), but more as exploratory ventures that probe particular regions of the terrain from multiple angles.[1] My hope is that, in combination with each other, this assemblage of exploratory ventures does provide an overview of sorts, but not one that loses sight of salient peculiarities caught sight of along the way.

The purpose of the study as a whole, as I have emphasized from the outset, has not been to try to settle questions such as whether rebirth happens or whether we or anyone else ought to believe that it does. Rather, it has been to indicate what it means for people who believe that it happens and how this belief relates to other dimensions, especially ethical dimensions, of a life lived in community with others. The relevant meanings and ethical connections are not uniform and do not lend themselves to concise summary; they are seen in the descriptions of specific cases.

While essentially hermeneutical, my approach has also served the critical objective of placing in question certain theses of a very general nature – theses which, by trying to say 'more than we know', tend to obfuscate aspects of the phenomena concerned.[2] Since these theses typically grow out of deep-rooted assumptions or 'pictures' that maintain a strong influence on much of our thinking, the task of unsettling the theses involves disrupting the assumptions or pictures that underlie them. I shall elaborate this point in relation to particular instances below.

Disrupting Assumptions

One of the theses to which I have given attention consists in the claim of a number of philosophers that believing in rebirth or believing that someone can remember a previous life must be excluded on logical grounds, these grounds being that the belief in question violates some rational norm associated with the concepts of personal identity and memory. As I pointed out in Chapters 2 and 3, the debate surrounding this exclusionary thesis relies heavily on rather thinly described thought experiments intended to reveal relevant characteristics of

---

1. Cf. Wittgenstein (2009a: 3e): 'The philosophical remarks in this book are, as it were, a number of sketches of landscapes which were made in the course of … long and meandering journeys.'

2. 'The difficulty in philosophy is to say no more than we know' (Wittgenstein 1969: 45).

the concepts at issue. In the background of the debate is a picture of concepts as entities whose criteria of application can be determined in virtual isolation from the complex cultural environments in which the concepts have their natural homes. When we turn from thought experiments to life, however, we see that the conceptual situation is far less tidy than some philosophers might imagine. Instead of adjudicating that what is said by believers in rebirth cannot logically make sense – or indeed ricocheting to the other extreme and supposing that it must make sense merely because people say it – I have proposed that we look to see what sense it makes in the communities of discourse in which the words are used.

Underlying both the exclusionary conceptual thesis to which I have just referred and the theses concerning the historical development of karmic conceptions of rebirth that I examined in Chapter 4 is a certain picture of the relation between metaphysics and ethics. As David Cockburn, among others, has noted, it is often assumed in philosophical discussions that metaphysics is logically prior to ethical thought and action, and that such thought and action must be 'grounded in' metaphysical beliefs or theories (Cockburn 1990: 11). This assumption can be challenged by showing that, in many areas of our lives, it is not clear what it would even mean to form a metaphysical conception of what something is – of what a human being is, for example – prior to, and hence independently of, particular ethical attitudes that we adopt.

Of most direct relevance to the concerns of this study are Cockburn's reflections on what it means to regard someone as the reincarnation of a deceased sibling. As we saw in Chapter 3, he argues that there is a sense in which, even if 'all the facts' are available, two or more people might continue to disagree over whether a child who previously died has been reborn as the child who is now alive. What they would be disagreeing about is not well described as either a purely ethical or a purely metaphysical matter, for each of those characteristics would be present. So when Cockburn says, for instance, that 'we must think of a metaphysical picture of persons as an *expression* of an ethical outlook' (1990: 206), we need not suppose – as some philosophers would be prone to do – that 'expression' is here being used to denote a kind of epiphenomenon that stands in a merely contingent relation to the ethical outlook with which it is associated. Rather, we can see the ethical outlook and the metaphysical picture as mutually informing – as two aspects of an integrated conception. Despite Cockburn's own categorical-sounding 'must', a viable way of hearing his contention is precisely as a caution *against* the assumption that the direction of dependence has to be one way.

The context in which this question of the relation between ethics and metaphysics arose in Chapter 4 was that of conceptions of rebirth or transmigration in ancient societies. The tendency in at least some of Catherine Osborne's pronouncements on the issue is towards the view that, in the case of some notable proponents of transmigration in ancient Greece, the metaphysical theory is a product of prior ethical commitments. Meanwhile, with reference to South Asian traditions in particular, Gananath Obeyesekere affirms the more common thesis that it was from the metaphysical conception of rebirth that the ethically infused notion of retributive karma emerged. Once the assumption that there must be an order of priority between metaphysics and ethics is abandoned, however, the temptation to say more than we know about how these ancient beliefs developed can also be relinquished. We are then free to wait on relevant historical evidence without being constrained by a theoretical assumption that the development 'must logically' have followed one particular course rather than another. We are also free to observe the variety of ways in which ethical attitudes are articulated in terms of rebirth and in which conceptions of rebirth manifest in ethical attitudes, rather than having to designate non-karmic versions of rebirth as 'non-ethicized' merely because they do not conform to a linear model, which purports to represent a logically impelled historical development.

Diversity and Dispute

A pervasive theme, evident throughout this study, is the emphasis on multiplicity as opposed to homogeneity. A reasonable response to anyone who is inclined to dismiss rebirth beliefs as confused or logically defective would be to ask which version of belief in rebirth the dismissal is targeted at. What we have seen is that, not only do conceptions of rebirth come in many varieties, but there is ongoing dispute within certain traditions as well as in the scholarly literature surrounding those traditions over how rebirth is best to be understood.

The focus of Chapter 5 was the efforts of particular exponents of rebirth to find a meaning in the traditional sources that does not require a commitment to elaborate mythological worldviews. Although my discussion there was centred upon the work of interpreters of Buddhism that has been carried out within the last century, we should not assume that these interpretive debates are only a recent phenomenon. As Rupert Gethin reminds us, 'the Buddhist tradition itself at an early date was quite capable of demythologizing' (1997: 189), and hence to speak of 'demythologizing' at all would be misleading if it were taken to imply that only modern interpreters have sought psychological and ethical significance in ostensibly cosmological imagery. While it remains difficult to see how disputes over what counts as an authentic interpretation of the original sources can be resolved satisfactorily, it is clear that those original sources have themselves given rise to vibrant traditions of interpretation. The possibilities of sense that we encounter in those traditions should again give us pause before assuming that belief in rebirth is all of one kind and that determining what it consists in is a fairly straightforward affair.

Meanwhile, in debates concerning the morality of the doctrine of retributive karma, which we considered in Chapter 6, there are important disagreements not only about the key concepts of karma and rebirth, but also about what is and what is not a morally significant attitude. Central to the position of prominent defenders of belief in karma is a distinction, whether implicit or explicit, between evaluative and non-evaluative aspects of the belief. Such defenders maintain, for instance, that believing of someone that her physical or psychological impairment or socio-economic disadvantage is necessarily the result of past misdeeds does not amount to holding a morally significant attitude towards the person in question; it amounts merely to affirming a truth or fact which is in itself value-neutral. According to such defenders of karma, the morally significant question does not arise when one considers *whether* the person one is faced with deserves her plight; it arises only when one asks how, given the fact that she has ended up in that plight, one ought to respond, or, as Arvind Sharma (1999) puts it, 'Given the situation, what is my duty?'

Critics who raise moral objections to the karma doctrine tend not to divide up the evaluative and non-evaluative elements of the belief along the same lines as its defenders. Instead, they regard the belief that someone deserves her plight as itself carrying moral significance; moreover, since they can see no good reason for crediting this belief, they denounce it as adding insult to injury, cruelly blaming the victim, and so forth. Another observation of Cockburn's, though not itself a direct contribution to debates over karma, nonetheless bears upon these debates. Writing of 'the significance which another's treatment of me has for me', Cockburn remarks that it 'does not lie solely in the "effects" which their behaviour has on me; where "effects" are understood as states which could have been brought about in a way which did not involve another human being' (1990: 202–3). Rather, Cockburn continues, it is at least to some extent 'in the attitude towards me which it expresses' that the behaviour's moral significance resides:

> It makes a significant difference whether another's apparent acts of kindness towards me flow from physical compulsion by a third party, a sense of duty, or something more akin to love. I suppose that to most people this kind of thing matters a great deal. They would rather undergo a substantial measure of unpleasant 'effects' than lose the affection and goodwill of others. (203)

Although these thoughts of Cockburn's do not of course immediately settle the dispute concerning the morality of the karma doctrine, they illustrate one way in which a critic of the doctrine might begin to soften the demarcation that defenders such as Arvind Sharma try to maintain between the attitude of holding someone responsible for her own suffering on the one hand and one's way of acting towards her on the other (cf. Sharma 2008: 573). What Cockburn is highlighting is how one's attitude towards, or perception of, the person to whom one is responding affects the moral character of the response itself, for there is a sense in which the attitude is indeed *part of* the response. Once we notice that underlying the debate between defenders and critics of karma there is this basic disagreement – a disagreement about whether perceiving someone as deserving of her plight has any moral significance in itself – then the depth of the dispute and the difficulty of resolving it become more apparent.

One of the impressive features of the case of Ani Pachen, which I touched on towards the end of Chapter 6, is the way in which her actions embody a synthesis of the view that each of us is karmicly responsible for our misery and the view that committing evil is itself a profound, perhaps the profoundest, form of misery. This synthesis opens up the possibility not only of her forgiving those by whom she is imprisoned and tortured, but also – remarkably and relatedly – of feeling deep compassion for them. By shifting the emphasis from doing one's duty to acting out of compassion even towards one's own abusers, Pachen exhibits a moral possibility within the framework of a belief in karma that usually goes unnoticed, albeit one that Pachen herself admits to be extremely hard to put into practice.

Methodological Reflections

Finally in this concluding chapter let me offer a few further thoughts on methodological matters. In addition to exploring the cultural landscape of rebirth from a number of different vantage points, my aim has been to contribute towards an expanded conception of philosophy of religion. Intrinsic to this conception is the cultivation of mutual engagement between philosophy and other relevant disciplines – notably theology, anthropology and religious studies – along with the enhancement of cross-cultural modes of inquiry that such interdisciplinarity makes possible. The present study exemplifies certain ways in which this expanded conception can be put into effect while also retaining an awareness of the conception's potential drawbacks.

The comparisons in Chapter 5 between aspects of Rudolf Bultmann's demythologizing project in biblical hermeneutics on the one hand, and the efforts of certain exponents of Buddhism to find or recover a psychologically and soteriologically satisfactory conception of karma and rebirth on the other, illustrate one means by which theological resources can usefully be drawn upon in the context of a cross-cultural investigation. In earlier chapters, meanwhile, the turn from thought experiments to life, which I mentioned above, is part of a reorientation towards a more extensive use of anthropological and biographical sources of information, albeit a reorientation that harbours potentially negative as well as positive implications. On the positive side, consulting material derived from anthropological and biographical sources, alongside more doctrinally focused texts, offers a means of broadening the scope of inquiry to encompass a wide range of religious and cultural traditions, many of which are routinely neglected in philosophy of religion. Wittgenstein's work provides one valuable interface, having had an influence within both philosophy and anthropology. Also exemplifying fruitful approaches are those anthropologists, such as Geertz (to whom I referred in Chapter 4) and Needham (whom I mentioned earlier in this one), whose anthropological studies are directly informed by philosophical ways of thinking.[3]

On the negative side, a danger that comes with doing philosophy in a more anthropological style – a danger common to most forms of interdisciplinary inquiry – is that the result may turn out to be neither

---

3. Also important in this regard is Stanley Tambiah, who successfully integrates ethnographic, textual, historical and philosophical perspectives into much of his work; see esp. Tambiah (1990).

one thing nor the other: too philosophical to be anthropology and too anthropological to be philosophy. No doubt some critical readers will judge that parts of the present study suffer from this shortcoming. One recurrent difficulty is that of giving enough space to ethnographic description to illuminate the topic under discussion while also retaining a clear view of the philosophical job at hand. Another difficulty is that of finding points at which ethnographic or other anthropological material can be brought into productive dialogue with existing philosophical debates. Both of these difficulties tend to militate against providing the sort of detailed treatment of a cultural tradition that is typified by anthropological studies with an ethnographic focus.

What I have endeavoured to do is to at least indicate some directions in which philosophy of religion can go, directions that give due attention to what sociologists and anthropologists are calling 'lived' or 'everyday' religion as well as to the rich textual heritage that the world's religious and philosophical traditions have to offer.[4] 'The stream of life, or the stream of the world, flows on', as Wittgenstein remarks (1975: §48); and as it does so, the proclivities and interests of philosophy of religion are inevitably transformed. Conceptions of rebirth, along with the manifold beliefs and values and forms of life with which they are intermingled, constitute a fertile area for continued research – research that goes to the heart of what it is to contemplate the sense of human life.

---

4. For representative sociological expositions of 'lived' and 'everyday' religion, see McGuire (2008) and Ammerman (2007).

BIBLIOGRAPHY

Abhedananda, Swami. 1957. *Reincarnation*, 7th edn. Calcutta: Ramakrishna Vedanta Math.
Allen, N. J. 1985. The Category of the Person: A Reading of Mauss's Last Essay. In *The Category of the Person*, ed. Michael Carrithers, Steven Collins and Steven Lukes. Cambridge: Cambridge University Press, 26–45.
Almeder, Robert. 1992. *Death and Personal Survival: The Evidence for Life after Death*. Lanham, MD: Rowman & Littlefield.
Almeder, Robert. 1997. Critique of Arguments Offered against Reincarnation. *Journal of Scientific Exploration* 11 (4): 499–526.
Almeder, Robert. 2000. Reincarnation Evidence: Stevenson's Research. Gold Thread Video Productions. www.youtube.com/watch?v=hZhMDU9GcVg (accessed 2 April 2013).
Almeder, Robert. 2001. On Reincarnation: A Reply to Hales. *Philosophia* 28 (1–4): 347–58.
Ammerman, Nancy T., ed. 2007. *Everyday Religion: Observing Modern Religious Lives*. Oxford: Oxford University Press.
Anuruddha, Ācariya. 2007. *A Comprehensive Manual of Abhidhamma: The Abhidhammattha Saṅgaha of Ācariya Anuruddha*, ed. Bhikkhu Bodhi, trans. Mahāthera Nārada and Bhikkhu Bodhi, 3rd edn. Kandy: Buddhist Publication Society.
Arnason, Johann P., S. N. Eisenstadt and Björn Wittrock, eds. 2005. *Axial Civilizations and World History*. Leiden: Brill.
Asad, Talal. 1983. Anthropological Conceptions of Religion: Reflections on Geertz. *Man*, n.s. 18 (2): 237–59.
Asad, Talal. 1993. *Genealogies of Religion: Discipline and Reasons of Power in Christianity and Islam*. Baltimore, MD: Johns Hopkins University Press.
Asher, Frederick M. 2006. Early Indian Art Reconsidered. In *Between the Empires: Society in India 300 BCE to 400 CE*, ed. Patrick Olivelle. Oxford: Oxford University Press, 51–66.
Aurobindo, Sri. 1978. *The Problem of Rebirth*, 3rd edn. Pondicherry: Sri Aurobindo Ashram.
Aurobindo, Sri. 2005 [1939–40]. *The Life Divine*. Pondicherry: Sri Aurobindo Ashram Trust.
Awolalu, J. Omosade. 1996. *Yorùbá Beliefs and Sacrificial Rites*. Brooklyn, NY: Athelia Henrietta Press.
Ayer, A. J. 1956. *The Problem of Knowledge*. Harmondsworth: Penguin.
Ayer, A. J. 1963. *The Concept of a Person and Other Essays*. London: Macmillan.
Baker, G. P., and P. M. S. Hacker. 2005. *Wittgenstein: Understanding and Meaning*, Part 2, 2nd edn, rev. by P. M. S. Hacker. Oxford: Blackwell.

Bartsch, Hans-Werner, ed. 1972. *Kerygma and Myth: A Theological Debate*, trans. Reginald H. Fuller, 2 vols. London: SPCK.
Basham, A. L. 1981. *History and Doctrines of the Ājīvikas: A Vanished Indian Religion*, 2nd edn. Delhi: Motilal Banarsidass.
Batchelor, Stephen. 1998. *Buddhism without Beliefs*. London: Bloomsbury.
Bechert, Heinz. 1966. *Buddhismus, Staat und Gesellschaft in den Ländern des Theravāda-Buddhismus*, Vol. 1. Frankfurt: Institut für Asienkunde in Hamburg.
Berger, Helen A., Evan A. Leach and Leigh S. Shaffer. 2003. *Voices from the Pagan Census: A National Survey of Witches and Neo-Pagans in the United States*. Columbia, SC: University of South Carolina Press.
Berger, Peter L. 1967. *The Sacred Canopy: Elements of a Sociological Theory of Religion*. Garden City, NY: Doubleday.
Besant, Annie. 1892. *Reincarnation*. London: Theosophical Publishing Society.
Besterman, Theodore. 1930. The Belief in Rebirth among the Natives of Africa (including Madagascar). *Folklore* 41 (1): 43–94.
Beyer, Stephan V. 1992. *The Classical Tibetan Language*. Albany, NY: State University of New York Press.
Bharati, Agehananda. 1965. *The Tantric Tradition*. London: Rider.
Bhāratī, Swāmī Veda, trans. 2001. *Yoga Sūtras of Patañjali with the Exposition of Vyāsa: A Translation and Commentary*, Vol. 2. Delhi: Motilal Banarsidass.
Bhattacharji, Sukumari. 1982. Fatalism – Its Roots and Effects. *Journal of Indian Philosophy* 10 (2): 135–54.
Black, Max. 1962. *Models and Metaphors: Studies in Language and Philosophy*. Ithaca, NY: Cornell University Press.
Blackman, Margaret B. 1992. *During My Time: Florence Edenshaw Davidson, a Haida Woman*, rev. edn. Seattle, WA: University of Washington Press.
Blavatsky, H. P. 1888. *The Secret Doctrine*, 2 vols. London: Theosophical Publishing Company.
Blavatsky, H. P. 1987 [1889]. *The Key to Theosophy*. Pasadena, CA: Theosophical University Press.
Bloch, Jon P. 1998. *New Spirituality, Self, and Belonging: How New Agers and Neo-Pagans Talk about Themselves*. Westport, CT: Praeger.
Boas, Franz. 1896. Sixth Report on the Indians of British Columbia. *Report of the Sixty-Sixth Meeting of the British Association for the Advancement of Science*. London: Murray, 569–91.
Bockmuehl, Klaus. 1988. *The Unreal God of Modern Theology: Bultmann, Barth, and the Theology of Atheism: A Call to Recovering the Truth of God's Reality*, trans. Geoffrey W. Bromiley. Colorado Springs, CO: Helmers & Howard.
Bodewitz, Hendrik W. 1997. The Hindu Doctrine of Transmigration: Its Origin and Background. *Indologica Taurinensia* 23-4: 583–605.
Bodhi, Bhikkhu, trans. 2000. *The Connected Discourses of the Buddha: A Translation of the Saṃyutta Nikāya*. Somerville, MA: Wisdom.

Bodhi, Bhikkhu. 2005 [2001]. Does Rebirth Make Sense? *Buddhist Publication Society Newsletter* 46-7: 1-7. www.accesstoinsight.org/lib/authors/bodhi/bps-essay_46.pdf (accessed 27 March 2013).
Bodhi, Bhikkhu. 2010. Dhamma without Rebirth? *Access to Insight*. www.accesstoinsight.org/lib/authors/bodhi/bps-essay_06.html (accessed 3 December 2013).
Bodhi, Bhikkhu, trans. 2012. *The Numerical Discourses of the Buddha: A Translation of the Aṅguttara Nikāya*. Somerville, MA: Wisdom.
Bogart, Elizabeth. 1866. *Driftings from the Stream of Life: A Collection of Fugitive Poems*. New York: Hurd and Houghton.
Broad, C. D. 1938. *An Examination of McTaggart's Philosophy*, Vol. 2, Part 2. Cambridge: Cambridge University Press.
Broido, Michael. 1982. Does Tibetan Hermeneutics Throw Any Light on Sandhābhāṣā? *Journal of the Tibet Society* 2: 5-39.
Bronkhorst, Johannes. 1998. Did the Buddha Believe in Karma and Rebirth? *Journal of the International Association of Buddhist Studies* 21 (1): 1-19.
Bronkhorst, Johannes. 2001. Etymology and Magic: Yāska's *Nirukta*, Plato's *Cratylus*, and the Riddle of Semantic Etymologies. *Numen* 48 (2): 147-203.
Bronkhorst, Johannes. 2007. *Greater Magadha: Studies in the Cultures of Early India*. Leiden: Brill.
Bryant, Edwin. 2001. *The Origins of Vedic Culture: The Indo-Aryan Migration Debate*. Oxford: Oxford University Press.
Bryant, Edwin, trans. 2009. *The Yoga Sūtras of Patañjali: A New Edition, Translation, and Commentary*. New York: North Point Press.
Bucknell, Roderick S., and Martin Stuart-Fox. 1983. The 'Three Knowledges' of Buddhism: Implications of Buddhadasa's Interpretation of Rebirth. *Religion* 13 (2): 99-112.
Bucknell, Roderick S., and Martin Stuart-Fox. 1986. *The Twilight Language: Explorations in Buddhist Meditation and Symbolism*. London: Curzon.
Buddhadāsa Bhikkhu. n.d. [1970?]. *Another Kind of Birth: A Lecture Delivered at Phatthalung, Thailand, 16 July 1969*, trans. R. B. [no further details given]. Bangkok: Sivaphorn.
Buddhadāsa Bhikkhu. 1971. *Toward the Truth*, ed. Donald K. Swearer. Philadelphia, PA: Westminster Press.
Buddhadāsa Bhikkhu. 1974. *Two Kinds of Language*, trans. Ariyananda Bhikkhu. Bangkok: Sublime Life Mission.
Buddhadatta. 1980 [1915, 1928]. *Buddhadatta's Manuals*, 2 parts, ed. A. P. Buddhadatta. London: Pali Text Society.
Buddhaghosa, Bhadantācariya. 2010 [fifth c. CE]. *The Path of Purification (Visuddhimagga)*, trans. Bhikkhu Ñāṇamoli, 5th edn. Onalaska, WA: Pariyatti.
Bultmann, Rudolf. 1957. *History and Eschatology: The Presence of Eternity*. New York: Harper and Brothers.
Bultmann, Rudolf. 1972a [1941]. New Testament and Mythology. In Bartsch (1972 I: 1-44).

Bultmann, Rudolf. 1972b [1952]. Bultmann Replies to His Critics. In Bartsch (1972 I: 191-211).
Burgess, Ruth Vassar. 2012. Religion's Influence on Social Justice Practices Relating to Those with Disabilities. In *The Wiley-Blackwell Companion to Religion and Social Justice*, ed. Michael D. Palmer and Stanley M. Burgess. Oxford: Wiley-Blackwell, 575-90.
Burley, Mikel. 2004. 'Aloneness' and the Problem of Realism in Classical Sāṃkhya and Yoga. *Asian Philosophy* 14 (3): 223-38.
Burley, Mikel. 2012a. *Contemplating Religious Forms of Life: Wittgenstein and D. Z. Phillips*. London: Continuum.
Burley, Mikel. 2012b. Self, Consciousness, and Liberation in Classical Sāṃkhya. In *Hindu and Buddhist Ideas in Dialogue: Self and No-Self*, ed. Irina Kutznetsover, Chakravarthi Ram-Prasad and Jonardon Ganeri. Farnham: Ashgate, 47-62.
Burley, Mikel. 2013. Retributive Karma and the Problem of Blaming the Victim. *International Journal for Philosophy of Religion* 74 (2): 149-65.
Burley, Mikel. 2014a. Conundrums of Buddhist Cosmology and Psychology. Paper presented at the *31st Annual STIMW [Sanskrit Tradition in the Modern World] Seminar*, University of Manchester, 23 May.
Burley, Mikel. 2014b. Taking Reincarnation Seriously: Critical Discussion of Some Central Ideas from John Hick. *International Journal of Philosophy and Theology* 75 (3): 236-53.
Burrow, T. 1949. Review of J. G. Jennings, *The Vedāntic Buddhism of the Buddha*. *Journal of the Royal Asiatic Society* 81 (3-4): 201-2.
Burton, David. 2013. Buddhism. In Meister and Copan (2013: 18-28).
Buswell, Robert E., Jr., and Donald S. Lopez Jr. 2014. *The Princeton Dictionary of Buddhism*. Princeton, NJ: Princeton University Press.
Butler, Joseph. 1736. Of Personal Identity. In his *The Analogy of Religion, Natural and Revealed, to the Constitution and Course of Nature*. London: Knapton, 301-8.
Campbell, Thomas. 1853. *The Poetical Works of Thomas Campbell*. London: Moxon.
Canada Tibet Committee. 2002. Ani Pachen Dolma: Tibet's 'Warrior Nun'. *World Tibet Network News*, 19 February. www.tibet.ca/en/newsroom/wtn/archive/old?y=2002&m=2&p=19_4 (accessed 1 January 2013).
Canto-Sperber, Monique. 2008. *Moral Disquiet and Human Life*, trans. Sylvia Pavel. Princeton, NJ: Princeton University Press.
Carpenter, Amber D. 2015. Persons Keeping Their *Karma* Together: The Reasons for the *Pudgalavāda* in Early Buddhism. In *The Moon Points Back*, ed. Koji Tanaka, Yasuo Deguchi, Jay L. Garfield and Graham Priest. New York: Oxford University Press, 1-44.
Carrithers, Michael. 1989. Naked Ascetics in Southern Digambar Jainism. *Man*, n.s. 24 (2): 219-35.

Carter, John Ross, and Mahinda Palihawadana, trans. 1987. *The Dhammapada*. New York: Oxford University Press.
Casadio, Giovanni. 1992. The Manichaean Metempsychosis: Typology and Historical Roots. In *Studia Manichaica II: Internationaler Kongress zum Manichäismus*, ed. Gernot Wiessner and Hans-Joachim Klimkeit. Wiesbaden: Harrassowitz, 105-30.
Cavalcanti, Maria Laura Viveiros de Castro. 2006. Life and Death in Kardecist Spiritism. *Religião & Sociedade* 1 (special edn): 1-15.
Cayce, Edgar. 2006. *Reincarnation and Karma*. Virginia Beach, VA: ARE Press.
Chadha, Monima, and Nick Trakakis. 2007. Karma and the Problem of Evil: A Response to Kaufman. *Philosophy East and West* 57 (4): 533-56.
Chakravarthi, S. C. 1967. Karma and Rebirth. *Indian Philosophical Annual* 1: 56-62.
Chattopadhyaya, S. K. 1967. Karma and Rebirth. *Indian Philosophical Annual* 1: 50-5.
Chomsky, Noam. 1972. Deep Structure, Surface Structure, and Semantic Interpretation. In his *Studies on Semantics in Generative Grammar*. The Hague: Mouton, 62-119.
Chrétien, Jean-Louis. 2002. *The Unforgettable and the Unhoped For*, trans. Jeffrey Bloechl. New York: Fordham University Press.
Christiano, Kevin J., William H. Swatos Jr. and Peter Kivisto. 2008. *Sociology of Religion: Contemporary Developments*, 2nd edn. Lanham, MD: Rowman & Littlefield.
Chryssides, George D. 2012. *Historical Dictionary of New Religious Movements*, 2nd edn. Lanham, MD: Scarecrow Press.
Churchill, John. 1984. Wittgenstein on the Phenomena of Belief. *International Journal for Philosophy of Religion* 16 (2): 139-52.
Clack, Brian R. 1995. D. Z. Phillips, Wittgenstein and Religion. *Religious Studies* 31 (1): 111-20.
Clack, Brian R. 1999. *Wittgenstein, Frazer and Religion*. Basingstoke: Macmillan.
Clarke, Peter, ed. 2006a. *Encyclopedia of New Religious Movements*. Abingdon: Routledge.
Clarke, Peter. 2006b. *New Religions in Global Perspective*. Abingdon: Routledge.
Clayton, John. 2006. *Religions, Reasons and Gods: Essays in Cross-Cultural Philosophy of Religion*. Cambridge: Cambridge University Press.
Cockburn, David. 1990. *Other Human Beings*. Basingstoke: Macmillan.
Cockburn, David. 1991. The Evidence for Reincarnation. *Religious Studies* 27 (2): 199-207.
Collins, Steven. 1982. *Selfless Persons: Imagery and Thought in Theravāda Buddhism*. Cambridge: Cambridge University Press.
Collins, Steven. 1994. What Are Buddhists *Doing* When They Deny the Self?

In *Religion and Practical Reason: New Essays in the Comparative Philosophy of Religions*, ed. Frank E. Reynolds and David Tracy. Albany, NY: State University of New York Press, 59–86.

Collins, Steven. 2009. Remarks on the *Visuddhimagga*, and on its Treatment of the Memory of Former Dwelling(s) (*pubbenivāsānussatiñāṇa*). *Journal of Indian Philosophy* 37 (5): 499–532.

Coomaraswamy, Ananda K. 1946. Gradation, Evolution and Reincarnation. *New Blackfriars* 27: 425–9.

Cowell, E. B. 1895. Preface. In *The Jātaka, or Stories of the Buddha's Former Births*, Vol. 1, trans. Robert Chalmers, ed. E. B. Cowell. Cambridge: Cambridge University Press, vii–xii.

Creider, Jane Tapsubei. 1986. *Two Lives: My Spirit and I*. London: Women's Press.

Creider, Jane Tapsubei, and Chet A. Creider. 1984. The Past in the Present: Living Biographies of the Nandi. *Anthropos* 79 (4–6): 537–44.

Dalal, Ajit K. 2000. Living with a Chronic Disease: Healing and Psychological Adjustment in Indian Society. *Psychology and Developing Societies* 12 (1): 67–82.

Dalton, Jacob. 2004. The Early Development of the Padmasambhava Legend in Tibet: A Study of IOL Tib J 644 and Pelliot tibétain 307. *Journal of the American Oriental Society* 124 (4): 759–72.

Daniel, Sheryl B. 1983. The Tool Box Approach of the Tamil to the Issues of Moral Responsibility and Human Destiny. In Keyes and Daniel (1983: 27–62).

Daniels, Charles B. 1990. In Defence of Reincarnation. *Religious Studies* 26 (4): 501–4.

Dasgupta, Surama. 1965. *Development of Moral Philosophy in India*. New York: Ungar.

Dasgupta, Surendranath. 1927. *A History of Indian Philosophy*, Vol. 2. Cambridge: Cambridge University Press.

Davidson, Ronald M. 2002. *Indian Esoteric Buddhism: A Social History of the Tantric Movement*. New York: Columbia University Press.

Davis, Stephen T. 2001. Introduction. In *Encountering Evil: Live Options in Theodicy*, ed. Stephen T. Davis, new edn. Louisville, KY: Westminster John Knox Press, vii–xiii.

Davy, Barbara Jane. 2007. *Introduction to Pagan Studies*. Lanham, MD: AltaMira Press.

Dawkins, Richard. 1995. *River Out of Eden: A Darwinian View of Life*. London: Weidenfeld & Nicholson.

Deutsch, Eliot. 1966. The Self in Advaita Vedānta. *International Philosophical Quarterly* 6 (1): 5–21.

Dhammananda, K. Sri. 1973. *Do You Believe in Rebirth?* 2nd edn. Kuala Lumpur: Buddhist Missionary Society.

Dombrowski, Daniel A. 1984a. *The Philosophy of Vegetarianism*. Amherst, MA: University of Massachusetts Press.

Dombrowski, Daniel A. 1984b. Was Plato a Vegetarian? *Apeiron* 18 (1): 1–9.
Doniger, Wendy, and Brian K. Smith, trans. 1991. *The Laws of Manu*. London: Penguin.
Driberg, J. H. 1936. The Secular Aspect of Ancestor-Worship in Africa. *Journal of the Royal African Society* 35: 1–21.
Duff, Antony. 1976. Must a Good Man Be Invulnerable? *Ethics* 86 (4): 294–311.
Dumont, Louis. 1970. *Religion, Politics and History in India: Collected Papers in Indian Sociology*. Paris: Mouton.
During, Jean. 1998. A Critical Survey on Ahl-e Haqq Studies in Europe and Iran. In *Alevi Identity: Cultural, Religious and Social Perspectives*, ed. Tord Olsson, Elisabeth Özdalga and Catharina Raudvere. Istanbul: Swedish Research Institute, 105–25.
Eckel, Malcolm David. 1997. Is There a Buddhist Philosophy of Nature? In *Buddhism and Ecology: The Interconnection of Dharma and Deeds*, ed. Mary Evelyn Tucker and Duncan Ryūken Williams. Cambridge, MA: Harvard University Press, 327–49.
Edgerton, Franklin, trans. 1944. *The Bhagavad Gītā*, 2 vols. Cambridge, MA: Harvard University Press.
Edwards, Paul. 1996. *Reincarnation: A Critical Examination*. Amherst, NY: Prometheus.
Eggeling, Julius, trans. 1882–1900. *The Śatapatha-Brâhmana according to the Text of the Mâdhyandina School*, 5 vols. Oxford: Clarendon Press.
Ehnmark, Erland. 1957. Transmigration in Plato. *Harvard Theological Review* 50 (1): 1–20.
Einarsdóttir, Jónína. 2004. *Tired of Weeping: Mother Love, Child Death, and Poverty in Guinea-Bissau*, 2nd edn. Madison, WI: University of Wisconsin Press.
Eliade, Mircea, ed. 1987. *The Encyclopedia of Religion*, 16 vols. New York: Macmillan.
Eshleman, Andrew, ed. 2008. *Readings in Philosophy of Religion: East Meets West*. Oxford: Blackwell.
Evans-Wentz, W. Y. 2000 [1927]. *The Tibetan Book of the Dead*, 4th edn. Oxford: Oxford University Press.
Evers, Sandra J. T. M. 2002. *Constructing History, Culture and Inequality: The Betsileo in the Extreme Southern Highlands of Madagascar*. Leiden: Brill.
Eylon, Dina Ripsman. 2003. *Reincarnation in Jewish Mysticism and Gnosticism*. Lewiston, NY: Mellen Press.
Farrar, Janet, and Stewart Farrar. 1985. *The Witches' Way: Principles, Rituals and Beliefs of Modern Witchcraft*. London: Guild.
Federman, Asaf. 2010. What Kind of Free Will Did the Buddha Teach? *Philosophy East and West* 60 (1): 1–19.
Feer, M. Leon, ed. 1884–98. *Saṃyutta-Nikāya*, 5 vols. London: Pali Text Society.

Filice, Carlo. 2006. The Moral Case for Reincarnation. *Religious Studies* 42 (1): 45–61.
Fisher, Joe. 2001. *Coming Back: The Case for Reincarnation*. London: Souvenir Press.
Flanagan, Owen. 2011. *The Bodhisattva's Brain: Buddhism Naturalized*. Cambridge, MA: MIT Press.
Flew, Antony. 1951. Locke and the Problem of Personal Identity. *Philosophy* 26: 53–68.
Fort, Andrew O. 1998. *Jīvanmukti in Transformation: Embodied Liberation in Advaita and Neo-Vedanta*. Albany, NY: State University of New York Press.
Frankfurt, Harry G. 1969. Alternate Possibilities and Moral Responsibility. *Journal of Philosophy* 66 (23): 829–39.
Freuchen, Peter. 1961. *Peter Freuchen's Book of the Eskimos*, ed. Dagmar Freuchen. Cleveland, OH: World Publishing Co.
Garrett, William. 2005. *Bad Karma: Thinking Twice about the Social Consequences of Reincarnation Theory*. Lanham, MD: University Press of America.
Gasser, Georg, ed. 2010. *Personal Identity and Resurrection: How Do We Survive Our Death?* Farnham: Ashgate.
Geertz, Clifford. 1973. *The Interpretation of Cultures*. New York: Basic Books.
Geertz, Clifford. 1983. *Local Knowledge: Further Essays in Interpretive Anthropology*. New York: Basic Books.
Geertz, Clifford. 2000. *Available Light: Anthropological Reflections on Philosophical Topics*. Princeton, NJ: Princeton University Press.
Gelblum, Tuvia. 1986. Review of Robert J. Zydenbos, *Mokṣa in Jainism, according to Umāsvāti*. *Bulletin of the School of Oriental and African Studies* 49 (1): 229–30.
Gernet, Alexander von. 1994. Saving the Souls: Reincarnation Beliefs of the Seventeenth-Century Huron. In Mills and Slobodin (1994: 38–54).
Gethin, Rupert. 1997. Cosmology and Meditation: From the Aggañña Sutta to the Mahāyāna. *History of Religions* 36 (3): 183–217.
Gethin, Rupert. 1998. *The Foundations of Buddhism*. Oxford: Oxford University Press.
Gethin, Rupert, trans. 2008. *Sayings of the Buddha: A Selection of Suttas from the Pāli Nikāyas*. Oxford: Oxford University Press.
Ghai, Anita. 2010. The Psychology of Disabled People. In *Psychology in India*, Vol. 3, ed. Girishwar Misra. Noida: Dorling Kindersley, 107–84.
Gimaret, Daniel. 2000. Tanāsukh. In *The Encyclopaedia of Islam*, new edn, ed. P. J. Bearman, Th. Bianquis, C. E. Bosworth, E. Van Donzel and W. P. Heinrichs, Vol. 10. Leiden: Brill, 181–3.
Gippert, Jost, ed. 2008. *White Yajur-Veda: Śatapatha-Brāhmaṇa (Mādhyandiniya)*. Frankfurt: Thesaurus Indogermanischer Text- und Sprachmaterialien. http://titus.uni-frankfurt.de/texte/etcs/ind/aind/ved/yvv/sbm/sbm.htm (accessed 9 November 2013).

Glasenapp, Helmuth von. 2003 [1942]. *The Doctrine of Karman in Jain Philosophy*, trans. G. Barry Gifford, ed. Hiralal R. Kapadia. Fremont, CA: Asian Humanities Press.

Glock, Hans-Johann. 1996. *A Wittgenstein Dictionary*. Oxford: Blackwell.

Goethe, Johann Wolfgang von. 1998 [1833]. *Maxims and Reflections*, trans. Elisabeth Stopp, ed. Peter Hutchinson. London: Penguin.

Goldman, Robert P. 1985. Karma, Guilt, and Buried Memories: Public Fantasy and Private Reality in Traditional India. *Journal of the American Oriental Society* 105 (3): 413–25.

Goldschmidt, Tyron and Beth Seacord. 2013. Judaism, Reincarnation, and Theodicy. *Faith and Philosophy* 30 (4): 393–417.

Gombrich, Richard F. 1971. *Precept and Practice: Traditional Buddhism in the Rural Highlands of Ceylon*. Oxford: Clarendon Press.

Gombrich, Richard F. 2006. *How Buddhism Began: The Conditioned Genesis of the Early Teachings*, 2nd edn. London: Routledge.

Gombrich, Richard F. 2013. *What the Buddha Thought*. Sheffield: Equinox.

Gonda, Jan. 1955-6. The Etymologies in the Ancient Indian Brāhmaṇas. *Lingua* 5: 61–86.

Gonda, Jan. 1975. *Selected Studies*, Vol. 4: *History of Ancient Indian Religion*. Leiden: Brill.

Goodman, Charles. 2002. Resentment and Reality: Buddhism on Moral Responsibility. *American Philosophical Quarterly* 39 (4): 359–72.

Gottlieb, Alma. 1998. Do Infants Have Religion? The Spiritual Lives of Beng Babies. *American Anthropologist*, n.s. 10 (1): 122–35.

Gottlieb, Alma. 2004. *The Afterlife Is Where We Come From: The Culture of Infancy in West Africa*. Chicago, IL: University of Chicago Press.

Gottlieb, Alma. 2006. Non-Western Approaches to Spiritual Development among Infants and Young Children: A Case Study from West Africa. In *The Handbook of Spiritual Development in Childhood and Adolescence*, ed. Eugene C. Roehlkepartain, Pamela Ebstyne King, Linda Wagener and Peter L. Benson. Thousand Oaks, CA: Sage, 150–62.

Goudey, R. F. 1928. *Reincarnation: A Universal Truth*. Los Angeles, CA: Aloha Press.

Gowans, Christopher W. 2003. *Philosophy of the Buddha: An Introduction*. London: Routledge.

Green, Dave. 2001–2. Death, Nature and Uncertain Spaces: A Commentary from Paganism. *Omega: Journal of Death and Dying* 44 (2): 127–49.

Griffith-Dickson, Gwen. 2005. *The Philosophy of Religion*. London: SCM Press.

Griffiths, Paul J. 1982. Notes towards a Critique of Buddhist Karmic Theory. *Religious Studies* 18 (3): 277–91.

Gudmunsen, Chris. 1977. *Wittgenstein and Buddhism*. Basingstoke: Macmillan.

Gupta, Akhil. 2002. Reliving Childhood? The Temporality of Childhood and Narratives of Reincarnation. *Ethnos* 67 (1): 33–55.

Guthrie, W. K. C. 1993 [1952]. *Orpheus and Greek Religion: A Study of the Orphic Movement*. Princeton, NJ: Princeton University Press.

Gyatso, Janet B. 1996. Drawn from the Tibetan Treasury: The *gTer ma* Literature. In *Tibetan Literature: Studies in Genre*, ed. José Ignacio Cabezón and Roger R. Jackson. Ithaca, NY: Snow Lion, 147–69.

Habermas, Jürgen. 1993. *Justification and Application: Remarks on Discourse Ethics*, trans. Ciaran Cronin. Cambridge, MA: MIT Press.

Hacker, P. M. S. 2004. *Wittgenstein: Connections and Controversies*. Oxford: Oxford University Press.

Hacker, P. M. S. 2007. *Human Nature: The Categorial Framework*. Oxford: Blackwell.

Halbfass, Wilhelm. 1980. Karma, *Apūrva*, and 'Natural' Causes: Observations on the Growth and Limits of the Theory of *Saṃsāra*. In O'Flaherty (1980: 268–302).

Hammer, Olav. 2004. *Claiming Knowledge: Strategies of Epistemology from Theosophy to the New Age*. Leiden: Brill.

Hanegraaff, Wouter J. 1998. *New Age Religion and Western Culture: Esotericism in the Mirror of Secular Thought*. Albany, NY: State University of New York Press.

Haraldsson, Erlendur and Majd Abu-Izzeddin. 2004. Three Randomly Selected Lebanese Cases of Children Who Claim Memories of a Previous Life. *Journal of the Society for Psychical Research* 68 (2): 65–85.

Häring, Hermann and Johann-Baptist Metz, eds. 1993. *Reincarnation or Resurrection?* London: SCM Press.

Harvey, Peter. 2013a. The Conditioned Co-Arising of Mental and Bodily Processes within Life and Between Lives. In *A Companion to Buddhist Philosophy*, ed. Steven M. Emmanuel. Chichester: Wiley, 46–68.

Harvey, Peter. 2013b. *An Introduction to Buddhism: Teachings, History and Practices*, 2nd edn. Cambridge: Cambridge University Press.

Hay, Louise L. 2004 [1984]. *You Can Heal Your Life*. Carlsbad, CA: Hay House.

Hayes, Richard P. 1998. *Land of No Buddha: Reflections of a Sceptical Buddhist*. Birmingham: Windhorse.

Hazra, R. C. 1940. *Studies in the Purāṇic Records on Hindu Rites and Customs*. Dacca: University of Dacca.

Heelas, Paul. 1996. *The New Age Movement*. Oxford: Blackwell.

Heijke, Jan. 1993. Belief in Reincarnation in Africa. In Häring and Metz (1993: 46–53).

Hemacandra. 2002 [twelfth c. CE]. *The Yogaśāstra of Hemacandra: A Twelfth Century Handbook on Śvetāmbara Jainism*, trans. Olle Quarnström. Cambridge, MA: Harvard University Press.

Herman, Arthur L. 1987. Karmadicy: Karma and Evil in Indian Thought. In Pappu (1987a: 221–48).

Herman, Arthur L. 1993. *The Problem of Evil and Indian Thought*, 2nd edn. Delhi: Motilal Banarsidass.

Hick, John. 1973. *Philosophy of Religion*, 2nd edn. Englewood Cliffs, NJ: Prentice-Hall.
Hick, John. 1976. *Death and Eternal Life*. London: Collins.
Hick, John. 1990. *Philosophy of Religion*, 4th edn. Upper Saddle River, NJ: Prentice-Hall.
Hick, John. 2006. *The New Frontier of Religion and Science: Religious Experience, Neuroscience, and the Transcendent*. Basingstoke: Palgrave Macmillan.
Hick, John. 2010. *Dialogues in the Philosophy of Religion*. Basingstoke: Palgrave Macmillan.
Hiebert, Paul G. 1983. Karma and Other Explanation Traditions in a South Indian Village. In Keyes and Daniel (1983: 119–30).
Hiltebeitel, Alf. 2011. *Dharma: Its Early History in Law, Religion, and Narrative*. Oxford: Oxford University Press.
Hiriyanna, Mysore. 1949. *Essentials of Indian Philosophy*. London: Allen & Unwin.
Hodgson, Marshall G. S. 1962. Al-Darazî and Ḥamza in the Origin of the Druze Religion. *Journal of the American Oriental Society* 82 (1): 5–20.
Hogan, Joseph, and Rebecca Hogan. 1998. Autobiography in the Contact Zone: Cross-Cultural Identity in Jane Tapsubei Creider's *Two Lives*. In *True Relations: Essays on Autobiography and the Postmodern*, ed. G. Thomas Couser and Joseph Fichtelberg. Westport, CT: Greenwood Press, 83–95.
Horsch, Paul. 1971. Vorstufen der indischen Seelenwanderungslehre. *Asiatische Studien/Études Asiatiques* 25: 99–157.
Horton, Robin. 1993. *Patterns of Thought in Africa and the West: Essays on Magic, Religion and Science*. Cambridge: Cambridge University Press.
Hoynacki, George John. 1993. 'And the Word was Made Flesh': Incarnations in Religious Traditions. *Asia Journal of Theology* 7 (1): 12–34.
Hultkrantz, Åke. 1953. *Conceptions of the Soul among North American Indians: A Study in Religious Ethnology*. Stockholm: Ethnographical Museum of Sweden.
Humphreys, Christmas. 1983. *Karma and Rebirth*. London: Curzon.
Hutton, Ronald. 1999. *The Triumph of the Moon: A History of Modern Pagan Witchcraft*. Oxford: Oxford University Press.
Huxley, Julian. 1926. *The Stream of Life*. London: Watts.
Huxley, T. H. 1947 [1893]. Evolution and Ethics. In T. H. Huxley and Julian Huxley, *Evolution and Ethics, 1893–1943*. London: Pilot Press, 60–102.
Idowu, E. Bọlaji. 1966. *Olódùmarè: God in Yoruba Belief*. London: Longmans.
Idowu, E. Bọlaji. 1973. *African Traditional Religion: A Definition*. London: SCM Press.
Jackson, Peter A. 2003. *Buddhadāsa: Theravada Buddhism and Modernist Reform in Thailand*, 2nd edn. Chiang Mai: Silkworm Books.
Jaini, Padmanabh S. 1980. Karma and the Problem of Rebirth in Jainism. In O'Flaherty (1980: 217–38).

James, William. 1890. *The Principles of Psychology*, Vol. 1. New York: Holt.
Jamison, Stephanie W., and Joel P. Brereton, trans. 2014. *The Rigveda: The Earliest Religious Poetry of India*, 3 vols. Oxford: Oxford University Press.
Jantzen, Grace M. 1984. Do We Need Immortality? *Modern Theology* 1 (1): 33–44.
Jaspers, Karl. 2010 [1949]. *The Origin and Goal of History*, trans. Michael Bullock. Abingdon: Routledge.
Jayatilleke, K. N. 1963. *Early Buddhist Theory of Knowledge*. London: Allen & Unwin.
Jefferson, Warren. 2008. *Reincarnation Beliefs of North American Indians: Soul Journeys, Metamorphoses, and Near-Death Experiences*. Summerton, TN: Native Voices.
Jennings, J. G. 1947. *The Vedāntic Buddhism of the Buddha*. London: Oxford University Press.
Jennings, Pete. 2002. *Pagan Paths: A Guide to Wicca, Druidry, Asatru, Shamanism and Other Pagan Practices*. London: Rider.
Jha, Ganganatha, trans. 1939. *The Tattvasaṅgraha of Śāntarakṣita, with the Commentary of Kamalaśīla*, Vol. 2. Baroda: Oriental Institute.
Johnson, Roger A. 1974. *The Origins of Demythologizing: Philosophy and Historiography in the Theology of Rudolf Bultmann*. Leiden: Brill.
Johnson, Will. 1997. Transcending the World? Freedom (*Mokṣa*) and the *Bhagavadgītā*. In *The Fruits of Our Desiring: An Enquiry into the Ethics of the Bhagavadgītā for Our Times*, ed. Julius Lipner. Calgary: Bayeux, 92–104.
Jonas, Hans. 1930. *Augustin und das paulinische Freiheitsproblem: Ein philosophischer Beitrag zur Genesis der christlich-abendländischen Freiheitsidee*. Göttingen: Vandenhoeck & Ruprecht.
Jonas, Hans. 1965. *Augustin und das paulinische Freiheitsproblem: Eine philosophische Studie zum pelagianischen Streit*, 2nd edn. Göttingen: Vandenhoeck & Ruprecht.
Josephus, Flavius. 2008 [first c. CE]. *Judean War: Translation and Commentary*, trans. Steve Mason. Leiden: Brill.
Jurewicz, Joanna. 2004. Prajāpati, the Fire and the *Pañcâgni-vidyā*. In *Essays in Indian Philosophy, Religion and Literature*, ed. Piotr Balcerowicz and Marek Mejor. Delhi: Motilal Banarsidass, 45–60.
Kalghatgi, T. G. 1972. *Karma and Rebirth*. Ahmedabad: L. D. Institute of Indology.
Kane, Pandurang Vaman. 1977. *History of Dharmaśāstra*, Vol. 5, Part 2, 2nd edn. Poona: Bhandarkar Oriental Research Institute.
Kane, Robert. 1996. *The Significance of Free Will*. Oxford: Oxford University Press.
Katzenell, Jack. 2000. Rabbi Says Holocaust Victims were Sinners. *ABC News*, 6 August. http://abcnews.go.com/US/story?id=96252&page=1 (accessed 5 November 2011).

Kaufman, Whitley R. P. 2005. Karma, Rebirth, and the Problem of Evil. *Philosophy East and West* 55 (1): 15-32.
Kaufman, Whitley R. P. 2007. Karma, Rebirth, and the Problem of Evil: A Reply to Critics. *Philosophy East and West* 57 (4): 556-60.
Keith, Arthur Berriedale. 1925. *The Religion and Philosophy of the Vedas and Upanishads*, Part 2. Cambridge, MA: Harvard University Press.
Kemp, Daren. 2004. *New Age: A Guide*. Edinburgh: Edinburgh University Press.
Keown, Damien. 1996. Karma, Character, and Consequentialism. *Journal of Religious Ethics* 24 (2): 329-50.
Keown, Damien. 1998. Paternalism in the *Lotus Sūtra*. *Journal of Buddhist Ethics* 5: 190-207.
Keown, Damien. 2004. *A Dictionary of Buddhism*. Oxford: Oxford University Press.
Kern, Hendrik. 1898. *Manual of Indian Buddhism*. Strassburg: Trübner.
Kessler, Gary E., ed. 1999. *Philosophy of Religion: Toward a Global Perspective*. Belmont, CA: Wadsworth.
Keyes, Charles F. 1983a. Introduction: The Study of Popular Ideas of Karma. In Keyes and Daniel (1983: 1-24).
Keyes, Charles F. 1983b. Merit-Transference in the Kammic Theory of Popular Theravāda Buddhism. In Keyes and Daniel (1983: 261-86).
Keyes, Charles F. and E. Valentine Daniel, eds. 1983. *Karma: An Anthropological Inquiry*. Berkeley, CA: University of California Press.
King, Winston L. 1962. *Buddhism and Christianity: Some Bridges of Understanding*. Philadelphia, PA: Westminster Press.
Klostermaier, Klaus K. 2007. *A Survey of Hinduism*, 3rd edn. Albany, NY: State University of New York Press.
Kohn, Livia. 1998. Steal Holy Food and Come Back as a Viper: Conceptions of Karma and Rebirth in Medieval Daoism. *Early Medieval China* 4: 1-48.
Kohn, Livia. 2003. *Monastic Life in Medieval Daoism: A Cross-Cultural Perspective*. Honolulu, HI: University of Hawai'i Press.
Kolak, Daniel and Raymond Martin, eds. 2001. *The Experience of Philosophy*, 5th edn. Belmont, CA: Wadsworth/Thomson Learning.
Koller, John M. 1972. *Dharma*: An Expression of Universal Order. *Philosophy East and West* 22 (2): 131-44.
Krishan, Yuvraj. 1983. Karma Vipāka. *Numen* 30 (2): 199-214.
Krishan, Yuvraj. 1997. *The Doctrine of Karma: Its Origin and Development in Brāhmanical, Buddhist and Jaina Traditions*. Delhi: Motilal Banarsidass.
Kumar, Alok. 2010. Pythagoras. In *Cultural Encyclopedia of Vegetarianism*, ed. Margaret Puskar-Pasewicz. Santa Barbara, CA: Greenwood, 192-3.
Kuppuswamy, B. 1977. *Dharma and Society: A Study in Social Values*. Columbia, MI: South Asia Books.
Langmead, Ross. 2004. *The Word Made Flesh: Towards an Incarnational Missiology*. Lanham, MD: University Press of America.

Larson, Gerald James. 2003. Some New Perspectives on Karma and Rebirth. *Bulletin of the Ramakrishna Mission Institute of Culture* 54 (6): 251–61.
Larson, Paul. 2010. Karma. In *Encyclopedia of Psychology and Religion*, ed. David A. Leeming, Kathryn Madden and Stanton Marlan. New York: Springer, 499.
Lehrer, Keith. 2004. Freedom and the Power of Preference. In *Freedom and Determinism*, ed. Joseph Keim Campbell, Michael O'Rourke and David Shier. Cambridge, MA: MIT Press, 47–69.
Leibniz, G. W. 1991 [1686]. *Discourse on Metaphysics*. In *Discourse on Metaphysics and Other Essays*, trans. Daniel Garber and Roger Ariew. Indianapolis, IN: Hackett, 1–41.
Leslie-Smith, L. H. 1990. Karma and Reincarnation. In *Karma: Rhythmic Return to Harmony*, ed. Virginia Hanson, Rosemarie Stewart and Shirley J. Nicholson. Wheaton, IL: Theosophical Publishing House, 38–45.
Lin, Wei. 2003. Padmasambhava and His Eight Manifestations. In John C. Huntington and Dina Bangdel, *The Circle of Bliss: Buddhist Meditational Art*. Columbus, OH: Columbus Museum of Art, 150–2.
Lindquist, Steven E. 2011. Literary Lives and a Literal Death: Yājñavalkya, Śākalya, and an Upaniṣadic Death Sentence. *Journal of the American Academy of Religion* 79 (1): 33–57.
Lispector, Clarice. 1989 [1973]. *The Stream of Life*, trans. Elizabeth Lowe and Earl Fitz. Minneapolis, MN: University of Minnesota Press.
Locke, John. 1979 [1689]. *An Essay concerning Human Understanding*, ed. Peter H. Nidditch. Oxford: Clarendon Press.
Long, Herbert Strainge. 1948. *A Study of the Doctrine of Metempsychosis in Greece: From Pythagoras to Plato*. Princeton, NJ: Princeton University Press.
Long, J. Bruce. 1987. Reincarnation. In Eliade (1987 XII: 265–9).
Lopez, Donald S., Jr. 1988. *The Heart Sūtra Explained: Indian and Tibetan Commentaries*. Albany, NY: State University of New York Press.
Lopez, Donald S., Jr. 1998. *Prisoners of Shangri-La: Tibetan Buddhism and the West*. Chicago, IL: University of Chicago Press.
Lopez, Donald S., Jr. 2008. *Buddhism and Science: A Guide for the Perplexed*. Chicago, IL: University of Chicago Press.
Lopez, Donald S., Jr. 2012. *The Scientific Buddha: His Short and Happy Life*. New Haven, CT: Yale University Press.
Macdonell, Arthur Anthony. 1954 [1929]. *A Practical Sanskrit Dictionary*. Oxford: Oxford University Press.
MacGregor, Geddes. 1978. *Reincarnation in Christianity: A New Vision of the Role of Rebirth in Christian Thought*. Wheaton, IL: Theosophical Publishing House.
MacIntosh, J. J. 1989. Reincarnation and Relativized Identity. *Religious Studies* 25 (2): 153–65.
MacIntosh, J. J. 1992. Reincarnation, Closest Continuers, and the Three Card Trick: A Reply to Noonan and Daniels. *Religious Studies* 28 (2): 235–51.

Mahābhārata. 1999. *Mahābhārata: Critical Edition*, electronic text. Pune: Bhandarkar Oriental Research Institute. http://bombay.indology.info/mahabharata/statement.html (accessed 8 June 2013).

Mahadevan, T. M. P. 1967. An Overview. *Indian Philosophical Annual* 1: 16-19.

Malalasekera, G. P. 1957. *The Buddha and His Teachings*. Colombo: Buddhist Council of Ceylon.

Malcolm, Norman. 1977. *Memory and Mind*. Ithaca, NY: Cornell University Press.

Malcolm, Norman. 1984. *Ludwig Wittgenstein: A Memoir*, 2nd edn. Oxford: Clarendon Press.

Malinowski, Bronislaw. 1932. *The Sexual Life of Savages in North-Western Melanesia*, 3rd edn. London: Routledge.

Mantin, Ruth. 2004. Thealogies in Process: Re-Searching and Theorizing Spiritualities, Subjectivities, and Goddess-Talk. In *Researching Paganisms*, ed. Jenny Blain, Douglas Ezzy and Graham Harvey. Walnut Creek, CA: AltaMira Press, 147-70.

Martin, Douglas. 2002. Ani Pachen, Warrior Nun in Tibet Jail 21 Years, Dies. *New York Times*, 18 February: B7.

Martin, Raymond. 1992. Survival of Bodily Death: A Question of Values. *Religious Studies* 28 (2): 165-84.

Matthews, Bruce. 1986. Post-Classical Developments in the Concepts of Karma and Rebirth in Theravāda Buddhism. In Neufeldt (1986: 123-43).

Mauss, Marcel. 1969 [1906]. Extrait de l'*Année sociologique*, 9. In *Oeuvres*, Vol. 2: *Représentations collectives et diversité des civilisations*, ed. Victor Karady. Paris: Les Éditions de Minuit, 135-9.

Mayeda, Sengaku, ed. and trans. 1992. *A Thousand Teachings: The Upadeśasāhasrī of Śaṅkara*, rev. edn. Albany, NY: State University of New York Press.

Mbiti, John S. 1990. *African Religions and Philosophy*, 2nd edn. Oxford: Heinemann.

McClelland, Norman C. 2010. *Encyclopedia of Reincarnation and Karma*. Jefferson, NC: McFarland & Co.

McDaniel, June. 1989. *The Madness of the Saints: Ecstatic Religion in Bengal*. Chicago, IL: University of Chicago Press.

McDermott, James P. 1976. Is There Group Karma in Theravāda Buddhism? *Numen* 23 (1): 67-80.

McDermott, James P. 1980. Karma and Rebirth in Early Buddhism. In O'Flaherty (1980: 165-92).

McGuire, Meredith B. 2008. *Lived Religion: Faith and Practice in Everyday Life*. Oxford: Oxford University Press.

McLeod, W. H., ed. and trans. 1984. *Textual Sources for the Study of Sikhism*. Manchester: Manchester University Press.

McMahan, David. 2004. Demythologization and the Core-versus-Accretions

Model of Buddhism. *Indian International Journal of Buddhism* 10 (5): 63–99.
McMahan, David. 2012. Buddhist Modernism. In *Buddhism in the Modern World*, ed. David L. McMahan. Abingdon: Routledge, 159–76.
Mead, G. R. S. 1912. The Doctrine of Reincarnation Ethically Considered. *International Journal of Ethics* 22 (2): 158–79.
Meenakshisundaram, T. P. 1967. Common Folk of Tamilnad and Theory of Karma and Rebirth. *Indian Philosophical Annual* 1: 24–31.
Megill, Allan. 1998. History, Memory, Identity. *History of the Human Sciences* 11 (3): 37–62.
Meister, Chad and Paul Copan, eds. 2013. *The Routledge Companion to Philosophy of Religion*, 2nd edn. London: Routledge.
Miles, M. 2002. Disability in an Eastern Religious Context. *Journal of Religion, Disability and Health* 6 (2–3): 53–76.
Mills, Antonia C. 1988. A Comparison of Wet'suwet'en Cases of the Reincarnation Type with Gitksan and Beaver. *Journal of Anthropological Research* 44 (4): 385–415.
Mills, Antonia C. 1994a. Rebirth and Identity: Three Gitksan Cases of Pierced-Ear Birthmarks. In Mills and Slobodin (1994: 211–41).
Mills, Antonia C. 1994b. Reincarnation Belief among North American Indians and Inuit: Context, Distribution, and Variation. In Mills and Slobodin (1994: 15–37).
Mills, Antonia C. 2001. Sacred Land and Coming Back: How Gitxsan and Witsuwit'en Reincarnation Stretches Western Boundaries. *Canadian Journal of Native Studies* 21 (2): 309–31.
Mills, Antonia and Richard Slobodin, eds. 1994. *Amerindian Rebirth: Reincarnation Belief among North American Indians and Inuit*. Toronto: University of Toronto Press.
Milton, J. L. 1864. *The Stream of Life on Our Globe: Its Archives, Traditions, and Laws*. London: Hardwicke.
Minor, Robert N. 1986. In Defense of Karma and Rebirth: Evolutionary Karma. In Neufeldt (1986: 15–40).
Mir-Hosseini, Ziba. 1994. Inner Truth and Outer History: The Two Worlds of the Ahl-i Haqq of Kurdistan. *International Journal of Middle East Studies* 26 (2): 267–85.
Monier-Williams, Monier. 1899. *A Sanskrit–English Dictionary*. Oxford: Oxford University Press.
Morris, Richard, A. K. Warder and E. Hardy, eds. 1885–1900. *The Aṅguttara-Nikāya*, 5 vols. London: Pali Text Society.
Mukerji, Bithika. 1983. *Neo-Vedanta and Modernity*. Varanasi: Ashutosh Prakashan Sansthan.
Mukherjee, Jugal Kishore. 2004. *Mysteries of Death, Fate, Karma and Rebirth: In the Light of the Teachings of Sri Aurobindo and the Mother*. Pondicherry: Sri Aurobindo Ashram.

Nadel, S. F. 1952. Witchcraft in Four African Societies: An Essay in Comparison. *American Anthropologist*, n.s. 54 (1): 18–29.
Nadel, S. F. 1954. *Nupe Religion: Traditional Beliefs and the Influence of Islam in a West African Chiefdom*. London: Routledge & Kegan Paul.
Nagapriya. 2004. *Exploring Karma and Rebirth*. Birmingham: Windhorse.
Nakagawa, Yoshiharu. 2010. Oriental Philosophy and Interreligious Education: Inspired by Toshihiko Izutsu's Reconstruction of 'Oriental Philosophy'. In *International Handbook of Inter-religious Education*, Vol. 4, ed. Kath Engebretson, Marian de Souza, Gloria Durka and Liam Gearon. Dordrecht: Springer, 325–39.
Ñāṇamoli, Bhikkhu, and Bhikkhu Bodhi, trans. 2009. *The Middle Length Discourses of the Buddha: A Translation of the Majjhima Nikāya*, 4th edn. Somerville, MA: Wisdom.
Nayak, G. C. 1993. *Evil and the Retributive Hypothesis*. Delhi: Motilal Banarsidass.
Needham, Rodney. 1972. *Belief, Language, and Experience*. Oxford: Blackwell.
Needham, Rodney. 1980. *Reconnaissances*. Toronto: University of Toronto Press.
Needham, Rodney. 1985. *Exemplars*. Berkeley, CA: University of California Press.
Nemoy, Leon. 1940. Biblical Quasi-Evidence for the Transmigration of Souls (From the Kitāb al-Anwār of Ya'qūb al-Qirqisānī). *Journal of Biblical Literature* 59 (2): 159–68.
Neufeldt, Ronald W., ed. 1986. *Karma and Rebirth: Post Classical Developments*. Albany, NY: State University of New York Press.
Newmyer, Stephen T. 2011. *Animals in Greek and Roman Thought: A Sourcebook*. Abingdon: Routledge.
Nidditch, Peter H. 1979. Foreword. In Locke (1979: vii–xxvi).
Nietzsche, Friedrich. 1998a [1886]. *Beyond Good and Evil*, trans. Marion Faber. Oxford: Oxford University Press.
Nietzsche, Friedrich. 1998b [1888]. *Twilight of the Idols*, trans. Duncan Large. Oxford: Oxford University Press.
Nietzsche, Friedrich. 2007 [1888]. *Ecce Homo*, trans. Duncan Large. Oxford: Oxford University Press.
Nimanong, Veechart. 1999. Renewal of Thai Buddhist Belief in *Kamma* and Rebirth. In *The Bases of Values in a Time of Change: Chinese and Western*, ed. Kirti Bunchua, Liu Fangtong, Yu Xuanmeng and Yu Wujin. Washington, DC: Council for Research in Values and Philosophy, 227–56.
Noon, John A. 1942. A Preliminary Examination of the Death Concepts of the Ibo. *American Anthropologist* 44 (4): 638–54.
Noonan, Harold W. 2003. *Personal Identity*, 2nd edn. London: Routledge.
Nyanatiloka. 1980. *Buddhist Dictionary: Manual of Buddhist Terms and Doctrines*, 4th edn, ed. Nyanaponika. Kandy: Buddhist Publication Society.
Obeyesekere, Gananath. 1968. Theodicy, Sin, and Salvation in a Sociology of

Buddhism. In *Dialectic in Practical Religion*, ed. E. R. Leach. Cambridge: Cambridge University Press, 7–40.
Obeyesekere, Gananath. 1980. The Rebirth Eschatology and Its Transformations: A Contribution to the Sociology of Early Buddhism. In O'Flaherty (1980: 137–64).
Obeyesekere, Gananath. 1994. Foreword: Reincarnation Eschatologies and the Comparative Study of Religions. In Mills and Slobodin (1994: xi–xxiv).
Obeyesekere, Gananath. 2002. *Imagining Karma: Ethical Transformation in Amerindian, Buddhist, and Greek Rebirth*. Berkeley, CA: University of California Press.
Oboler, Regina Smith. 1985. *Women, Power, and Economic Change: The Nandi of Kenya*. Stanford, CA: Stanford University Press.
Odin, Steve. 2011. Review of Peter A. Jackson, *Buddhadāsa: Theravada Buddhism and Modernist Reform in Thailand*. *Philosophy East and West* 61 (1): 221–31.
O'Flaherty, Wendy Doniger, ed. 1980. *Karma and Rebirth in Classical Indian Traditions*. Berkeley, CA: University of California Press.
O'Flaherty, Wendy Doniger, ed. and trans. 1988. *Textual Sources for the Study of Hinduism*. Manchester: Manchester University Press.
Ogren, Brian. 2009. *Renaissance and Rebirth: Reincarnation in Early Modern Italian Kabbalah*. Leiden: Brill.
Olivelle, Patrick, trans. and ed. 1998. *The Early Upaniṣads: Annotated Text and Translation*. Oxford: Oxford University Press.
Olivelle, Patrick, ed. and trans. 2005. *Manu's Code of Law: A Critical Edition and Translation of the Mānava-Dharmaśāstra*. Oxford: Oxford University Press.
Onyewuenyi, Innocent C. 1996. *African Belief in Reincarnation: A Philosophical Reappraisal*. Enugu: Snaap Press.
Osborne, Catherine. 2007. *Dumb Beasts and Dead Philosophers: Humanity and the Humane in Ancient Philosophy and Literature*. Oxford: Oxford University Press.
Oxford English Dictionary. 2013. reincarnation, n. Oxford: Oxford University Press. www.oed.com (accessed 15 December 2013).
Pachen, Ani, and Adelaide Donnelley. 2001. *Sorrow Mountain: The Remarkable Story of a Tibetan Warrior Nun*. London: Bantam.
Pagan Federation. 2013. www.paganfed.org/paganism.shtml (accessed 25 March 2015).
Panaïoti, Antoine. 2013. *Nietzsche and Buddhist Philosophy*. Cambridge: Cambridge University Press.
Panikkar, Raymond. 1972. The Law of *Karman* and the Historical Dimension of Man. *Philosophy East and West* 22 (1): 25–43.
Pappu, S. S. Rama Rao, ed. 1987a. *The Dimensions of Karma*. Delhi: Chanakya.
Pappu, S. S. Rama Rao. 1987b. Introduction. In Pappu (1987a: 1–19).

Pappu, S. S. Rama Rao. 1987c. Karma: Individual and Collective. In Pappu (1987a: 292–313).
Parfit, Derek. 1984. *Reasons and Persons*. Oxford: Oxford University Press.
Pargiter, F. Eden, trans. 1904. *Mārkaṇḍeya Purāṇa*. Calcutta: Asiatic Society of Bengal.
Parrinder, E. G. 1951. *West African Psychology: A Comparative Study of Psychological and Religious Thought*. Cambridge: Lutterworth Press.
Parrinder, E. G. 1956–7. Varieties of Belief in Reincarnation. *Hibbert Journal* 55: 260–7.
Parrinder, E. G. 1974. *African Traditional Religion*, 3rd edn. London: Sheldon Press.
Paul, Ellen Frankel, Fred D. Miller Jr. and Jeffrey Paul, eds. 2005. *Personal Identity*. Cambridge: Cambridge University Press.
Pegg, Mark Gregory. 2001. On Cathars, Albigenses, and Good Men of Languedoc. *Journal of Medieval History* 27 (2): 181–95.
Pegg, Mark Gregory. 2008. *A Most Holy War: The Albigensian Crusade and the Battle for Christendom*. Oxford: Oxford University Press.
Penelhum, Terence. 1970. *Survival and Disembodied Existence*. London: Routledge & Kegan Paul.
Perrett, Roy W. 1987. *Death and Immortality*. Dordrecht: Nijhoff.
Perry, John. 2002. *Identity, Personal Identity, and the Self*. Indianapolis, IN: Hackett.
Perry, John. 2008. The Problem of Personal Identity. In *Personal Identity*, ed. John Perry, 2nd edn. Berkeley, CA: California University Press, 3–30.
Phillips, D. Z. 1970a. *Death and Immortality*. London: Macmillan.
Phillips, D. Z. 1970b. *Faith and Philosophical Enquiry*. London: Routledge & Kegan Paul.
Phillips, D. Z. 1986. *Belief, Change and Forms of Life*. Basingstoke: Macmillan.
Phillips, D. Z. 1988. *Faith after Foundationalism*. London: Routledge.
Phillips, D. Z. 1995. Dislocating the Soul. *Religious Studies* 31 (4): 447–62.
Phillips, D. Z. 2001. *Religion and the Hermeneutics of Contemplation*. Cambridge: Cambridge University Press.
Phillips, D. Z. 2004a. *The Problem of Evil and the Problem of God*. London: SCM Press.
Phillips, D. Z. 2004b. *Religion and Friendly Fire: Examining Assumptions in Contemporary Philosophy of Religion*. Aldershot: Ashgate.
Pinson, DovBer. 2004. *Reincarnation in Judaism: The Journey of the Soul*. Lanham, MD: Rowman & Littlefield.
Plato. 1997. *Plato: Complete Works*, ed. John M. Cooper and D. S. Hutchinson. Indianapolis, IN: Hackett.
Plotinus. 1956. *The Enneads*, trans. Stephen MacKenna, 2nd edn, rev. by B. S. Page. London: Faber & Faber.
Plotinus. 1979. *Ennead III*, trans. A. H. Armstrong. Cambridge, MA: Harvard University Press.

Pope, Alexander. 1983 [1734]. *Essay on Man*. In *Alexander Pope: Collected Poems*, ed. Bonamy Dobrée. London: Dent, 181–215.
Potter, Karl H. 1987. Karma and Rebirth: Traditional Indian Arguments. In Pappu (1987a: 139–65).
Powers, John. 2007. *Introduction to Tibetan Buddhism*, 2nd edn. Ithaca, NY: Snow Lion.
Powers, John, and David Templeman. 2012. *Historical Dictionary of Tibet*. Lanham, MD: Scarecrow Press.
Prabhu, Joseph. 1989. The Idea of Reincarnation. In *Death and Afterlife*, ed. Stephen T. Davis. New York: St Martin's Press, 65–80.
Preuss, Peter. 1989. *Reincarnation: A Philosophical and Practical Analysis*. Lewiston, NY: Mellen Press.
Priestley, Leonard C. D. C. 1999. *Pudgalavāda Buddhism: The Reality of the Indeterminate Self*. Toronto: Centre for South Asian Studies, University of Toronto.
Purton, A. Campbell. 1992. Wittgenstein and Pictures of Rebirth. In *Buddhist Essays – A Miscellany: A Memorial Volume in Honour of Venerable Hammalawa Saddhatissa*. London: Sri Saddhatissa International Buddhist Centre, 253–61.
Quine, W. V. O. 1975. Replies. In *Words and Objections: Essays on the Work of W. V. O. Quine*, ed. Donald Davidson and Jaakko Hintikka, rev. edn. Dordrecht: Reidel, 292–352.
Quispel, Gilles. 2000. Reincarnation and Magic in the Asclepius. In *From Poimandres to Jacob Böhme: Gnosis, Hermetism and the Christian Tradition*, ed. Roelof van den Broek and Cis van Heertum. Leiden: Brill, 167–232.
Radhakrishnan, S. 1937. *An Idealist View of Life*, 2nd edn. London: Allen & Unwin.
Radhakrishnan, S. 1952. The Religion of the Spirit and the World's Need: Fragments of a Confession. In *The Philosophy of Sarvepalli Radhakrishnan*, ed. Paul Arthur Schilpp. New York: Tudor, 1–82.
Radhakrishnan, S., trans. 1960. *The Brahma Sūtra: The Philosophy of Spiritual Life*. London: Allen & Unwin.
Radhakrishnan, S. 2008 [1923, 1927]. *Indian Philosophy*, 2nd edn, 2 vols. New Delhi: Oxford University Press.
Rahula, Walpola. 1959. *What the Buddha Taught*. Bedford: Fraser.
Ramendra, Dr [Ramendra Nath]. 2011. *Why I am Not a Hindu*, 3rd edn. Patna: Buddhiwadi Foundation.
Rao, P. Nagaraja. 1967. Some Reflections and Remarks on Karma and Rebirth. *Indian Philosophical Annual* 1: 138–42.
Reichenbach, Bruce R. 1990. *The Law of Karma: A Philosophical Study*. Basingstoke: Macmillan.
Rhees, Rush. 1997. *Rush Rhees on Religion and Philosophy*, ed. D. Z. Phillips and Mario von der Ruhr. Cambridge: Cambridge University Press.

Rhys Davids, C. A. F. 1942. Animal Rebirth. In her *Wayfarer's Words*, Vol. 3. London: Luzac, 1093–6.
Rhys Davids, T. W. 1881. *Lectures on the Origin and Growth of Religion as Illustrated by Some Points in the History of Indian Buddhism*. London: Williams and Norgate.
Rhys Davids, T. W., trans. 1890. *The Questions of King Milinda*, Part 1. Oxford: Clarendon Press.
Rhys Davids, T. W. and J. Estlin Carpenter, eds. 1890–1911. *The Dīgha Nikāya*, 3 vols. London: Pali Text Society.
Roberts, Jane. 1970. *The Seth Material*. Cutchogue, NY: Buccaneer Books.
Robinson, Ian. 1975. *The New Grammarians' Funeral: A Critique of Noam Chomsky's Linguistics*. Cambridge: Cambridge University Press.
Rocher, Ludo. 1978. Hindu Conceptions of Law. *Hastings Law Journal* 29: 1283–305.
Rocher, Ludo. 1980. Karma and Rebirth in the Dharmaśāstras. In O'Flaherty (1980: 61–89).
Rogers, G. A. J. 2008. Locke, Plato and Platonism. In *Platonism at the Origins of Modernity: Studies on Platonism and Early Modern Philosophy*, ed. Douglas Hedley and Sarah Hutton. Dordrecht: Springer, 193–205.
Roos, Willen B. 1967. Is Rebirth in a Subhuman Kingdom Possible? *Maha-Bodhi* 75: 238–42.
Ross, John J. 2009. *Reading Wittgenstein's 'Philosophical Investigations': A Beginner's Guide*. Lanham, MD: Lexington.
Rundle, Bede. 2009. *Time, Space, and Metaphysics*. Oxford: Oxford University Press.
Ryle, Gilbert. 2009 [1949]. *The Concept of Mind*. London: Routledge.
Sadiku, Matthew N. O. 1996. The Yoruba. In *Ethnic and Cultural Diversity in Nigeria*, ed. Marcellina U. Okehie-Offoha and Matthew N. O. Sadiku. Trenton, NJ: Africa World Press, 125–48.
Salomon, Richard. 1982. Review of Wendy Doniger O'Flaherty, ed. *Karma and Rebirth in Classical Indian Traditions*. *Journal of the American Oriental Society* 102 (2): 407–10.
Samdhong Rinpoche. 2006. *Uncompromising Truth for a Compromised World: Tibetan Buddhism and Today's World*, ed. Donovan Roebert. Bloomington, IN: World Wisdom.
Sandford, Sir Daniel Keyte, Thomas Thomson and Allan Cunningham. 1841. *The Popular Encyclopedia*, Vol. 4. Glasgow: Blackie.
Śāntideva. 1922 [eighth c. CE]. *Śikshā-Samuccaya: A Compendium of Buddhist Doctrine*, trans. Cecil Bendall and W. H. D. Rouse. London: Murray.
Sarbacker, Stuart Ray. 2005. *Samādhi: The Numinous and Cessative in Indo-Tibetan Yoga*. Albany, NY: State University of New York Press.
Sastri, S. S. Suryanarayana. 1961. Karma and Fatalism. In *Collected Papers of Professor S. S. Suryanarayana Sastri*, ed. T. M. P. Mahadevan. Madras: University of Madras, 233–8.

Scheler, Max. 1992 [1963]. The Meaning of Suffering. In *On Feeling, Knowing, and Valuing: Selected Writings*, ed. Harold J. Bershady. Chicago, IL: University of Chicago Press, 82–115.

Scheper-Hughes, Nancy. 1992. *Death without Weeping: The Violence of Everyday Life in Brazil*. Berkeley, CA: University of California Press.

Schilbrack, Kevin. 2005. Religion, Models of, and Reality: Are We Through with Geertz? *Journal of the American Academy of Religion* 73 (2): 429–52.

Schilbrack, Kevin. 2014. *Philosophy and the Study of Religions: A Manifesto*. Oxford: Wiley-Blackwell.

Schlieter, Jens. 2013. Checking the Heavenly 'Bank Account of Karma': Cognitive Metaphors for Karma in Western Perception and Early Theravāda Buddhism. *Religion* 43 (4): 463–86.

Scholem, Gershom. 1974. *Kabbalah*. Jerusalem: Keter.

Schopenhauer, Arthur. 1966 [1818]. *The World as Will and Representation*, trans. E. F. J. Payne, 2 vols. New York: Dover.

Schopenhauer, Arthur. 1974 [1851]. *Parerga and Paralipomena*, trans. E. F. J. Payne, 2 vols. Oxford: Oxford University Press.

Sears, David. 2003. *The Vision of Eden: Animal Welfare and Vegetarianism in Jewish Law and Mysticism*. Spring Valley, NY: Orot.

Seneca. 1935 [first c. CE]. *De Beneficiis* [On Benefits]. *Moral Essays*, trans. John W. Basore, Vol. 3. London: Heinemann.

Sen Gupta, Anima. 1967. Karma and Rebirth. *Indian Philosophical Annual* 1: 108–16.

Service, Elman R. 1978. *Profiles in Ethnology*, 3rd edn. New York: Harper & Row.

Shakespeare, Tom. 2007. Disability and Equity: Should Difference Be Welcomed? In *Principles of Health Care Ethics*, ed. Richard Ashcroft, Angus Dawson, Heather Draper and John McMillan, 2nd edn. Chichester: Wiley, 421–6.

Sharf, Robert H. 1995. Buddhist Modernism and the Rhetoric of Meditative Experience. *Numen* 42 (3): 228–83.

Sharma, Arvind. 1979. Fate and Free Will in the Bhagavadgītā. *Religious Studies* 15 (4): 531–7.

Sharma, Arvind. 1999. Karma was Fouled! Why Hoddle Did No Wrong to the Disabled. *Hinduism Today*, September: p. 13.

Sharma, Arvind. 2008. Karma, Rebirth, and the Problem of Evil: An Interjection in the Debate between Whitley Kaufman and Monima Chadha and Nick Trakakis. *Philosophy East and West* 58 (4): 572–5.

Sharma, Ursula. 1973. Theodicy and the Doctrine of Karma. *Man*, n.s. 8 (3): 347–64.

Sharot, Stephen. 2001. *A Comparative Sociology of World Religions: Virtuosos, Priests, and Popular Religion*. New York: New York University Press.

Shastri, Swami Dwarikadas, ed. 1968. *Tattvasaṅgraha of Ācārya Shāntarakṣita, with the Commentary 'Pañjikā' of Shri Kamalashīla*, 2 vols. Varanasi: Bauddha Bharati.

Shearar, Cheryl. 2000. *Understanding Northwest Coast Art: A Guide to Crests, Beings and Symbols*. Vancouver: Douglas & McIntyre.
Shoemaker, Sydney. 1959. Personal Identity and Memory. *Journal of Philosophy* 56 (22): 868–82.
Shoemaker, Sydney. 1963. *Self-Knowledge and Self-Identity*. Ithaca, NY: Cornell University Press.
Shoemaker, Sydney. 1970. Persons and Their Pasts. *American Philosophical Quarterly* 7 (4): 269–85.
Shweder, Richard A., and Edmund J. Bourne. 1982. Does the Concept of the Person Vary Cross-Culturally? In *Cultural Conceptions of Mental Health and Therapy*, ed. Anthony J. Marsella and Geoffrey M. White. Dordrecht: Reidel, 97–137.
Siderits, Mark. 2003. *Personal Identity and Buddhist Philosophy: Empty Persons*. Aldershot: Ashgate.
Singh, Shamsher. 2005. The Concept of *Mukti*: A Comparative Study. *Sikh Review* 53 (3). www.sikhreview.org/pdf/march2005/pdf-files/philo1.pdf (accessed 18 October 2013).
Singha, H. S. 2005. *Encyclopedia of Sikhism*, 2nd edn. New Delhi: Hemkunt.
Skeat, Walter W. 1882. *A Concise Etymological Dictionary of the English Language*. Oxford: Clarendon Press.
Sorabji, Richard. 1993. *Animal Minds and Human Morals: The Origins of the Western Debate*. London: Duckworth.
Spencer, Colin. 1996. *The Heretic's Feast: A History of Vegetarianism*. Hanover, NH: University Press of New England.
Spiegel, Andrew, and Emile Boonzaier. 1988. Promoting Tradition: Images of the South African Past. In *South African Keywords: The Uses and Abuses of Political Concepts*, ed. Emile Boonzaier and John Sharp. Cape Town: Philip, 40–57.
Spiro, Melford E. 1982. *Buddhism and Society: A Great Tradition and Its Burmese Vicissitudes*, 2nd edn. Berkeley, CA: University of California Press.
Springs, Jason A. 2008. What Cultural Theorists of Religion Have to Learn from Wittgenstein; Or, How to Read Geertz as a Practice Theorist. *Journal of the American Academy of Religion* 76 (4): 934–69.
Staples, James. 2011. At the Intersection of Disability and Masculinity: Exploring Gender and Bodily Difference in India. *Journal of the Royal Anthropological Institute* 17 (3): 545–62.
Steiner, Rudolf. 1977. *Karmic Relationships: Esoteric Studies*, Vol. 3, 2nd edn. Forest Row: Rudolf Steiner Press.
Steinkraus, Warren E. 1965. Some Problems in Karma. *Philosophical Quarterly* [India] 38: 145–53.
Stevenson, Ian. 1961. *The Evidence for Survival from Claimed Memories of Former Incarnations*. Tadworth: Peto.
Stevenson, Ian. 1974. *Twenty Cases Suggestive of Reincarnation*, 2nd edn. Charlottesville, VA: University Press of Virginia.

Stevenson, Ian. 1977. The Explanatory Value of the Idea of Reincarnation. *Journal of Nervous and Mental Disease* 164 (5): 305–26.
Stevenson, Ian. 1985. The Belief in Reincarnation among the Igbo of Nigeria. *Journal of Asian and African Studies* 20 (1–2): 13–30.
Stevenson, Ian. 1986. Characteristics of Cases of the Reincarnation Type among the Igbo of Nigeria. *Journal of Asian and African Studies* 21 (3–4): 204–16.
Stevenson, Ian. 1997a. *Reincarnation and Biology: A Contribution to the Etiology of Birthmarks and Birth Defects*, 2 vols. Westport, CT: Praeger.
Stevenson, Ian. 1997b. *Where Reincarnation and Biology Intersect*. Westport, CT: Praeger.
Stevenson, Ian. 2000. Introduction. In Story (2000: ix–xiv).
Stevenson, Ian. 2001. *Children Who Remember Previous Lives: A Question of Reincarnation*, rev. edn. Jefferson, NC: McFarland & Co.
Stirling, M. W. 1938. *Historical and Ethnographical Material on the Jivaro Indians. Smithsonian Institution Bureau of American Ethnology Bulletin* 117. Washington, DC: United States Government Printing Office.
Story, Francis. 2000. *Rebirth as Doctrine and Experience: Essays and Case Studies*, 2nd edn. Kandy: Buddhist Publication Society.
Strawson, P. F. 1985. *Skepticism and Naturalism: Some Varieties*. New York: Columbia University Press.
Strawson, P. F. 1992. *Analysis and Metaphysics: An Introduction to Philosophy*. Oxford: Oxford University Press.
Swearer, Donald K. 2010. *The Buddhist World of Southeast Asia*, 2nd edn. Albany, NY: State University of New York Press.
Swedberg, Richard, and Ola Agevall. 2005. *The Max Weber Dictionary: Key Words and Central Concepts*. Stanford, CA: Stanford University Press.
Tagore, Rabindranath. 1917 [1913]. *Gitanjali (Song Offerings)*, new edn. New York: Macmillan.
Taliaferro, Charles, Paul Draper and Philip L. Quinn, eds. 2010. *A Companion to Philosophy of Religion*, 2nd edn. Oxford: Blackwell.
Talib, Gurbachan Singh. 1979. Expression of the Mystical Experience in Sikh Sacred Literature. *Panjab University Journal of Medieval Indian Literature* 3 (1–2): 31–58.
Tambiah, Stanley Jeyaraja. 1984. *The Buddhist Saints of the Forest and the Cult of Amulets*. Cambridge: Cambridge University Press.
Tambiah, Stanley Jeyaraja. 1990. *Magic, Science, Religion, and the Scope of Rationality*. Cambridge: Cambridge University Press.
Tanney, Julia. 2013a. *Rules, Reason, and Self-Knowledge*. Cambridge, MA: Harvard University Press.
Tanney, Julia. 2013b. Ryle's Conceptual Cartography. In *The Historical Turn in Analytic Philosophy*, ed. Erich H. Reck. Basingstoke: Palgrave Macmillan, 94–110.
Tatacharya, Agnihotram Ramanuja. 1967. Philosophy of Karma and Rebirth. *Indian Philosophical Annual* 1: 45–9.

Taylor, A. E. 1928. *A Commentary on Plato's Timaeus*. Oxford: Clarendon Press.
Thiselton, Anthony C. 2002. *A Concise Encyclopedia of the Philosophy of Religion*. Grand Rapids, MI: Baker.
Thomas, E. J. 1947. Review of J. G. Jennings, *The Vedāntic Buddhism of the Buddha*. *Philosophy* 22: 275-7.
Thomas, N. W. 1921. Transmigration (Introductory and Primitive). In *Encyclopædia of Religion and Ethics*, ed. James Hastings with the assistance of John A. Selbie and Louis H. Grey, Vol. 12. Edinburgh: Clark, 425-9.
Toolan, David S. 1993. Reincarnation and Modern Gnosis. In Häring and Metz (1993: 32-45).
Trenckner, Vilhelm, ed. 1880. *The Milindapañho: Being Dialogues between King Milinda and the Buddhist Sage Nāgasena*. London: Williams and Norgate.
Trenckner, Vilhelm and Robert Chalmers, eds. 1888-1902. *The Majjhima-Nikāya*, 3 vols. London: Pali Text Society.
Trevelyan, George. 2012 [1977]. *A Vision of the Aquarian Age: The Emerging Spiritual Worldview*. Guildford: White Crow Books.
Tripathi, C. L. 1982. The Influence of Indian Philosophy on Neoplatonism. In *Neoplatonism and Indian Thought*, ed. R. Baine Harris. Albany, NY: State University of New York Press, 273-92.
Triratna NYC. 2010. The Wheel of Life: The Six Realms. http://triratna-nyc.org/files-6/wp-content/uploads/2010/10/week-3-Six-Realms_screen.pdf (accessed 3 December 2013).
Trungpa, Chögyam. 2002 [1976]. *The Myth of Freedom and the Way of Meditation*. Boston, MA: Shambhala.
Tucker, Jim B. 2009. *Life Before Life: A Scientific Investigation of Children's Memories of Previous Lives*. London: Piatkus.
Tull, Herman W. 1989. *The Vedic Origins of Karma: Cosmos as Man in Ancient Indian Myth and Ritual*. Albany, NY: State University of New York Press.
Vajira, Sister, and Francis Story, trans. 1998. *Last Days of the Buddha: The Mahāparinibbāna Sutta*, 2nd rev. edn. Kandy: Buddhist Publication Society.
Van Buitenen, J. A. B. 1957. Dharma and Moksa. *Philosophy East and West* 7 (1-2): 33-40.
Van Rossum, Rogier. 1993. Reincarnation in Connection with Spiritism and Umbanda. In Häring and Metz (1993: 54-64).
Vasubandhu. 1991 [fourth c. CE]. *Abhidharmakośabhāṣyam*, trans. into French by Louis de La Vallée Poussin, English version by Leo M. Pruden, 4 vols. Berkeley, CA: Asian Humanities Press.
Vroom, Hendrik M. 2006. *A Spectrum of Worldviews: An Introduction to Philosophy of Religion in a Pluralistic World*. Amsterdam: Rodopi.
Wadia, A. R. 1965. Philosophical Implications of the Doctrine of Karma. *Philosophy East and West* 15 (2): 145-52.

Walker, E. D. 1923. *Reincarnation: A Study of Forgotten Truth*. Point Loma, CA: Aryan Theosophical Press.

Wallace, B. Alan. 2011. A Buddhist View of Free Will: Beyond Determinism and Indeterminism. *Journal of Consciousness Studies* 18 (3–4): 217–33.

Waller, Bruce N. 2011. *Against Moral Responsibility*. Cambridge, MA: MIT Press.

Walshe, Maurice, trans. 1995. *The Long Discourses of the Buddha: A Translation of the Dīgha Nikāya*. Somerville, MA: Wisdom.

Walters, Kerry S., and Lisa Portmess. 2001. Introduction: Ambiguous Permission, Journeying Souls, Resplendent Life. In *Religious Vegetarianism: From Hesiod to the Dalai Lama*, ed. Kerry S. Walters and Lisa Portmess. Albany, NY: State University of New York Press, 1–12.

Warren, Donald, Jr. 1968. Spiritism in Brazil. *Journal of Inter-American Studies* 10 (3): 393–405.

Warren, Henry Clarke, trans. 1896. *Buddhism in Translations*. Cambridge, MA: Harvard University Press.

Waterhouse, Helen. 1999. Reincarnation Belief in Britain: New Age Orientation or Mainstream Option? *Journal of Contemporary Religion* 14 (1): 97–109.

Wayman, Alex. 1968. Concerning saṃdhā-bhāṣā/saṃdhi-bhāṣā/saṃdhyā-bhāṣā. *Mélanges d'indianisme à la mémoire de Louis Renou*. Paris: de Boccard, 789–96.

Weber, Max. 1949 [1905]. Critical Studies in the Logic of the Cultural Sciences. In *The Methodology of the Social Sciences*, trans. and ed. Edward A. Shils and Henry A. Finch. New York: Free Press, 113–88.

Weber, Max. 1958 [1916]. *The Religion of India: The Sociology of Hinduism and Buddhism*, ed. and trans. Hans H. Gerth and Don Martindale. New York: Free Press.

Weber, Max. 1963 [1922]. *The Sociology of Religion*, trans. Ephraim Fischoff. Boston, MA: Beacon Press.

Weber, Max. 2009 [1915]. The Social Psychology of the World Religions. In *From Max Weber: Essays in Sociology*, trans. and ed. H. H. Gerth and C. Wright Mills. Abingdon: Routledge, 267–301.

Werblowsky, R. J. Zwi. 1987. Transmigration. In Eliade (1987 XV: 21–6).

Whitney, William Dwight. 1874. *Oriental and Linguistic Studies: The Veda; the Avesta; the Science of Language*. New York: Scribner, Armstrong, and Co.

Wiggins, David. 1967. *Identity and Spatio-Temporal Continuity*. Oxford: Blackwell.

Wiggins, David. 2001. *Sameness and Substance Renewed*. Cambridge: Cambridge University Press.

Wilkes, Kathleen V. 1988. *Real People: Personal Identity without Thought Experiments*. Oxford: Clarendon Press.

Williams, Bernard. 1973. *Problems of the Self: Philosophical Papers 1956–1972*. Cambridge: Cambridge University Press.

Williams, Bernard. 2011 [1985]. *Ethics and the Limits of Philosophy.* Abingdon: Routledge.
Williams, George M. 2008. *Handbook of Hindu Mythology.* Oxford: Oxford University Press.
Williams, Paul, Anthony Tribe and Alexander Wynne. 2012. *Buddhist Thought: A Complete Introduction to the Indian Tradition*, 2nd edn. London: Routledge.
Williams Jackson, A. V. 1925. The Doctrine of Metempsychosis in Manichaeism. *Journal of the American Oriental Society* 45: 246–68.
Willson, Martin. 1987. *Rebirth and the Western Buddhist*, 2nd edn. London: Wisdom.
Winch, Peter. 1964. Understanding a Primitive Society. *American Philosophical Quarterly* 1 (4): 307–24.
Winch, Peter. 1972. *Ethics and Action.* London: Routledge & Kegan Paul.
Winch, Peter. 2008 [1958]. *The Idea of a Social Science and Its Relation to Philosophy*, 2nd edn. Abingdon: Routledge.
Wittgenstein, Ludwig. 1966. *Lectures and Conversations on Aesthetics, Psychology and Religious Belief*, ed. Cyril Barrett. Oxford: Blackwell.
Wittgenstein, Ludwig. 1967. *Philosophical Investigations*, 3rd edn, trans. G. E. M. Anscombe. Oxford: Blackwell.
Wittgenstein, Ludwig. 1969. *The Blue and Brown Books: Preliminary Studies for the 'Philosophical Investigations'*, 2nd edn. Oxford: Blackwell.
Wittgenstein, Ludwig. 1970. *Eine philosophische Betrachtung*, ed. Rush Rhees. *Schriften* 5. Frankfurt am Main: Suhrkamp Verlag, 117–237.
Wittgenstein, Ludwig. 1975. *Philosophical Remarks*, ed. Rush Rhees, trans. Raymond Hargreaves and Roger White. Oxford: Blackwell.
Wittgenstein, Ludwig. 1980. *Remarks on the Philosophy of Psychology*, Vol. 2, ed. G. H. von Wright and Heikki Nyman, trans. C. G. Luckhardt and M. A. E. Aue. Oxford: Blackwell.
Wittgenstein, Ludwig. 1981. *Zettel*, ed. G. E. M. Anscombe and G. H. von Wright, trans. G. E. M. Anscombe, 2nd edn. Oxford: Blackwell.
Wittgenstein, Ludwig. 1982. *Last Writings on the Philosophy of Psychology*, Vol. 1, ed. G. H. von Wright and Heikki Nyman, trans. C. G. Luckhardt and Maximilian A. E. Aue. Oxford: Blackwell.
Wittgenstein, Ludwig. 1992. *Last Writings on the Philosophy of Psychology*, Vol. 2, ed. G. H. von Wright and Heikki Nyman, trans. C. G. Luckhardt and Maximilian A. E. Aue. Oxford: Blackwell.
Wittgenstein, Ludwig. 1993. Remarks on Frazer's *Golden Bough*. In *Philosophical Occasions, 1912-1951*, ed. James C. Klagge and Alfred Nordmann. Indianapolis, IN: Hackett, 115–55.
Wittgenstein, Ludwig. 1998. *Culture and Value*, ed. G. H. von Wright and Heikki Nyman, rev. by Alois Pichler, trans. Peter Winch. Oxford: Blackwell.
Wittgenstein, Ludwig. 2000. *Wittgenstein's Nachlass: The Bergen Electronic Edition.* Oxford and Bergen: Oxford University Press, University of Bergen and Wittgenstein Trustees.

Wittgenstein, Ludwig. 2009a [1953]. *Philosophical Investigations*, 4th edn, trans. G. E. M. Anscombe, P. M. S. Hacker and Joachim Schulte. Oxford: Wiley-Blackwell.

Wittgenstein, Ludwig. 2009b [1953]. Philosophy of Psychology – A Fragment. In Wittgenstein (2009a: 182–243).

Wurm, Stephen Adolphe, Peter Mühlhäusler and Darrel T. Tryon, eds. 1996. *Atlas of Languages of Intercultural Communication in the Pacific, Asia and the Americas*. Berlin: De Gruyter.

Wylie, Turrell V. 1977. Etymology of Tibetan: *Bla-ma*. *Central Asiatic Journal* 21 (2): 145–8.

Wynn, Mark. 1995. Religious Language. In *Companion Encyclopedia of Theology*, ed. Peter Byrne and Leslie Houlden. London: Routledge, 413–32.

Yamunacharya, M. 1967. Karma and Rebirth. *Indian Philosophical Annual* 1: 66–74.

Yelle, Robert A. 2010. Hindu Law as Performance: Ritual and Poetic Elements in Dharmaśāstra. In *Hinduism and Law: An Introduction*, ed. Timothy Lubin, Donald R. Davis Jr. and Jayanth K. Krishnan. Cambridge: Cambridge University Press, 183–92.

Yelle, Robert A. 2011. Punishing Puns: Etymology as Linguistic Ideology in Hindu and British Traditions. In *Religion and Identity in South Asia and Beyond: Essays in Honor of Patrick Olivelle*, ed. Steven E. Lindquist. London: Anthem, 129–45.

York, Michael. 1995. *The Emerging Network: A Sociology of the New Age and Neo-Pagan Movements*. Lanham, MD: Rowman & Littlefield.

Zydenbos, Robert J. 1983. *Mokṣa in Jainism, according to Umāsvāti*. Wiesbaden: Steiner.

INDEX

Abhedananda, Swami 6, 8 n.20, 136
Abrahamic faiths 9
Africa, African traditions 2, 4, 9, 16,
   24–6, 35–6, 37, 38, 62, 75–7, 81
   n.1, 101, 104
   Beng 16, 25–6
   Betsileo 16
   Igbo 16, 36
   Madagascar 16
   Nandi 16, 25–6, 36
   Nupe 76–7
   Papel 101
   Yorùbá 16, 24, 35–6
Ahl-e Haqq 16
Ājīvikas 97
'Alawites *see* Nuṣayrīyah
Alevis 16
Almeder, Robert 44, 49–50, 51, 52, 58–9,
   63–4 n.1
Alto (people) 101
Americans, Native *see* Native Americans
Amerindians *see* Native Americans
anattā/anātman see non-self
ancestors 24 n.29, 25, 27, 36–7, 76–7,
   98, 100
Ancient Mystical Order of the Rosy
   Cross 17 n.16
animals
   attitudes towards (and treatment of)
     84–9, 92–3, 98–9, 102
   descent from 90
   rebirth as/of 5–6, 32–3, 85–9, 92, 93,
     98–9, 113, 139
anthropodicy 137
anthropology, anthropologists 9, 12, 30
   n.42, 47, 50, 58, 62, 71, 75, 78, 82,
   97 n.18, 99 n.20, 117, 155, 161–2
   see also ethnography
Anthroposophy 29 n.37
Anuruddha, Ācariya 57
Arjuna 132, 133 n.6
Asad, Talal 83

asceticism 46
Aśoka (Emperor) 110
Association for Research and
   Enlightenment 17 n.16
ātman 6, 20, 28
Aurobindo, Sri 6, 7–8, 15 n.1, 22, 29, 30
Avalokiteśvara 149
axial age 96 n.16
Ayer, A. J. 42–5, 49, 50, 78

Batchelor, Stephen 110
belief(s)
   and action/practice 9, 10, 65, 79,
     90–1, 92, 96, 97 n.18, 101, 104,
     107, 110
   and (ethical) values 1, 10, 77, 83–4,
     91–2, 95, 100, 103, 156, 162
   factual 121, 123
   in karma 13, 29, 30, 55, 103, 130–40,
     143, 145–6, 148, 153–4, 159, 160
   metaphysical 12, 83, 84, 157
   and rationality 58–9, 65–6, 156
   in rebirth *passim*
   religious 9, 10, 65, 66, 97 n.18, 105,
     146 *et passim*
   and wishful thinking 72
Bendre, Padmashree 8
Besant, Annie 5 n.11
Bhagavad Gītā 132, 133 n.6
bhavaṅga(-sota) 6, 7 n.15
Bible, the
   biblical hermeneutics 105, 161
   biblical phrase 22
   biblical studies 93
   New Testament 105, 106, 116
biology 3, 58, 86–7
   biological evolution 136
Black, Max 122
Blackman, Margaret 72, 100
Blavatsky, Helena 5–6 n.11, 29 n.37
Bloch, Jon 23
Boas, Franz 99

192　Index

Bockmuehl, Klaus 117
Bodewitz, Hendrik 27 n.32, 28
Bodhi, Bhikkhu 113, 114, 119, 121–2, 124, 145
bodhisattvas 31, 149
Brahma Kumaris 17 n.16
Brahmaloka 113
brahman 20, 28
Brahmanism, Brahmanical religion 27–8, 32, 99, 114
Broad, C. D. 145 n.24
Bronkhorst, Johannes 27, 28, 33 n.50, 35 n.53
Brotherhood of the Cross and Star 17 n.16
Bucknell, Roderick 106, 114–17, 119, 122–7
Buddha, the
　awakening of 46, 114
　and awareness 112 n.42
　cult 107
　divine eye 46, 55, 114
　and free will 134–5
　and karma 55, 57, 141, 145
　and *nirvāṇa* 20 n.21, 119 n.55
　powers of 46, 55
　recollection of former lives 46, 114–15, 120, 123, 127
　teachings of 31–2, 46–7, 106, 107, 109, 111, 113–14, 116, 118, 126–7
　see also Buddhism; Buddhist texts
Buddhadāsa Bhikkhu 106, 108, 111–16, 117, 119, 122–7
Buddhaghosa 31 n.43, 47, 109 n.33, 123 n.60
Buddhism, Buddhists 2, 3, 4, 6–7, 8, 9, 81, 82, 92, 96 n.16, 97, 98, 102, 105–27, 131 n.4
　Abhidharma 57
　and Christianity 150
　cosmology 113, 119, 125
　and Daoism 15
　and demythologization 105–6, 107–8, 112 n.42, 116, 121, 125–6, 158–9
　esoteric 21 n.27, 106, 113–14
　and ethics 82, 98, 102, 112, 122, 134, 145
　and evolution 136
　Hindu influence on 111, 114, 118
　and *kamma*/*karma* 21, 26, 30, 31–2, 55–7, 129, 133, 136, 139, 145
　Mahāyāna 31
　and meditation 18, 46–7, 114, 122–3
　modernism/-izers 107, 112 n.42, 113
　and *nibbāna*/*nirvāṇa* 20, 21, 112 n.42, 121
　and not-self 6–7, 108–9, 114, 118, 122–3
　and Pagans 23
　philosophy/-ers 107, 109, 122, 125, 137 n.10
　and psychology/psychotherapy 113, 119, 122, 134, 161
　Theravāda 21
　Tibetan 140–1, 148–50, 152–3
　and Vedānta 110
　see also Buddha, the; Buddhist texts; *dharma*
Buddhist texts 111, 114, 139
　Abhidhammāvatāra (Buddhadatta) 113 n.44
　Abhidharmakośa (*Bhāṣya*) 30, 123
　Aṅguttara Nikāya 30 n.40, 55, 118 n.53, 139 n.16, 141
　Cūḷakammavibhaṅga Sutta 139 n.16
　Dhammapada 30 n.39, 31 n.43
　Dīgha Nikāya 46 n.13, 113, 114, 115
　Mahāparinibbāna Sutta 113
　Majjhima Nikāya 46–7, 114, 115, 127, 139 n.16
　Milindapañha 109
　Pāli Canon 6, 115, 118
　Sāmaññaphala Sutta 46 n.13
　Saṃyutta Nikāya 20 n.21, 30 n.39, 46, 114, 115, 139 n.16
　Tattvasaṃgraha (Śāntarakṣita) 108–9
　Visuddhimagga (Buddhaghosa) 47, 109 n.33, 123 n.60
　Zuiye yingbao jing 31–2
Bultmann, Rudolf 105, 106–7, 116–17, 123–4, 125, 161
Burgess, Ruth 57
Burma, Burmese 21, 35
Burnouf, Eugène 111 n.39
Burton, David 57
Butler, Joseph 47

Index

Campbell, Thomas 76 n.12
Carpenter, Amber 108 n.31, 118 n.53
Carrithers, Michael 21
Cartesian(ism) 43, 91 n.13
Cathars 16
Cayce, Edgar 24
Chadha, Monima 138 n.12, 143
Chakravarthi, S. C. 145 n.24
Chattopadhyaya, S. K. 46 n.11
children, childhood 35–7, 62, 67, 68–70, 77, 100–1, 139, 141, 153, 157
  naming of 35–6, 100
  past-life memories of 11, 43, 54, 74, 77
China, Chinese 15, 31, 45, 142–3, 148–9
Chomsky, Noam 112 n.41
Christianity, Christians 1, 9, 16, 83, 105, 106–7, 109, 118, 145 n.25, 150
Church Universal and Triumphant 17 n.16
Cockburn, David 62, 67–70, 71, 76–8, 83, 89 n.8, 157–8, 159–60
Collins, Steven 4, 47 n.14, 108 n.30, 109, 114 n.49, 122
compassion 148, 149, 151, 152, 153, 160
conceptual
  amorphousness, fluidity 52
  analysis, inquiry, investigation, etc. 2, 10, 11, 17, 50, 52, 97
  confusion, incoherence 124, 134
  dispute 58
  evolution 93–4
  imperialism 50
  justice 58, 126
  maps, geography 96
  possibility, impossibility 35, 49, 59
Confucianism 9
connective analysis 96–7
consciousness
  equality across species 98
  of past lives 42, 121
  pure 20 n.22
  states of 21
  stream of 4, 6
Cosmodicy 137
cosmology 106, 107, 113, 119, 122, 124–5, 126, 159
  realms of existence 110, 113, 122, 125

Cowell, E. B. 46
craving *see* desire
Creider, Jane Tapsubei 16 n.10, 25–6, 36–7

Dalai Lama 149
Daniels, Charles 41
Daoism, Daoists 9, 15
Darwinian theory 136
Dasgupta, Surama 19, 22, 102
Dasgupta, Surendranath 27 n.35
Davidson, Florence Edenshaw 100
Davis, Stephen T. 137
Davy, Barbara Jane 23
Dawkins, Richard 3
death 29 n.37, 35, 53, 56, 73, 93, 113, 115, 119, 150, 151, 152
  existence/life after 19, 22, 45, 63, 66, 94, 116, 118, 126
  and rebirth 18, 19, 26, 72, 76, 110, 114, 115, 122, 125, 127
  and suffering 119, 151
  wishing for 31, 150
demythologizing 12, 105–8, 112 n.42, 116–17, 121, 123–7, 159, 161
desire, craving
  to believe 72
  for continued existence 19, 22, 46
  desirability of rebirth 45–6
  extinction of 21
  flow/recurrence of 4, 110, 115, 122, 126
  for reward 145
  for salvation 24 n.29
  selfish 110, 112, 115, 122, 126
  sensual 4, 32
Dhammananda, K. Sri 4 n.6
dharma, dhamma 111–12, 113, 119, 122, 131, 149
Dharma Śāstras 32 *see also: Mānava Dharmaśāstra*
DNA 3
Doniger (O'Flaherty), Wendy 19, 33 n.49
Donnelley, Adelaide 149
Dowding, Hugh 141 n.20
dreams, dream-life 73, 149
Driberg, J. H. 16 n.10
Druze 16
Dumont, Louis 119 n.55

Eckel, Malcolm David 150
Edwards, Paul 130–3, 135, 136, 138, 148, 154
Ehnmark, Erland 151
Einarsdóttir, Jónína 101
Empedocles 84, 86, 88, 89, 94
Enneads see Plotinus
eschatology 92–8, 102–3, 107, 119, 145
ethicization 12, 82–4, 92–8, 100, 103, 124
ethics
    Buddhist 111–12, 116, 117, 134, 145
    Christian 150
    and cosmology 124
    ethical action, attitudes, values, etc. 1, 12–13, 20, 21, 26, 28, 34, 61, 62, 67–9, 77, 81–4, 89, 91–5, 98–104, 106, 111–13, 115–18, 122–6, 134, 136, 145, 156–9
    ethical life 126
    ethical mastery 47
    ethical philosophy 2
    ethical texts 10
    ethical theory 154
    foundation of 145
    and metaphysics 13, 83, 157–8
    and meditation 21, 122, 123, 125
    and morality 84 n.4
    and relationships 71, 77, 101
    Socrates' 152
    and soteriology 112
    see also ethicization; morality
ethnography, ethnographic studies 10, 12, 35 n.53, 59, 62, 74, 161 n.3, 162 *see also* anthropology
eudaimonia 152
evil
    depths of 143
    doing 29, 144 n.23
    karma and 12, 129–30, 135, 139
    as misfortune (for the perpetrator) 153, 160
    mystery of 153
    necessary 22
    prevalence of 137
    problem of 10, 138, 153
    rebirth as 46 n.11
    and suffering 130, 154
Eylon, Dina Ripsman 15 n.1

Farrar, Janet and Stewart 16 n.14, 23
fatalism 13, 130, 132–3, 144
Flanagan, Owen 116–17
Flew, Antony 40 n.1
form(s) of life 6, 54, 104, 140, 146–7, 155, 162
    disagreement in 146–7
    religious 13, 65
Fort, Andrew 20
Frazer, James 89–90
free will 13, 132 n.5, 133, 134–6
Freuchen, Peter 36

Gandharva 28
Garrett, William 130
Geertz, Clifford 83, 97 n.18, 102, 104 n.25, 161
Gernet, Alexander von 73 n.9
Gethin, Rupert 113 n.44, 114–15, 125, 126, 159
Ghai, Anita 57
gilgul 9 n.21
Glasenapp, Helmuth von 20 nn.23, 24
Glock, Hans-Johann 111 n.41
God, gods 28, 29 n.37, 31, 75 n.10, 113, 117, 123, 136, 137, 138
Goethe, J. W. von 33 n.51
Gombrich, Richard 20 n.21, 107 n.28, 118 n.52, 135
Gonda, Jan 4, 33 n.50
Gottlieb, Alma 16 n.10, 25–6, 77
Goudey, R. F. 5 n.11, 6
Goulder, Michael 93
Gowans, Christopher 123 n.59
grammar
    depth–surface distinction 111–12
    of Vedic funeral hymn 27
Great White Brotherhood 17 n.16
Greece, ancient 2, 4, 8, 12, 15, 26, 81, 82, 84, 89 n.9, 95, 99, 102, 158
Greek (language) 5, 18 n.18
Green, Dave 23
Greenland 36
Griffiths, Paul 30, 131 n.3
Gupta, Akhil 37, 101
Gyalsay Rinpoche 151

Hacker, Peter 40–1, 47, 50–1, 58, 96–7
Halbfass, Wilhelm 18 n.18

Index 195

Hami, H. A. Wijeratne 56–8
Hanegraaff, Wouter 17 n.15, 22
Häring, Hermann 22
Harvey, Peter 6 n.14, 122
Hay, Louise 23, 24
Hayes, Richard 140–2
heaven(s), heavenly beings 22, 28, 94, 106, 111, 113
Heelas, Paul 17 n.15
hell(s) 31 n.44, 57, 94, 106, 111, 113, 122, 125
Hemacandra 33 n.48
Herman, Arthur 138
hermeneutics 111, 125, 156
  biblical 105, 161
  of contemplation 1
  hermeneutical charity 41, 118
  religious 116
Hick, John 1, 9, 38 n.56, 93, 107–8, 119–21, 123, 124
Hiltebeitel, Alf 131 n.4
Hindu(ism) 2, 3, 4, 6, 7, 9, 32–3, 81, 82, 92, 96 n.16, 102, 109, 114, 121
  customs 54
  and *dharma* 131
  as an 'ethicized' religion 98, 100
  'Hinduization' 111, 118
  and karma 26, 30, 129, 134
  and meditation 18
  reformers 107
  texts 99, 132
  see also Brahmanism; Veda(s)
Hiriyanna, Mysore 103
Hodgson, Marshall 16 n.6
Horsch, Paul 27, 28
Horton, Robin 24
Hultkrantz, Åke 72–3
Humphreys, Christmas 6 n.13, 103 n.23, 139, 144
Huxley, Julian 3
Huxley, Thomas 136, 137

identity, personal *see* personal identity
Idowu, E. Bọlaji 24–5, 36, 76
infanticide 101
injustice 99, 142, 152 *see also* justice
International Church of Ageless Wisdom 17 n.16

International Society for Krishna Consciousness 17 n.16
Inuit 2, 16, 35, 36, 62, 71, 72–3, 82, 98, 100
Islam 9, 16, 109
Ismāʿīlīs 16

Jainism, Jains 2, 3, 7, 20, 30, 33 n.48, 81, 82, 92, 96 n.16, 102, 109, 129
James, William 4
Jantzen, Grace 145 n.25
Jaspers, Karl 96 n.16
Jayatilleke, K. N. 118 n.54
Jefferson, Warren 24 n.29
Jennings, J. G. 106, 107–8, 110–13, 115–19, 123–6, 143 n.21
Jennings, Pete 16 n.14, 23
Jívaro 16
Jonas, Hans 106
Josephus, Flavius 15 n.5
Judaism, Jews 1, 9, 15, 141–2 *see also* Kabbalists
Jurewicz, Joanna 27
justice
  natural 131
  poetic 32
  retributive 102
  and suffering 144
  universal 131–2, 135
  see also injustice

Kabbalists 15, 85 n.5 *see also* Judaism
Kalghatgi, T. G. 8
Kalupahana, David 107
karma (*kamma, karman*)
  bank account of 30
  and 'blaming the victim' 13, 130, 139–44, 148, 159
  in Buddhism 21, 26, 30, 31–2, 55–7, 129, 133, 136, 139, 145
  collective 110, 141–3
  and determinism/fatalism 133–4, 144
  developmental 34
  doctrine of 10, 12–13, 26–30, 57, 102–3, 110, 117, 124, 129–31, 133–9, 142, 143, 144, 146, 152, 153–4, 159–60
  and education 23, 138
  and emotion 115–16

and ethical/moral action 12–13, 34, 98, 109, 123–4, 126, 129, 131–3
and evil 12, 129–30, 135, 139, 154
and intention/volition 29–30
in Jainism 20
karmic energy 6
karmic eschatology 93–4, 96, 102–3
karmic inheritance 133
and knowledge 20, 23, 28
law of 30, 31, 129, 133–6
and memory/recollection 55, 120, 127
in New Age 23
and purification 150–1
and rebirth 3, 10, 12, 23, 26–7, 32, 57, 96, 103, 105, 108–10, 116–18, 124–6, 136–7, 140, 145, 152, 158, 159, 161
retributive 11, 12, 26–32, 34, 35, 55–8, 82, 103, 129–30, 135, 139–40, 143–8, 158, 159
and science 136–7
the term 29–30
and theodicy 137–8
and wordplay 33
karmadicy 138
Kaufman, Whitley 130, 135–6, 137, 138, 143–4, 154 n.36
Kemp, Daren 17 n.15
Keown, Damien 6, 19 n.20, 31 n.43, 118
Kern, Hendrik 109
Keyes, Charles 30 n.39, 129
King, Winston 150
Kofuku-no-kagaku 17 n.16
Kohn, Livia 15 n.4, 31
Koller, John 131
Krishan, Yuvraj 30
Kuppuswamy, B. 130
Kurdistan 16

lamas (Tibetan) 140, 142–3, 149 see also monastics
language
  agreement in 146
  and culture 103–4
  dislocation of 65, 66
  everyday–Dhamma distinction 106, 111–12
  intentional (*saṃdhābhāṣā*) 114
  theological 117

twilight (*saṃdhyābhāṣā*) 114
Larson, Gerald 137
Larson, Paul 131
Lati Rimpoche 140–3, 152–3
Laws of Manu see: Mānava Dharmaśāstra
Leibniz, G. W. 45
Liberal Catholic Church 17 n.16
Lin, Wei 149
Lindquist, Steven 29
Locke, John 41–2, 44, 45, 47, 51
logical
  absurdity, confusion 64, 65, 79
  (im)possibility 12, 67, 73–4, 79
  'must' (necessity) 93, 95–6, 97, 103, 158
  principle 71
Long, J. Bruce 15
Lopez, Donald 30 n.41, 109 n.33, 111 n.39, 117–18, 129, 136 n.9, 149
love 68, 124, 160
  of life 19, 22
  power of 142

Macdonell, Arthur 7 n.16
MacIntosh, J. J. 7 n.19, 41
Mahābhārata 33 n.48
Mahadevan, T. M. P. 2
Malalasekera, G. P. 108
Malcolm, Norman 3 n.4, 39, 54, 66 n.2
Malinowski, Bronislaw 16 n.13
Mānava Dharmaśāstra 32–3, 46, 99, 139
Manichaeans 15
Mantin, Ruth 23
Manu see: *Mānava Dharmaśāstra*
Mārkaṇḍeya Purāṇa 19
Martin, Douglas 148 n.29, 150 n.32
Martin, Raymond 40, 41 n.3, 45
Mauss, Marcel 35 n.53
Mbiti, John 24
McClelland, Norman 35, 71–2
McDaniel, June 19
McMahan, David 107, 111
Mead, G. R. S. 26 n.31, 82
meditation, meditative discipline 18–19, 20, 21, 46–7, 114, 116, 122–3, 124, 125, 127, 152
Meenakshisundaram, T. P. 129, 138 n.15
Melanesia, Melanesians 2, 16

memory
    concept of 39-40, 47, 49-54, 55, 61, 156
    as criterion of personal identity 47-8, 65, 68
    fallibility of 48
    link of 120-1, 123
    of past-life 11, 13, 39-60, 61, 69, 77, 127, 156
    reliving the past 36, 39
    similarity of memories 64, 120
mental health/illness 56-7
metaphors 3, 4, 31, 96 n.17, 118, 122, 155
metaphysics 2, 7, 8, 65, 116-17, 120
    Cartesian 91
    Discourse on Metaphysics (Leibniz) 45
    and ethics 12, 13, 83-4, 89 n.8, 91, 157-8
    metaphysical baggage 8, 116
    of personhood/personal identity 40, 109 (*see also* personal identity)
    and religion 83
metempsychosis 5, 6, 8, 41 *see also* metensomatosis; rebirth; transmigration
metensomatosis 5, 8 *see also* metempsychosis; rebirth; transmigration
Metz, Johann-Baptist 22
Mills, Antonia 16 n.9, 35, 36, 37, 72, 74, 98, 99 n.21, 100
Mishra, Swarnlata 53-4
Moggallāna 31
mokṣa, mukti 19
monastics, monks, nuns 20-1, 31, 46, 106, 109, 129, 142, 148-9
Monier-Williams, Monier 7 n.16
morality
    and action/behaviour 26, 30, 93-4, 110, 129-31, 134, 135, 145
    and desert 30, 35, 129, 132, 135, 142-4, 148, 159-60
    and ethics 84 n.4
    moral advice, guidance, instruction, etc. 13, 23, 32, 33, 85, 126, 130-4, 144, 154
    moral compliment 57
    moral goodness/integrity/virtues 29, 122, 152
    moral law/order 111, 136
    moral meaning/value(s) 87-9, 91, 131, 147
    moral objections (to karma) 131, 138, 140, 142, 144-5, 148, 153-4, 159-60
    moral outlook/understanding 84-9, 91-2, 94-5, 99, 102, 104, 147
    moral responsibility 70, 74, 109, 132 n.5, 134-6
    moral sphere 34
    moral universe 124
    and pleasure 29
    see also ethics
Myth of Er (Plato) 23, 151 n.34
mythology 99 n.21, 110, 125
    mythic conception (of rebirth) 120, 124
    mythological accretions 105
    mythological pictures/worldviews 106, 158
    and New Testament 106, 116
    see also demythologizing

Nadel, S. F. 76 n.11
Nagapriya 57 n.22, 113 n.45
Nāgārjuna 137 n.10
Nāgasena 109
Native Americans, Amerindians 2, 4, 16, 24 n.29, 35, 37, 62, 71-2, 82, 98-100, 104
    Beaver (people) 98
    Gitxsan 72, 74, 75, 98
    Haida 72, 100
    Kwakwaka'wakw 99-100
    Wet'suwet'en 98
Nayak, G. C. 129, 138 n.12, 144
Nazi holocaust 141-2, 143
near-death experience 23
Needham, Rodney 90 n.12, 155, 161
Neo-Pagans *see* Pagans
New Age 4, 16-17, 22-4
New Religious Movements 17
Nietzsche, Friedrich 151
Nimanong, Veechart 6-7
nirvāṇa, nibbāna 20, 21, 112 n.42, 119, 121
non-cognitivism 91
non-realism 91

non-self, not-self 108–9, 118, 123, 126
numinous 18
Nuṣayrīyah 16
Nyanatiloka 7 n.15

Obeyesekere, Gananath 12, 16 n.13, 26, 82–4, 92–8, 102–3, 158
Oboler, Regina Smith 37
O'Flaherty, Wendy Doniger see Doniger (O'Flaherty), Wendy
Olivelle, Patrick 28, 29, 33, 46, 139
omniscience 20
Onyewuenyi, Innocent 24–5, 36
Orphics 15
Osborne, Catherine 12, 84–92, 94–5, 99, 102, 158

Pachen, Ani 148–53, 160
Padmasambhava 149
Pagans, Paganism, Neo-Paganism 4, 16, 22–3
    Ásatrú (Odinism) 16 n.14
    Druidry 16 n.14
    Shamanism 16 n.14
    Wicca 16 n.14
Pāli Canon see under Buddhist texts
palingenesis 5, 8 see also metempsychosis; metensomatosis; rebirth; transmigration
Panikkar, Raymond 30 n.41
Pappu, S. S. Rama Rao 29–30, 131, 143 n.21
paramattha-sacca (absolute truth) 7
Parfit, Derek 42–3, 44, 48 n.15, 64, 68
Parrinder, E. G. 16 n.10, 24 n.29, 25 n.30, 35, 36 n.54
Penelhum, Terence 48–50, 64
Perrett, Roy 108 n.29
Perry, John 42 n.4, 50
personal identity, personhood 10, 11, 12, 40–5, 47–8, 50–2, 61–5, 67–79, 83–4, 100, 109, 120–3, 126, 156–7
Pharisees 15 n.5 see also Judaism
Phillips, D. Z. 1, 62–7, 78, 96–7 n.18
philosophy, philosophers
    Buddhist 106, 107, 109, 122, 125, 137 n.10

contemplative 65–6
cross-cultural 1, 78 n.14
Greek 4, 12, 84–9, 91, 94, 99, 102
Indian 2, 6, 46 n.11, 107, 136–7
interdisciplinary 1, 9–10, 161–2
moral 140 n.18 (see also ethics)
philosophical hermeneutics 1
philosophical thought experiments (see thought experiments)
and 'primitive tribes' 82
and psychology 4
of religion 1–3, 9–11, 65, 107, 108 n.29, 161–2 *et passim*
of science 2
Plato, Platonism 15, 23, 32, 45, 81, 84–9, 94, 99–100, 151–2
Neoplatonism 32 see also Plotinus
Plotinus 5 n.7, 32
poisoned arrow, parable of 127
Pope, Alexander 132
Potter, Karl 136–7
Powers, John 47, 140 n.19
Prabhu, Joseph 139
Prajāpati 28
Preuss, Peter 44
'primitive' societies/tribes 81–2, 103 n.24
problem of evil see under evil
psychological
    abuse 149
    accounts, explanations, etc. 72, 76, 106, 113, 115–16, 118
    capacities, characteristics, etc. 73, 85–6, 134–5, 152
    continuity 120, 122
    impairment 159
    troubles 56
    well-being 121
psychology
    and cosmology 106, 119, 122, 124–5, 126, 159
    and karma/rebirth 12, 34, 58, 161
    and philosophy 4
psychotherapy 113, 119, 122 see also mental health/illness
pudgala(vāda) 108 n.31
punabbhava, ponobbhavikā, punarbhava 6, 110 see also rebirth
punarjanman 7 see also rebirth
pūrvajanman 7 n.16 see also rebirth

Pythagoras, Pythagoreans 15, 81, 84, 86, 88, 89, 91, 92, 94

Quine, W. V. O. 41 n.2

Radhakrishnan, Sarvepalli 3, 6, 22, 107, 129
Radhasoami 17 n.16
Rahula, Walpola 107, 108 n.30
Ramendra (Nath) 130
Rao, P. Nagaraja 130 n.1, 131
realms of existence *see under* cosmology
rebirth, reincarnation
   affinitive 33–5
   as/of animals 5–6, 32–3, 85–9, 92, 93, 98–100, 113
   cessation of 4 n.6, 19, 21–2, 46, 119, 121–2, 129
   consanguineous 33–7, 98, 100
   cycle/round/wheel of 3–4, 19, 21, 22, 24, 94
   destinations (*gatis*) 113, 114
   demythologizing 12, 105–27, 159
   eschatologies 92–8, 102
   and ethics/morality 12, 67–71, 77, 81–104, 106, 109–18, 122–6, 129–48, 152–4, 156–60
   and karma 3, 10, 12, 23, 26–33, 55–8, 82, 93–6, 102–3, 105–10, 115–27, 129–54, 157–61
   minimalist reincarnation thesis 52
   multiple simultaneous 26, 62, 71–5
   partial 24–5
   as recurrence of desires 110, 112, 115, 122, 126
   and remembering 11, 13, 39–60, 61, 69, 77, 127, 156
   and science 52, 58–9, 69, 136–7, 140
   and the spirit world 25–6, 75–7
   terms for 5–8
   varieties of 11, 15–38, 61, 158 *et passim*
   see also metempsychosis; metensomatosis; palingenesis; *punabbhava, ponobbhavikā, punarbhava; punarjanman*; transmigration
Reichenbach, Bruce 138 n.12, 145
reincarnation *see* rebirth

religion(s)
   African 9, 38
   Brahmanical, Vedic 27–8 (*see also* Brahmanism)
   ethicized 93 n.14, 98, 103
   everyday, lived 162
   historians of 16 n.8
   historical 96 n.16
   philosophy of (*see under* philosophy)
   religiosity 20 n.25
   South Asian 2, 3, 8, 11, 15, 19–21, 26–30, 45–7, 55, 57, 81, 92–6, 102–4, 129, 158 *et passim*
   see also names of particular religions
religious
   beliefs 9, 10, 65, 66, 97 n.18, 105, 146 *et passim*
   conversion 140
   disagreement 147
   reformers 107, 111
   truth 66, 125
   virtuosos 20–1, 55, 129
religious studies, study of religions 2 n.2, 9–10, 83, 92 n.13, 96 n.18, 106–8, 125, 161
remembering *see* memory
resurrection 48–9 n.17
R̥gveda 27 *see also* Veda(s)
Rhys Davids, T. W. 109, 136 n.9
River of Forgetfulness 45
Roberts, Jane 23
Rocher, Ludo 32, 132 n.4
Ross, John 146 n.27
Rowett, Catherine *see* Osborne, Catherine
Roy, Rammohan 107
Ryle, Gilbert 39, 89 n.8, 91–2 n.13, 96

salvation 18, 21, 24 n.29 *see also* soteriology
Samdhong Rinpoche 142
Sāṃkhya 20
saṃsāra 3–4, 19, 22, 116, 129
Śaṅkara 20 n.22
Śāntarakṣita 108–9
Śāntideva 139 n.16
Saraswati, Swami Dayananda 107
Sarbacker, Stuart 18–19
Sastri, Suryanarayana 134

Śatapatha Brāhmaṇa 27–8
Sathya Sai Baba movement 17 n.16
Scheler, Max 150
Schilbrack, Kevin 2 n.2, 9 n.24, 83 n.2
schizophrenia 56, 57 n.22 *see also* mental health/illness
Schlieter, Jens 30
Schopenhauer, Arthur 5 n.8
science 3, 52, 58–9, 69, 85, 87 n.7, 91, 97, 106, 107, 112, 136–7, 138, 140
   philosopher of 2
science fiction 11, 40
self
   ātman 20, 28
   deconstruction of 122
   denial of a persisting 6, 108–9, 114, 122–3, 126 (*see also* non-self)
   -denying life 46, 116
   depth of the 20
   evolving 8
   as process 123
   -purification 148
   -serving desires/actions 103 n.23, 110, 112, 115, 122, 126, 145, 151
   -understanding 124
   see also soul(s)
selfless altruism 116 *see also* compassion
Self-Realization Fellowship 17 n.16
Seneca 145 n.26
Sen Gupta, Anima 47
Shamanism *see under* Pagans
Sharma, Arvind 133 n.6, 138 n.12, 139 n.17, 159, 160
Sharot, Stephen 20 n.25, 21
Shoemaker, Sydney 40 n.1, 42 n.4, 48, 50
Sikhism, Sikhs 2, 3, 7, 30, 81, 129
sin, original 153
sociology, sociologists 10, 162
Socrates 23, 32, 99, 151–2
Soka Gakkai 17 n.16
soteriology 11, 17, 18–26, 112, 116, 119, 121, 122, 161
soul(s)
   born without 101
   choosing next life 23
   denial of 7
   different types of 72–3, 76
   evolving 7
   immortal 6
   inhabiting body 8
   kept fresh 90
   living 20
   and person 42
   shared 71–2
   and suffering 150
   the term 65, 73
   transference/transmigration of 5, 6, 25, 41, 45, 63, 81–2, 84–9 (*see also* transmigration)
   see also self; spirit(s)
Spencer, Colin 85 n.5
Spiritists 16
spirit(s)
   disembodied 63
   intervening 138
   measure of 32
   of non-human species 98
   Transcendent 8
   spirit world 25–6, 75–6
   see also soul(s)
spiritual
   activity of children 77
   adept 19
   awakening, enlightenment, liberation, etc. 18, 23, 46, 114, 120–2, 123, 127
   depth, profundity 106, 154
   development, evolution, etc. 5–6, 8, 22–4, 28, 31, 46–7, 129, 136, 150–1
   elements 142
   meaning, value 22, 147
   message 105
   orientation 11
   teachers 151
Spiritual Science Church 17 n.16
spirituality 17 n.15
Spiro, Melford 21, 129, 138 n.13
Steiner, Rudolf 29 n.37
Steinkraus, Warren 143, 154
Stevenson, Ian 16 nn.6, 10, 24 n.29, 34–5, 36, 37, 43–4, 47, 50, 52–8, 59 n.23, 62, 69
Stoicism 145 n.26
Story, Francis 6 n.13, 7, 55 n.21, 113, 133
Strawson, Peter 96 n.17
stream
   of becoming (*bhavaṅga-sota*) 6–7

Index 201

of consciousness/thought 3, 4, 6, 116
of happenings 3
of life 2–5, 20, 75, 129, 155, 162 (*see also: saṃsāra*)
Stuart-Fox, Martin 106, 114–17, 119, 122–7
suffering
  cessation/relief of 119, 121, 127, 129, 151, 152
  cycle of 121
  consequence of wrongdoing 30–2, 55, 131, 139–40, 143–5, 148, 150, 160
  and dissatisfaction 153
  and evil 130, 154
  future 115, 131, 145, 152
  of hell beings 57 n.22
  path of 22
  as purifying 150–1
Swearer, Donald 107, 112 n.42

Tagore, Rabindranath 3
Talib, Gurbachan Singh 19
Tambiah, Stanley 138 n.13, 161 n.3
tanāsukh 9 n.21
taṇhā (thirst, desire) 110 *see also* desire
Tanney, Julia 52, 96 n.17
tašpikha 9 n.21
Tatacharya, Agnihotram R. 26 n.31, 82
Taylor, A. E. 87 n.7
theodicy 137
theology, theologians 9, 10, 105, 106, 117, 125, 145 n.25, 161
Theosophical Society, Theosophists 5–6, 8, 17 n.16, 29 n.37, 141 n.20
Thiselton, Anthony 117
Thomas, N. W. 25
thought experiments 11–12, 40–3, 44, 47, 49, 51, 54, 59, 61–4, 70, 71, 73, 75, 78, 156–7, 161
Tibet, Tibetans 71, 140–3, 148–53
Toolan, David 17 n.17, 153
Trakakis, Nick 138 n.12, 143
transitivity of identity 71
transmigration (of souls) 5–6, 8, 41, 45, 69, 81, 84–92, 102–3, 119 n.55, 136 n.9, 158
  see also metempsychosis; metensomatosis; rebirth
Trevelyan, George 22

Tribe, Anthony 119
Trobriand Islanders 16
Trungpa, Chögyam 57 n.22, 113
truth
  absolute 7
  conventional 137
  religious 66
Tull, Herman 27

Umbanda 16
Upaniṣads 27–9, 97, 139
  Bṛhadāraṇyaka 28–9
  Chāndogya 28, 139
  Śvetāśvatara 29 n.37

Vasubandhu 30 n.40, 113 n.43, 123 n.60
Vedānta, Neo-Vedānta 6, 7–8, 20, 110 n.37
Veda(s), Vedic religion 27–8, 46 *see also* Brahmanism
vegetarianism, abstaining from meat 33, 85–6, 92, 102

Wadia, A. R. 130 n.1, 134–5
Walker, E. D. 6
Waller, Bruce 136
Walshe, Maurice 46 n.13, 113 n.46, 114 n.49, 115
Weber, Max 20 n.25, 95 n.15, 137
Weberian 129
well-being 30, 55, 121
Werblowsky, R. J. Zwi 5 nn.7, 10, 9 n.21, 16 n.6, 85 n.5
Whitney, William Dwight 27
Wicca *see under* Pagans
Wiggins, David 45 n.10, 48 n.15
Wilkes, Kathleen 78 n.13
Williams, Bernard 12, 62–5, 67–8, 70–1, 73–5, 84 n.4, 120
Williams, Paul 119
Winch, Peter 61, 75 n.10, 140 n.18
Wittgenstein, Ludwig
  and anthropology 161
  on aspect perception 54
  on belief and practice 90, 91–2 n.13, 95, 96–7 n.18
  and Buddhism 137 n.10
  conception of philosophy 65–6, 156 n.2

conceptual map 96
'craving for generality' 97
'family resemblances' 38
on forms of life 146
on *Golden Bough* 89–90
on illness and punishment 146
on language and meaning 3, 4, 8, 51 n.18, 103–4, 155
Lectures on Religious Belief 146
'stream of life' 3, 4, 155, 162
on surface and depth grammar 111–12
world, outlook on the 10, 84–5, 88–91, 102, 149

Wynn, Mark 96–7 n.18
Wynne, Alexander 119

Yājñavalkya 29
Yamunacharya, M. 77, 130 n.1
Yelle, Robert 33
yoga, yogins 18, 20, 46, 47
Yoga Bhāṣya 129
Yoga Sūtra 46
Yosef, Rabbi Ovadia 141 n.20

Zedong, Mao 150, 152

www.ingramcontent.com/pod-product-compliance
Lightning Source LLC
Chambersburg PA
CBHW061827300426
44115CB00013B/2282